Life Is Good!
A Personal Journey

By Richard Hébert
2009

Out of Your Mind Publishing LLC
Palm Coast, Florida

Life Is Good! A Personal Journey
By Richard Hébert

Copyright © 2009 By Richard Hébert.

First Printing, 2009
Black Collegiate Press
Baltimore, MD

Second Printing, 2012
Out of Your Mind Publishing LLC
PO Box 353431
Palm Coast, FL 32135-3431
www.outofyourmindpublishing.com

ISBN: 978-1-935795-89-6   LCCN: 2011918145

All Rights Reserved. No part of this book may be reproduced, stored in a retrieval system, or transmitted, in any form or by any means, electronic, mechanical, photocopying, recording, or otherwise, without permission in writing from Out of Your Mind Publishing LLC.

<u>Also by Richard Hébert</u>

Highways to Nowhere: The politics of City Transportation
The Questing Beast, A Novel
MindWarp, A Novella…And Other Strange Tales*

*Named to Kirkus Reviews' "Best of 2011" and recipient,
First Prize, Royal Palm Literary Awards, Novella—2011

Printed in the United States of America

Table of Contents

Preface	i
One: Our Heritage	1
Two: Early Scars	7
Three: Other Early Memories	10
Four: Hinsdale Street	14
Five: Fun and Games	25
Six: Old Time Religion	31
Seven: Tiny	36
Eight: My Kingdom for a Horse!	40
Nine: No More Nuns	46
Ten: Heading South	51
Eleven: Normandy Isle	55
Twelve: High School Hi-jinks	62
Thirteen: The Seminary	68
Fourteen: Reaping the Whirlwind	79
Fifteen: Campus Life	88
Sixteen: 'Stormy'	97
Seventeen: Jailbird	106
Eighteen: Guy Gone Wild	112
Nineteen: Goodbye to All That	120

Twenty: Hello, D.C.	132
Twenty-One: *Parlez-vous*	145
Twenty-Two: On the Road Again	157
Twenty-Three: South of the Border	171
Twenty-Four: Steeped in History	177
Twenty-Five: Castle in Spain	183
Twenty-Six: Beginning (Again)	195
Twenty-Seven: Back to D.C.	201
Twenty-Eight: Playing Politics	215
Twenty-Nine: Reunions & the Grim Reaper	227
Thirty: Innkeeping	237
Thirty-One: Retirement	250
Epilogue: What's It All Mean?	254

Appendices

Appendix A: Canada's First Colonist	265
Appendix B: My Father's Diary	268
Appendix C: Belize, December 2005	273
Appendix D: Peru, June-July 2007	291

Grow old along with me!
The best is yet to be,
The last of life, for which the first was made:
Our times are in His hand
Who saith "A whole I planned,
Youth shows but half; trust God:
    see all, nor be afraid!"

— Robert Browning
Rabbi Ben Ezra

Preface

This is my second attempt to record what it's been like being — no, *becoming* — me all these years. It isn't intended to be so much an autobiography (although it does chronicle what I did and saw) as a reflection on those events that shaped who I am. I'll try to hold an honest mirror up to myself; perhaps others might manage to avoid some of the pitfalls (and pratfalls) I didn't.

A caveat: Memory is a malleable substance. It can trick us, but more often than not, it's we who trick our memories. After we've lived a moment and it has gone to memory's parking lot in our brains, we subtly alter it, reshape it a little to comport with our own image of ourselves. We all do it. It isn't that we lie to ourselves so much as that we erase any dissonance that might exist between what actually happened and how we think someone like us would have acted. Self-justification? In all likelihood. And, as the years accumulate, so do the reshaped memories. Our self-image progresses as we age, and the memories trail along obediently, nudging that image here and there, and in turn, being nudged by the image. I will try as hard as I can to stick with what really happened to me and what I did and felt, and not be lured into what lingers of what I wish had happened, what I wish I'd done, or how I wish I'd done it. Others will have to judge whether I succeed or not.

Authenticity is that for which I strive. To that end, at least the photographs herein are true. They are originals, taken from family albums, mine and others'. A few in the earliest chapters approach 100 years of age, some quite fragile, much abused as they moved over the years from one family album to the next. Their quality (or lack of it) is a badge of their age, and of their agelessness.

One more caveat: Some years ago, I wrote and published my only novel, The Questing Beast. It, too, was built from some of my memories. But I said then and repeat now: it was and is fiction. The memories provided the skeleton upon which to flesh out a story, a made-up story. Some in my family couldn't quite understand the distinction. If you read the novel after reading this, you will see where my real life story intersects it and where they stray apart, often quite dramatically. That one was fiction. This is a serious attempt at "faction."

I say this is my second attempt because in my first, in the spring of 2000, I tried to do it longhand in a "memory book" my daughter Teri had given me for Christmas. That proved far too painful. I was unable to write more than a few sentences at a sitting without weeping over the memories it stirred. I guess I didn't realize how painful the past can be when you look closely at it. The task forced me to remember too much of the pain and loss of the early years, and there were plenty of both. By the time I entered the University of Florida in 1959, not quite 19 years old, I'd lost a brother, my father, the only grandparent I'd ever known, several friends, the only pet I'd ever had…and my innocence. (Do not be misled: losing innocence is quite different from losing one's virginity, and much more important. The latter was not to be lost for several years yet.)

I had already by age 19 come to what I considered some pretty hard conclusions about my life: it would be lived hard, it would be fast, it would be short. I'd be dead by age 50, as so many men of my father's line had died young, so I had better win a Pulitzer Prize, if not a Nobel Prize for literature, by age 40, so I'd have at least a decade to enjoy its fruits. I would never get too attached to anything or anyone again because life had a cruel way of snatching away the ones you most love. What happened after college — a busted marriage, more lost best-friends to suicides and cancer at young ages, much aimlessness and rootlessness — only confirmed me in my angst.

I now know I was wrong on all scores. Now in my early 70s as this second edition is being prepared for press, I'm still alive, still living life at full bore if not so swiftly anymore. No Nobel or Pulitzer (although I was nominated for the latter back in 1967), but with honors and awards enough that I am fairly satisfied with my achievements, if not entirely ready to rest on my laurels. Resting does not come naturally to me, anyway. Importantly, I am devotedly attached to several people, the loss of any one of whom would be devastating to me. I have found comfort and abiding love in family and friends. The friends may be few, but they are true. And family is my anchorage in the storms of life, even when they might not think so.

Above everything else, I have learned to look forward, not backward. The legendary pitcher Satchel Paige used to say, "Don't look back, someone may be gaining on you." I understand that now, and that the "someone" gaining on me may well be myself, my own angst-ridden past. So I try to live in the moment and trust in the future. Perhaps it is all the pain and loss of yesteryear that turned my focus toward tomorrow. If so, then the pain and loss served me well.

Because I now know: life is good. Damn good.

One: Our Heritage

The Héberts are descended from Louis Hébert, the very first French person to settle in Québec. He first came with Samuel Champlain, the famous explorer, and a group of other settlers in 1604, settling near the mouth of the St. Lawrence River. Winters were harsh and promised support from France never arrived. In 1607, the colonists returned to Paris, but Louis tried again in 1611, only to be forced to return to France after the village at Port Royal was destroyed by the British from Virginia. Finally in 1617, Louis agreed to try again with Champlain, this time settling upriver, at what is now the City of Québec. (A brief biography of Louis based on information I gleaned from the Internet is at Appendix A.)

    I mention this because our roots deep in Québec history were important to my father, and through him to me as well. He almost never spoke of it, but he didn't have to. He lived it. Canada to us growing up was not the vast open land to the north, it was French Canada, it was Québec. It was the homeland. It was Montreal and Québec City, "the nuns" and the asbestos pits of Thetford Mines. It is a family heritage I treasure, as he did. Throughout my childhood, until we moved to Florida in 1954, my father and mother would return to Québec for summer vacations, leaving us children with babysitters until we were old enough to go with them. There is a photo in my family album of my brother and me in a rowboat on Lac Huitre (Oyster Lake) near Thetford Mines, where my aunt and uncle (Antoinette and Albert Cloutier, who inherited the family hotel) had a lovely vacation cottage.

    It was in Thetford Mines, where he was born, that my father died on his last visit there, in 1959, two weeks after his 50th birthday. (He would have turned 100 in 2009.) His death was the fulcrum event of my life. Everything else hinged on it. It shaped me and my anger for years, and continues to have a profound influence over me in ways I still do not completely comprehend. I will get to that eventually. Suffice to say here, it also provided the impetus for my one published novel, The Questing Beast.

My father, Leopold Joseph Hébert (with a bunch of other "middle names" thrown in that only he could remember, let alone recite – such was the propensity of French Canadian Catholics back then to bestow lineage upon their sons), was born June 3, 1909, one of 15 children. I never knew either of my grandparents on his side, Rose deLima Blais Hébert and Salomon Hébert. They both died at age 54, in March 1922 and March 1923 respectively, when my father was 12 and 13. Salomon died as the result of a hernia operation.

My grandparents owned and lived in the Central Hotel in Thetford Mines, Québec, an asbestos mining town on the edge of the Green Mountains. All 15 children were born and lived in that hotel. In 1921, they sold it and built the Manoir Hébert, which stayed in the family until it was destroyed by fire in the late 1970s. I did learn my grandfather was a strict disciplinarian. There's a tale told of how he once received a report that two of his sons, my father and Uncle Dan, were at the movies. He rushed to the theater just outside the town limits and ordered the owner of the theater to turn up the lights. Movies were considered sinful "foreign entertainments" in those silent movie days, and not permitted inside the town. Salomon thundered down the aisle, found his sons, not yet teenagers, and marched them out by their ears. At least that's how I remember my father telling about it years ago. I also read in an old history book of the mining town how Salomon Hébert led the temperance league in Thetford Mines, trying to banish "demon rum" from the lives of all those sinful asbestos miners. I don't think I would have liked old Salomon.

Salomon Hébert

Rose deLima Hébert

After my father died, we found among his belongings a payroll envelope tightly wrapped in cellophane tape. Inside were handwritten index cards: the diary of his life until 1934, when he met my mother. I cannot read them without tears. (Their original wording is reproduced in Appendix B.)

In brief, after he was orphaned he was sent by his older sister, Marianne, to a boarding school, then to a novitiate to study to become a Christian brother (a male nun). We have a 1924 photo of him at a novitiate chess meet. He's in the back row, second from the right.

At 18, he met a girl, Ivonne Florent, had a crush on her and kissed her in church. He appears to have been gradually coming to grips with the fact that he was not very pious. He left the brotherhood after his first vows (his gravesite had been earmarked for him by the brotherhood at that point), worked a while, then hitchhiked and walked to the United States to join his older brother Adelard in Waterbury, Connecticut, having squandered all but $2 of the $100 Adelard had sent him for the trip. Partying in Montreal apparently accounted for most of that money, as I recall his telling me.

Yes, today he would be considered an "illegal alien" and possibly deported. If that had been the case, he would never have gone to work in the Rhode Island mill or met and married my mother. If I had turned out to be his son anyway, I'd be a Canadian, my novel published in Canada would have been eligible for a $6,000 prize as the best first novel of the year by a Canadian (it was nominated but ruled ineligible), and my mother might well be Ivonne Florent. I toyed cavalierly with this notion in the novel, The Questing Beast. I don't think my mother ever understood it was meant as pure fiction. Many, many years later, she received a strange phone call from a woman that led her to believe I "knew" this stranger had had a child by my father. I swear I knew no such thing. It is and was always a fiction concocted in my imagination.

As a young immigrant, Dad went to work in a factory and almost lost his right hand in an accident with a buzz-saw and contracted blood-poisoning. After the hand was sewn back together, he was sent to rehabilitate it by milking cows at a dairy farm. After that, his life became a blur of jobs, girlfriends, dances, joblessness, instability. He appears to have been something of a dapper party animal. He eventually found his way to Rhode Island and another brother, Daniel, his favorite. Then, in 1934, he got a job at the Guyan Mills, a textile plant in Pawtucket, Rhode Island. There he met my mother. I came along six years later.

On my mother's side, I have only a vague recollection of an elderly, rather round-bellied woman who may have been her mother, Laura Dugas Malo, but more likely was a family friend who sometimes took care of us, I'm told. My mother's father, Noë Malo (Noë is French for Noah), is the only one of my grandparents I recall ever meeting. Pépère, as we knew him, was a small, lean man with white hair who stayed with us a while in Swansea, Massachusetts, before his death while visiting my Aunt Lorraine and Uncle Roland in Florida. My only clear memory of Pépère is of his sitting in our back yard whittling wood. I used to watch him do it, fascinated by how he transformed a shapeless chunk of wood into something beautiful. He whittled me a wooden canoe paddle. I still have it. Thanks to Pépère, I will never, ever be up a creek without a paddle.

His death, when I was about 7, was my first encounter with the concept of mortality. I was taken to the funeral parlor. I saw him lying in the casket, so still, so peaceful. I touched him, his hand I think, and he was so cold. Like marble. It shook me in some profound but silent way. I remember having great difficulty understanding what this was. I was told the usual stuff about his being in heaven, of course, but I could see him, right there in front of me, as cold and hard as stone. I think a tiny piece of me died that day.

My mother's maiden name was Malo, but not really. The true family name was Hayet. They were a family from St. Malo, France, a walled pirate town on the Brittany coast. (Ann and I visited there with her in 1976, after her visit to us in Spain, and she loved it! A drunk made a pass at her in a bar after we walked the walls.) There must have been more than one Hayet family where they settled in Québec — first Pointe-aux-Trembles (1639), then L'île Ste. Thérèse, Varennes, St. Marc, and finally Beloeil, because they became known as "Hayet de St. Malo" and, eventually, simply Malo.

My mother was born in Chicago on September 15, 1910, but grew up in Waltham, Massachusetts, near Boston. She had a younger sister, Lorraine, and two brothers, Robert and Richard. Like my father, she never finished high school, dropping out after the ninth grade to go to work. She, too, ended up at the Guyan Mills.

This chapter couldn't end on a more fitting note than these final words my father wrote on his autobiographical index cards. It's the entry for 1934. I think my father had finally discovered that life is good.

> *July: Have a big date for the 4th. Go to Revere Beach all night.*
> *September: Lill is quite sick…goes to the hospital. She doesn't die….*
> *Christmas: Best one I ever had. I get a wristwatch from Lillian.*
> *I don't think I'll…go…back…to…be…a…Brother.*

Two: Early Scars

I started collecting scars quite early in life, at age two and three. My memories of the events that produced the scars are built on what adults later told me. I have absolutely no recollection of them of my own, though I carry the scars still, and quite visibly.

Our first homes were a succession of tenements in Pawtucket, Rhode Island. The term "tenement" has fallen out of use, I think. Back then, they were flats in rather nondescript buildings where the laboring classes lived, offering little more than the basics of life. We three children were each born in a different tenement house — Elaine first (1937) on Anthony Avenue, then myself (1940) on Sisson Street, then Ronald (1942) on Garden Street, which Elaine remembers as "rundown."

Dad was then working with his brother, Uncle Dan, who owned a nursery and did landscape gardening on the side. Among their customers were some of those millionaire mansions in Newport, Rhode Island, where the mega-wealthy resided. I don't know if he actually worked on any of the famous ones that are on the waterfront, much ogled by tourists today, but he may have. I know he fell in love with working the land, building yard structures of stone, and growing plants that flower. They became his life's passions.

I suppose I was a somewhat uncontrollable toddler, always poking around where I shouldn't, looking for adventure. One day when I was about two, I decided to explore the kitchen trash can. What could go wrong? A place like that could be full of hidden treasures. My mother was at the kitchen stove, boiling a ham. She carried the pot to the sink to drain off the boiling fat just as I toppled the trash can. Instinctively, she reached down to "save" me from hurting myself. Unfortunately, the pot was perched on the edge of the sink. It fell, dumping the ham and boiling grease on the back of my neck and left shoulder.

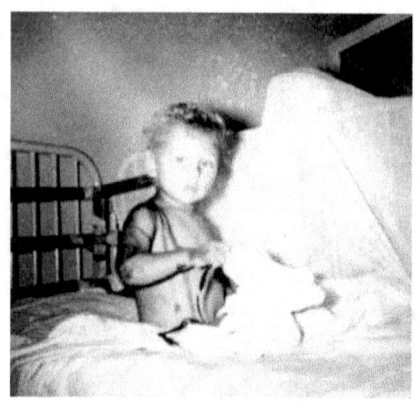
One of the photos I retain of me in the hospital tells the tale, if in reverse: streaks of blackened flesh down my chest from the shoulder, splats of burned skin on my arm. (The photo must have been printed in reverse, because it shows the burns on my right side, but the scars are still clearly on my left.) The scalding also spread across the back of my neck. Skin had to be grafted to my shoulder, where the scar is still most visible. Later in life, I kidded my mother about trying to kill me off. Not funny!

Some years later, when the family moved to Miami Beach and I started running around without a shirt, I tanned easily and quickly, but not the scarred shoulder. Totally melanin-deprived, it would burn instead, and the white flesh would become soft. I poked it tenderly once and it started oozing blood. After that I started covering it in the sun — wearing a shirt, tossing a towel over my shoulder, even wearing a bandage over it at times. Later, I told tales of using it to attract girls' revulsion by lifting a flap of skin off my shoulder to display my shoulder bone. Pure fabrication. Never happened. (At least I don't think it did. This is where memory and fable get blurred.) The people I told this to must have thought me a real jerk, both the ones who believed me and the ones who didn't. Such is the callowness of youth.

It wasn't long after my recuperation from the scalding that I decided to explore the landing of the wooden staircase outside our second-story tenement. This time it was my father who was in the kitchen. He told me this is how it happened: he saw me crawling around out there just as I started toward the edge of the landing. He stuck his head out the window to shout at me to get back from the edge. Unfortunately for him, the window was still closed. His face crashed through the glass. He spent the rest of his life with a curious bump across the bridge of his nose where it had done battle with the window.

As for me, I landed, appropriately enough, in a large trash can (again!) at the foot of the stairs. This one was metal and had a rusty rim that caught my right wrist as I fell, nearly severing my hand as if to mimic my father's earlier scar. The scar there is permanent as well, about two inches long and still showing where the stitches went.

I think I was about 4, maybe 5, when we moved out of the tenements and into the big rented house on Gardner's Neck Road in Swansea, Massachusetts. There I had my third encounter with grave physical harm — and one which I do remember, indelibly. It is probably my earliest true memory.

What I remember most is the scream. Or rather, the merger of two screams. There is the scream of a car's brakes right next to me, and from farther away my name being screamed by my sister. The next thing I remember is being in the hospital. I think that was the time (or was it when I had the mumps?) that on a visit to the hospital my father brought me a detailed drawing of one of his mill's trucks. (He'd gone to work at Smith Textile in Fall River by this time.) I vividly remember being fascinated by the drawing and its incredible detail. In my memory, the drawing has all the clarity of a professional draftsman's work. The event itself is a little murky.

It was the eggs. Our big white house (it had become a funeral parlor the last time I visited the area) was the second from the four-lane highway we used to call the "Grand Army Highway" because it had been built to move troops, if necessary, during World War II. The chicken farm where we bought our eggs was a short distance away on the other side of the highway. (This, remember, was a good 10 years before Dwight Eisenhower started construction of the Interstate Highway System. I-95 now slices through that area, but that is now; this was then.)

I had gone to the egg farm with my sister and we were on our way back. Elaine carried the eggs and held my hand, as she was told to do. As we approached the highway, I could clearly see our home and bolted from her. I think I made it two or three lanes across the highway before the shriek of brakes joined that of my sister screaming my name. "RICH—ID!!!"

I woke up in the hospital. Brain concussion was the diagnosis. I was kidded fairly often about that supposed brain damage as my childhood rolled by.

It turned out it would take much more than boiling hams, rusting trash cans and screeching cars to get rid of me. Considering the alternative, life was far better.

Three: Other Early Memories

I harbor a few other early memories from those years on Gardner's Neck Road. Scattered memories, like snapshots.

Justin E. Smith had been one of Dad's and Uncle Dan's gardening customers. He also owned a mill in Fall River that trafficked in rags, cloth remnants and waste cotton. Good male workers were hard to find during World War II. My father had become a U.S. citizen in 1942 and had tried to enlist in the Navy even before then but was rejected because he had already suffered a heart attack, although still in his early 30s. Mr. Smith (he was always "Mr. Smith" to us), impressed by how thorough and conscientious my father was about his yard work at the mansion in Seekonk, Massachusetts, invited him to learn the textile trade. My father drove a truck for the mill for a month or so, and then was promoted to manager. It nearly killed him. In a way, years later, maybe it did.

It was probably the switch from gardening to managing the mill that prompted the move out of tenements in Pawtucket and into the white house on Gardner's Neck Road.

It was a huge house, at least it seemed so to me, with a broad front yard. It had one of those sloping cellar doors that opened upward like wings. In the basement was a bin where potatoes were stored over the winter. And a coal chute, I think. I vaguely recall being scolded more than once for playing around the coal chute and trying to use it as a playground slide.

In front of the house my father dug two deep holes in which to plant evergreens. His first mistake: he dug the holes before he had the bushes. His second mistake: he left me and my brother Ronald at home with those gaping holes while he went to get the bushes.

Two tykes are not going to leave two such beautiful holes unabused. They make perfect forts for pitched battles with cap pistols, or maybe foxholes for all-out war. Clambering in and out and around them, we managed to topple much of the dirt he'd excavated back into the holes. He was furious when he reached home with his shrubs. We were appropriately scolded, I'm sure, but again it's the mortification I felt that I remember most. Many years later, driving by during the 1980s, I saw those evergreens again — grown into towering trees in front of what is now the Birchcrest Home of Waring, a funeral parlor.

(They aren't there any longer. The big yard has been turned into a parking lot. I know this because I recently zoomed in on that lot with Google Earth. Trees perish. Death goes on.)

Another memory of life there also concerns a tree, this an aging one at the front of our broad yard. I have no idea what kind of tree it was. Back then, to me, trees were simply that: trees. Bushes were small, trees were big. And this one was big, too big to put my arms around. A hurricane swept through and toppled it. My father sweated and worked for hours to prop that tree up again, pulling it up with a truck from the textile mill and then propping it up with wooden two-by-fours, or maybe they were four-by-eights. He said something about the tree being worth saving, and thus worth the effort. I remember thinking that was probably a pretty important lesson, right up there with boys should never hit girls and you should never talk back to your mother or play in traffic.

Then there were "The Sisters," two kindly (if spooky) elderly ladies who lived in the first house beside the Grand Army Highway and pretty much kept to themselves. As did most people during World War II, they had a Victory Garden in their back yard, where they grew vegetables. We had one as well, but theirs was far more inviting, probably because, as everyone knows, forbidden fruit is better. Also, their rows of crops were all so neat and straight and weeded compared to ours, I thought. I sneaked into their garden (fencing yards was unheard of back then) and made off with a handful of fresh green beans, which I proceeded to eat raw. I was caught, of course, red-handed. I must have been about 5 or 6, because as I remember it, this was one of the first "sins" I had to confess when I finally reached the designated "Age of Reason" to start going to confession and receiving communion. Once again, it's the mortification I remember most, this time the mortification of imagining the shock on the hidden priest's face as I, at my tender age, confessed to the mortal sin of theft.

Elaine, three years older than I, started school while we were on Gardner's Neck Road. That memory is (painfully) all hers, but it's relevant to how our childhood went, so I'll let her describe it:

I began kindergarten at Dominican Academy boarding school. I stayed there Monday through Friday and came home weekends. The nuns complained to Dad that I wet the bed every night, so at Christmas he took me out and placed me in a public school. I spoke no English. That did not work either and for the first grade I was placed at St. Louis de France, where they spoke English and French.

St. Louis de France was the French Catholic grade school in Swansea. That's where I did my kindergarten. It was quite a long walk to the corner where the school bus picked us up. Sometimes Dad would drive us to the corner, but on many occasions we had to walk, especially on the return trip home in the afternoon. The streets were lined with chestnut trees — an ideal place for a youngster to collect buckeyes and, even more delightful, those seedpods that drift down like spinning helicopter blades. What we did with these was peel open the bulbous end, remove the seeds, then stick the flaps on the tip of our noses and make faces at each other. Why? Because we could, I guess.

I can't leave these first five or so years of my life without noting that, however dramatic they may have seemed for me, they were far more so for the world around me: these were the war years. I was but a year old when the Japanese bombed Pearl Harbor, and I was still a few weeks shy of my fifth birthday when we dropped the world's first two atom bombs on Japan to end the war in 1945. In the process, we forever changed the course of history. During the years between those two world-shaking events, humanity was in turmoil, but I was unaware of it. I didn't know about the rationing of everything from sugar and flour to gasoline; about war bonds being sold to pay for the war; about Civilian Defense volunteers watching the skies at night for incoming bombers from Japan on the Pacific coast and for U-boats from Germany off our Atlantic coast. I didn't know that in the beginning German submarines were sinking our merchant ships in our own harbors. Most of all, I was blissfully unaware of the bleeding and the dying being visited upon humanity by the millions, or of the hatred and inhumanity being committed on all sides, ours included.

Writing this now, more than a half century later, I am awed and saddened by the crazy quilt of horror, hardship and heroism of it all. How young men and women died in the muck and mud of a war they didn't choose, for a cause they truly believed in, with good reason. And how we as a society acted much less humanely than we'd like to think we did. How we often abjectly failed to live up to our own principles at the very time we were defending them before the world.

My own country could fight the Nazis and their concentration camps and the world-domination agenda of imperialist Japan while we ourselves sent more than a hundred thousand of our citizens to our own concentration camps, simply because they had been born of Japanese parents. We also sent our African-descent citizens to fight and die for us while we kept them in segregated lives of insulting deprivation and stripped them of pride — from back-of-the-bus rules to separate water fountains to "no niggers" signs at public establishments throughout the South. Blacks stepped out of line at grave risk of lynching and worse.

These were years and events of which we had much to be proud, but also much to be ashamed. For now their lessons waited in the wings, waiting to clobber me with the impact of a sledgehammer when I became old enough to understand them, during the 1960s. About all that later.

Elaine remembers more than I do about those years, how all lights had to be turned out in our homes at night and the windows covered with "blackout curtains" to prevent even candlelight from leaking out, so the Germans wouldn't know we were there, I suppose. I do recall vaguely something like that, too. It must have happened at Gardner's Neck Road, because by the time we moved away from there, the war had ended.

I became aware that the war had happened only a few years after it ended, from my namesake, Uncle Dick, Mom's brother, for whom I'd been named. (Despite my later claims that they'd given me "Leo" as a middle name in honor of Richard the Lion-heart, the "Leo" was from my Dad. While Dad was indeed a "lion-hearted" man, it was not the medieval — and womanizing drunk — crusader for whom I was named, but my Uncle Dick and my Dad, Leopold, known by everyone as Leo.)

Uncle Dick had gone to war and come back whole, with an "Eisenhower" jacket and a khaki GI knapsack. He gave both to me. I wore that jacket and carried that knapsack as my schoolbook bag proudly every day for years, through high school, I think. Without knowing what they truly stood for, I sensed, somehow in the recesses of my mind, that they linked me to something important that had happened. It would be many more years before I would understand just how important, but I think I was already beginning to sense that war was bad, and life was good.

Four: Hinsdale Street

My first coherent string of memories begins at 50 Hinsdale Street, where we moved in 1946, my first year in school. (We didn't consider kindergarten as "real school" back then. It was more like "play school.") My memories of that time are not a string in any chronological sense, actually, but a kaleidoscope, patterns of things that gradually emerged. Disentangling them into a chronological account of my youth would be an exercise in futility now, and probably not very useful. Instead, allow me to skip back and forth thematically across those years on Hinsdale Street, from age 6 to 13.

When The Big War ended in 1945, its reformation of life didn't screech to a stop. The wartime lifestyle continued, out of both habit and the continued necessity of paying for the more than three and a half years of bloodshed in Europe and the Pacific. Women were in the workplace to stay. Backyard "victory gardens" continued on for years (ours certainly did). At the movies, what are now popcorn and Coca-Cola commercials were celebrity-loaded promotions to buy war bonds. Regular "paper drives" and "scrap iron drives" and similar collections of used goods also continued, not out of ecological considerations such as saving the planet, which would come decades later, but out of economic necessity. Recycling was a statement of support for the war effort, long before it became a political statement in support of Mother Earth. Dad used an open-bed tractor-trailer from the mill to make the rounds on weekends, collecting from street-sides bundled up old newspapers or discarded rags and clothing or heaps of scrap iron — old bed frames and bedsprings and discarded bicycles; rusting wagons and old rakes and shovels; and a multitude of random bits of twisted and mangled metal. I accompanied him on several such collecting adventures. I know it wasn't weekly, but there were enough such drives that they seemed routine, and I found them oddly exciting, a grown-up thing to do.

The house number on Hinsdale was 326 when we moved there, until the town decided to renumber everything and confuse us kids. I found it strange that they could actually "move" you that way, without even asking, from 326 Hinsdale to 50 Hinsdale. And why would they do it? To this day I don't know. Hinsdale ran just one block, downhill from Hot and Cold Lane at the top to Bark Street below. (Yes, the house still stands and is visible on Google Earth.) The hill was ideal for sledding in winter, until the nasty snow plows and sand trucks arrived to spoil our fun. I think the only people who lived in the area were we second-generation French Canadians and the Portuguese descendants of the whaling men who had come to New Bedford from the Azores a century before.

Across the street from us lived the Furtados, Johnny's family. Once, while we were playing, his pants tore and I saw he didn't have any underwear on. I figured that meant they were poor. Other evidence: they lived in a rickety old unpainted house that would today be called a shanty. It had no running water, just a well with a handpump and an outhouse out back.

Uphill from them, beyond an empty field, were the Arudas and their pig farm. We carried our garbage — we called it "swill" — up there a few times a week to donate to the pigs' trough. In return, when they'd butcher a pig or two in the fall, amid much squealing and screaming and the smell of singed hair, we'd get perhaps a pork roast or at least some sausage. We watched them slaughter one of the pigs once. Elaine cried for the pig. I have to admit I didn't enjoy it either, but back then boys weren't supposed to cry.

One of the Aruda girls, Lorraine, was a few years older than I. When I was perhaps 7 or 8, we were sitting together unseen (we thought) on the front veranda of our house. She hiked up her skirt to prove to me she didn't have a "peanut" and invited me to touch her there. My mother chose that moment to look out the parlor window and saw us. She knocked on the window and we ran. Once again, I was mortified. I didn't particularly know why it was wrong to do what I'd done, but I did comprehend that I wasn't supposed to do it. No one ever mentioned the incident to me, but I'm almost sure Mom knew what was going on. And told Dad. Lorraine Aruda didn't seem to come around much anymore after that.

The Benevides family (Bobby was my age, but bigger, probably twice my skimpy weight) lived just uphill from us, and at the top of the hill were the French, the Castonguays and the Babins. Jeanine Babin was my age and my chief rival in the competition for top grades at St. Louis de France. Her brother, Leonard, whom everyone called "Boy" Babin as though there were some doubt as to his gender, was a couple years younger, about my brother's age. He used to brag how he could eat poison ivy and never get sick. I saw him do it once. And he didn't get sick, at least not that I know of.

Our family "car" was a huge GMC tractor from the mill until well after the war, when we finally bought our first automobile – a 1941 Cadillac! I think that car was my father's attempt to leapfrog out of his laborer's socioeconomic status. We were what today would be called the working poor, but we didn't know it.

Mom made most of our clothes. If we got "store bought" clothes, it meant it was Easter. Socks and underwear came from the store, of course, but were darned and sewn until there was no room left to put a stitch. Our shirts, shorts, trousers — all came whirring from her faithful old Singer, made out of bolts of cloth Dad brought home from the mill. She washed our clothes by hand on a scrub board in a tub with one of those sturdy old roller-wringers. Drying, of course, was done on clotheslines strung from tree to tree in the back yard, the three pear trees, whose straight trunks were more suited to the task than were the crabapple trees.

Eventually, those clotheslines were often draped with nothing but white rags. What I didn't know then but would discover many years later is that Elaine had entered puberty, and rather than buy sanitary pads for her, Dad would bring pieces of white cloth home from the mill and Mom would

With Elaine, Ronald, Gary

With Ronald and our 1941 Caddy

wash them after each use. Elaine says she was mortified by the public display. I barely noticed it at the time. (We spent a lot of time being mortified back then.) Another thing about those trees: some of the kids would eat the green pears but I found them hard and relatively tasteless. Instead, I loved scampering up among the branches of our crabapple trees, trying to reach the farthest (and by definition, best) apples to toss down to my brother and friends. I fell out of that tree more than once. But those bitter apples did taste good when you needed a power boost in mid-afternoon.

Meals were healthy but not lavish, and never "fast food" (it didn't exist) or "carry-out," and almost never in restaurants. It was a rare treat when Dad took the family out for a feast at Brook Manor, where it was usually lobster, to this day my favorite meal. Fridays were Boston baked beans or fish. Catholics didn't eat meat on Fridays. I never quite understood why. Meatloaf was on the menu all too often, I thought. When it was, I knew it meant I'd be eating cold meatloaf sandwiches at school for several days. To this day I will never order meatloaf at a restaurant or have it in my home. Mom was a child of the Great Depression. Money was to be saved, never spent unless absolutely necessary. No scrap of food was ever wasted. Hence meatloaf. Every shred of ham was stripped from its bone and passed through a hand-cranked grinder, to be turned into more sandwich fodder. We were constantly reminded of the "starving children in China," as though we owed it to them to clean our plates. I still do to this day. Some habits are hard to break.

The house itself was an old clapboard barn when we moved in. Little by little, sometimes almost by dint of his stubborn will and sweat,

Dad transformed it. He repainted it several times, once a beautiful aquamarine.

The basement was a damp, dark place before he transformed it. Coal was piled behind a furnace there. He carved half the basement away from the rest and turned it into a rumpus room — a wonderful recreational area. He gave it a new, polished cement floor and painted it caramel brown, with a huge ship's compass painted at the center. The walls were a blue and white seascape, here and there some seagulls in flight amid puffs of cloud above the waves. He built a large stone fireplace against the wall, just behind the furnace in the other room and connected it to the chimney that ran up through the kitchen to the attic.

In the Rumpus Room with Queenie

At the rumpus room entrance he hung a rustic wooden sign he'd made, welcoming all comers to "The Ripples." At a back corner of The Ripples he built a bar, stocked with fancy glasses. One set had the Hébert "H" on them. My mother kept those for years, as breakage slowly shrank their number. I broke the last one several years ago. Another set of bar glasses was decorated with drawings of scantily clad ladies, that is if you looked at them from the front of the glass. If you turned the glass around and looked from the back, they were naked. I used to sneak back there and admire the lovely rumps when I thought no one was looking. Elaine put an end to that. She says one day she scratched all the pictures off the glasses, but "I don't believe Dad ever approached me about this."

The rumpus room was also where the Christmas tree went each winter, where the upright and, later, baby grand piano went, and where all partying was done. It's also where I used to like to go and sit by myself to read, or simply be alone.

Dad would retreat down there too, to play the piano. He could read music, but he didn't need to. Music seemed to flow in his veins. He could play anything he wanted by ear, from boogie-woogie to the classics. He'd sit Elaine on bench beside him and play and sing to her, *Daddy's Little Girl*, a song made popular by the Mills Brothers. All I usually got was *Open the Door, Richard*, sung usually to a chorus of laughter, although I do remember once — a mighty proud once — when he sat me on the bench beside him and sang *Danny Boy*. It was only many, many years later that I actually paid attention to the words — how the father in the song is pining for his son's return from war but knows he will probably be in his grave by then. To this day, some 60 years later, the song never fails to make my eyes sting and tear up.

Dad turned another part of the basement into his tool room, and the rest became home to the furnace that eventually replaced the coal stove in the kitchen. One wall of that room was lined with shelves for the preserves my mother would "put up" each summer. Mom was the old-fashioned type, always cooking, canning, sewing, doing laundry. I don't think I ever saw her sit down and simply do "nothing."

I remember (because Elaine recently reminded me) that Mom once burned her face and hair trying to light the coal stove in the kitchen, probably by pouring lighter fluid or kerosene on already burning coals. That stove was an all-purpose appliance: it heated the house via the chimney that went up through the attic; it cooked our food; it heated the water that was dumped into our bathtub for our once-a-week baths — each Saturday, one tub of water for all three kids. If the water cooled too much for proper cleansing by the unlucky third child, another pot of boiling water would be added. The intention appeared to be to scald us clean. We never had showers or hot running water (or air conditioning for that matter) until we moved to Florida in 1954. We didn't understand that to be a misfortune, only the natural order of things. Having to use an outhouse, like Johnny Furtado, that was poverty.

Dad also carved the attic into two bedrooms, one at either end with a common room of storage cabinets between them. Ronald and I shared one bedroom, my sister had the other. The chimney ran up through that central space and warmed the entire attic through vents.

While the attic reconstruction was going on, my sister decided to play doctor one day. I was her "patient." Pronouncing me ill of I don't know what, she fed me her "medicine" from a bottle of turpentine Dad had left there. They had to rush me to the hospital for real then, to have my stomach pumped out. I tell you, my childhood was perilous.

The other major modification Dad made to the house, after we kids were consigned to the attic, was to convert what had been our downstairs bedroom into a den. That was done while Mom was in St. Petersburg, Florida, staying with her sister Lorraine and Uncle Roland, recuperating from a hysterectomy, I believe. This would have been after her fourth pregnancy ended in stillbirth. When she came home, she found the kitchen wall demolished and replaced by an archway, and our former bedroom turned into a family den. It was there, a few years later, that our first television set was installed, a 12-inch black-and-white Philco. The first program we watched on it, constantly reaching behind to readjust the tiny knob that kept the screen from rolling or turning into lightening-like scribbles, was *Howdy Doody*. Howdy and Captain Bob and Clarabell the Clown and Captain Phineas T. Bluster became daily constants in my life, preceded by a half hour of Beanie and Cecil, the Seasick Sea Serpent, whom I considered far more serious.

My introduction to television had preceded that by a year or so, however, because a friend several blocks away was the first in our neighborhood that I knew who acquired that magic box, and every Thursday evening I was allowed to go to his house (he had a cute sister, I recall, though I can't remember her name or his) to watch *Martin Kane, Private Eye*, starring Ralph Bellamy. It was a classic detective series that captivated my young imagination.

At either side of our driveway entrance stood huge boulders, nature's leftovers from long ago glacier movement across New England. My father turned the sloping front of the larger of these into a planter, with the word "Welcome" spelled out in ribbons of grass. He planted flowers on the hollowed-out top of the other.

Dad loved working in stone, probably from his earlier days with Uncle Dan on those millionaires' stone-walled yards in Newport. A veranda extended across most of the front of our house and half the downhill side, the very veranda where I was caught examining Lorraine Aruda's genitalia, but because of the hill's steep slope the veranda was high and ungainly. Dad banked it half-way up with earth, then built a stone retaining wall. We kept firewood stacked under that veranda, beside the basement door, leaving ample hiding room beyond it for a young boy. Dad also built a stone terrace attached to the back of the house and eventually walled it in with windows, then added a stone fireplace in the back yard that seemed to grow more elaborate each year as

This Ole House

...as bought...

...in mid-modification...

...chicken coop and fireplace (before it got its chimney)

The terrace before it was enclosed

he gave it a chimney, then warming ovens at either side, and even wing-benches to sit on.

The stones — as for all Dad's constructions, whether fireplaces, terraces or retaining walls — were collected at the seaside near Newport. We kids usually were recruited to go "help" him collect the stones, but of course Ronald and I spent most of our collecting time chasing each other from rock to rock.

Yet another boulder poked out of the ground in our back yard. He hollowed out its crown to create a birdbath. Grape arbors abounded, but he got rid of all except one of those, saving the one to provide shade and a place for weather-protected parties and cook-outs. He cleared a large area near the cesspool and planted a Victory Garden, although the war had been long over. He planted, and it fell to us kids to weed, rows of potatoes, string beans, carrots, radishes, tomatoes, cucumbers and strawberries. Mom would can vegetables and preserves, all stored on those shelves in the cellar for the winter months.

A small chicken coop at a back corner of our yard successively became a dollhouse for Elaine then a gym for me. I was a rather skinny, bookish kid, and Dad was adamant about toughening me up with things like a punching bag and exercise springs. An empty lot behind us, which we also owned, was cleared and became a baseball field, complete with a chain-link backstop.

Along the dirt lane beyond our ballpark, yet more boulders plowed up and pushed aside to make room for housing provided a wonderful setting for young war games or just going to hide from everyone and think about stuff. Uphill from us, on the other side of Hot and Cold Lane, was a jungle — well maybe it was just a wooded area – but it was also suitable for playing Cowboys and Indians and other young activities that involved running and hiding and shooting arrows at each other, arrows we would make ourselves out of dried reeds.

Summers, when Mom and Dad went to Canada, we would be left with baby-sitters, usually the Carons, who owned a farm on Gardner's Neck Road, at its other end from where we had lived. The Carons had chickens and a few cows and a cornfield. Of the two grown sons, Norman would take me out in the pre-dawn hours to show me how to fish for eel in the creek that ran through their property. Mrs. Caron, a grandmotherly figure, would sit and cut out pictures like dolls from magazines and make us paste them on sheets of paper. I much preferred spending my time with Norman and his older brother, Junior, in the barn or in the mud down by the creek.

Family came to visit often. Our home seemed always full of people talking loudly, singing, laughing. My mother's brothers, Uncle Bob and Uncle Dick, came with their wives, Jeannette and Fay, and my cousins on that side — Bobby, Sandy, and Beverly. (We lost Sandy to cancer a few years ago.) Mom's sister, Lorraine, had by then married Roland Choinière and moved to St. Petersburg, Florida, but even they came north to visit once in a while. No matter what the season, Lorraine always seemed cold, needing at least a sweater in even the mildest summer weather. I imagined Florida as a sweat tank, designed to make you think everywhere else was the Arctic.

My father's sisters and brothers would also gather at our place from near and far with their families at least once each summer, and Dad would make a good old New England clam bake. He'd dug a deep pit in the back yard, then lined it with rocks we'd collected at Newport and hauled home in a makeshift trailer he hitched behind that Cadillac (and the 1951 Hudson that succeeded it). Food was heaped inside and layered with wet seaweed we'd also collected, then he covered it all with a final layer of rocks. After the guests started arriving on Friday, a massive bonfire was built on top of all this and kept burning through the night. The heat seeped down into the underground "oven" and made the seaweed steam the clams, ears of corn, lobsters, even chicken legs and breasts. When the bonfire finally burned down, the hot rocks were raked aside and serious eating could begin.

Meanwhile, of course, there were always hot dogs and hamburgers being grilled on the backyard fireplace, and quahog chowder cooking in the kitchen (every time I smell clam chowder now, I recall that scent coming from Mom's kitchen). If Dad took a break from the cooking, he'd go to the upright piano and start banging away. I recall that at one such family gathering he parked one of the open trailers from Smith Textile in the driveway, put the upright piano in it, and turned it into a dance floor.

If Dad loved anything more than flowers and plants and yard work, it was people and being surrounded by the laughter and loud conversations of a fun-loving family. He loved a party more than anyone I've ever known. I believe it's because he lost his own family at such a young age.

There was a famous New Year's Eve party that no one came to, at least not on New Year's Eve. That was the year Pépère Malo was living with us. The relatives were all stranded in Rhode Island by a blizzard. Dad decided to open the Southern Comfort while he, Mom and Pépère waited for the company to arrive. They must have put away a lot of Southern Comfort-and-ginger ale "highballs" (not an advisable way to consume Southern Comfort, by the way; the sweet ginger ale gives the alcohol one heck of a kick), because when the company did finally arrive the next morning, they were all passed out. The story became part of family lore, no doubt embellished over the years.

Five: Fun and Games

I knew fun on Hinsdale Street, before I became aware that life was not supposed to be all fun, and made my first friends who weren't relatives. First among these was Billy Cain. He went to our "French" school but was different: he wasn't French. He lived perhaps a mile away, downhill from Bark Street, toward the Taunton River. I'd bicycle to his home to play every chance I could. It was a long way for a little runt like me to bicycle, but his friendship was worth it. Then, only a very few years into our friendship, his family moved away. He never said goodbye. I was told they'd moved to Arizona. I thought moving to Arizona must be something like dying, going away and never coming back, the way Pépère had.

Nancy was my first "crush." Damn, she was cute, in a Shirley Temple way, with blonde curls and dimpled cheeks. Come to think of it, I'm not even sure her name was Nancy, and I sure don't remember her last name. She may not even have been blonde or have had dimples. All I remember is she lived in the house right next to St. Louis de France, and I had to walk or bicycle past it every day on my way to and from school. Every time I passed it I hoped to get a glimpse of her. I don't think she knew I existed.

"Fun" consisted mostly of pick-up baseball games in the field behind our house; cowboys and Indians with blazing cap pistols and homemade bows and arrows in the woods up the hill or along the ridge of boulders dredged up behind our property; Saturday matinee movies in Fall River starring Whip Wilson and Lash Larue and Hopalong Cassidy and the Red Rider, and, of course, Roy Rogers and Dale Evans and Gabby Hayes, and the Lone Ranger and Tonto; in summer, going to nearby Ocean Grove beach with the family and learning how to dig with our toes in the squishy sand for littlenecks and longnecks and quahogs;

and racing down our hill in our homemade buggies — mine a heavy, clunky, slow-moving thing that looked like a jeep. My father had built it out of discarded parts from the mill, right down to the heavy steel wheels from the mill's discarded handtrucks. I never did win any of those races, but I had the fanciest looking vehicle, especially when compared to the others, typically a plank, four "real" wheels like those on baby carriages, a swiveling axle in front and a rope to steer by. Mine even had a proper steering wheel! A lot of good that did. My lumbering fat SUV was downright embarrassing.

In winter, we built snow forts in the back yard and staged all-out snowball wars. We sleighed down Hinsdale Street after snowfalls and then peppered sand trucks and snow plows with snowballs when they came to ruin everything. A few times my father even agreed to drive his car up and down the hill to pack down the snow for us if it was too soft for our sleds.

Christmas was a big deal. In November, Dad would take us kids to the woods beyond the Carons' farm to collect buckets of moss. Lawn furniture and boxes would be heaped on the floor of the backyard terrace, a mountainside cascading down from one corner. Then the entire mountainside was covered with bedsheets.

Party Time!
Dad at the piano, Gary clowning. Others (l-r): Gary's father, Uncle Leonard; family friends Violet and Henry Pelletier; Mom (one of the few times ever photographed with a big smile!), and Gary's grandfather.

A tin trough snaked down the mountainside to an upturned garbage can lid, and then out of that to the wall. Sand was glued to the tin and the lid to turn them into a stream and lake bed, and a garden hose trickled water down the stream to the lake and then drained outside through a hole poked in the wall behind the set. The manger was located just above the stream. Two or three villages of small wooden houses sprouted on the hillside in the distance, with the steepled country churches typical of New England and Québec, if not Israel. Plaster of Paris sheep grazed on patches of moss, watched over by their plaster shepherds. Slowly, day by day, the Magi would inch their way from the distance to the manger – the *crèche* –and as Christmas neared, Joseph and Mary would appear in the manger with a few cows and sheep. Baby Jesus never arrived until Christmas morning, of course. Every year that display seemed to grow larger, until it consumed almost half of the terrace. I wish I had a photo of it, because it was truly spectacular, but apparently none has survived.

Dad would also have us rehearse a play to perform for visiting relatives on Christmas Day, down in the rumpus room. I remember nothing more than scraps from two of them. One was in French, and we had to sing a song announcing that the Three Kings were coming. All I remember is the line, *"Voici la-bas, la-bas, la-bas!"* (Look over there, over there, over there!) In the other, a war-time story, I actually had a speaking part. As I arrived at an encampment, I was challenged by someone demanding to know the password. My line was the password: "Chicken feathers blowing in the wind." Now how could anybody forget a performance like that?

Music was also a constant. Dad could come back from a musical play, sit down at the piano and play the tunes from it as though he'd known them his whole life. He insisted we kids each learn to play an instrument. Elaine studied piano under a nun at the school until she grew tired of the classical music they insisted on teaching. Ronald took up the mandolin. For me, he brought home a violin. I hated it. All I could get out of it was scratchy noises, and the chin cup hurt my neck.

Memory gets a little murky here. I've told any number of people that I was so angry about the violin that I hit my father over the head with it one day when his back was turned, but in all honesty I can't see myself as having mustered the courage to do something like that. The wish must have been father to the memory. What I may have done is slammed the poor instrument down a little too hard a few times. I do remember my father being very diplomatic about it. Okay, so I didn't like the violin. I was going to play some instrument, no getting out of that, so what instrument did I want to learn to play? Drums, I said. That, he said, is not an instrument; it's a noisemaker. I shifted to Plan B: guitar. He bought me an acoustic guitar with classical nylon and silver strings.

Ronald and I were dispatched to a music teacher, a *classical* music teacher. I progressed by fits and starts from *Twinkle, Twinkle, Little Star* through *Hear the Wind Blow* and *Red River Valley* and eventually to some vague semblance of *Malagueña* and *Claire de Lune*, even a little Bach. But I was never very good; I simply repeated by rote what I'd been taught and practiced. Pure muscle memory. We played in an orchestra assembled by the music teacher, and then they even asked Ronald and me, along with Armand Lambert, another mandolin player in Ronald's class, to play at a St. Louis de France commencement exercise. We made an interesting if amateurish trio.

It would be my one public performance of any note. Backstage, before the show, I nervously tripped over a bucket, the guitar hit the floor, cracking its underbelly rather seriously. Frightened how he'd react, I circled out into the audience and found my father. In tears, I told him what I'd done. He went backstage, played a few notes and knew the instrument was seriously out of tune. He re-tuned it, or at least five of its six strings. I think the high-E string was broken. He told me to fake it, to just pretend that string was there, which it wasn't, on the piece, *Santa Lucia*. At the end, the adults politely applauded as though nothing were amiss.

The most memorable summer events on Hinsdale Street were the movies at Bark Street School. Except, back then, I thought it was "Box Street" School. This was a small wooden structure on Buffington Street, not even on Bark Street. To get there we had to go up Hinsdale Street, pass the Arudas' pig farm, and follow a dirt trail through the woods for a mile or so, until it exited at the back of the schoolyard. They hung a bedsheet on the outside wall of the schoolhouse for a screen, and when it grew dark enough, we'd all sit on the grass and watch black-and-white movies which, almost always, would break and have to be spliced back together before the movie could resume.

We watched the *Dead End Kids* and *Spanky and The Gang, The Count of Monte Cristo, The Man in the Iron Mask, Robinson Crusoe* and *Treasure Island*. Every year, it seemed, the same movies returned, but we loved them all the more for their familiarity. Much the way today I still love to watch *It's a Wonderful Life* or *The Hustler* or *Casablanca*. And when the movie was done, we had to face the perilous walk home through the deep dark forest, where the slightest unusual sound could make our hearts race. It was enough to make a young boy's imagination run rampant. Everyone knew danger lurked in the deepest shadows.

There were afternoons wiled away in summer laziness, when we would graze like cows. I ate something we called sourgrass, a weed in the yard; ate clover buds and berries and those tender tendrils that the grapevine sent out to grab a nearby branch or support post; chewed the green bark off new-growth branches of the spindly sassafras trees that grew behind our lot. That kind of diet today would probably be outlawed by the Food and Drug Administration.

Weekends, Dad might go out to Mr. Smith's estate in Seekonk, where he'd once been the caretaker, and help out his replacement, "Lefty," who was a war veteran. Mr. Smith's place seemed a palace to us kids, with a Renaissance-looking swimming pool to match. Running the length of the pool on the back side was a baroque edifice of columns with fountains cascading down to the pool itself, some of the water spouting out of lions' mouths, some running down little finger canals between flagstones. There were so many places from which to jump or dive into the pool it was often hard to decide which you wanted to do next. Those were great days.

But the most fun of all were those Saturdays when Dad had to go to the mill to work for a few hours. He'd turn us and our friends loose in the huge back room stacked with bales of waste cotton. It was like having our private mountain range upon which to enact our personal version of the wild west, romping and fighting and shooting and yelling to our hearts' content. Rails were anchored to the high ceiling as tracks for the dollies that grappled bales and moved them about the cavernous expanse to lift them into stacks. This we also turned into a Tarzan-like terrain where you could run across the bale-tops with the dolly chain and then swing out over space. There was never any fear we would hurt ourselves because there were bales of waste cotton everywhere for soft landings. Dad made sure we knew never to go near the fenced area that held the baling press.

Life was not entirely fun and games, though. We had our chores to do. Elaine had to work in the house helping Mom. Ronald and I had to mow the lawn, rake leaves, weed the vegetable garden and the ever-present flower beds my father couldn't live without.

When I was 11 or 12, weeding the garden against my will and further disgruntled at some request from my mother that I no longer remember, I did what I'd seen other angry kids do at school: I flipped her my middle finger. I don't think it was more than 15 minutes before a truck from the mill pulled into our driveway and I was told to get in with one of Dad's drivers, Mark Petty. I was taken to the mill and sent up to my father's office. He put me in his personal office and left me there, alone, to stew and think about what I'd done for I don't know how long while he went on about his mill-managing duties. The office walls were knotty pine. The knots in the boards seemed like devil's eyes staring down at me for hours.

Only when the workers had gone home did he come in to me. He raised his middle finger and asked me if I knew what it meant. I shook my head. I truly didn't. "It means up your ass!" he snapped, his voice knife-edged with anger, and then — disappointment. "You did that to your mother!?" He didn't have to slap me, didn't have to take away any privileges, or even say another word. This was true mortification. I've never forgotten that afternoon.

Of course, being siblings, we fought. Usually it was my younger brother and I, fighting over the most inconsequential things. But the fight that sticks most indelibly in my mind — and my sister's — is the one she and I had. I have no recollection what it was about. We were yelling and hurling snowballs at each other from a safe distance. Elaine seems to have a clearer memory of it than I, and for good reason:

> *I grabbed a handful of snow and ran onto the terrace, slammed the door shut, opened it and attempted to throw the snow at you. I lost my balance and my left hand went through the glass door. I had a deep gash shaped like a horseshoe. I still have the scar. Mom scolded me in the car all the way to the emergency room.*

Life became better after that. I don't think we've had a good fight since.

Six: *Old Time Religion*

Ours was a religious home, deeply religious, in the way of French Canadian Catholics. It was Old School: daughters were raised to be nuns, first sons to be priests, or at least brothers — guys in dresses, the male version of nuns. My father had been sent to a novitiate as a young boy, to take vows as a brother. He didn't quite make it to his final vows — the part that included celibacy for life — but that didn't dilute his religiosity.

Even Elaine got into the act in a way some years later, thanks to the urgings of the good nuns at Notre Dame Academy in Miami, where she finished her high school. As she tells it, when she was in the 11th grade, one of the nuns "harassed me almost daily to consider becoming a nun. She had me so upset that Dad went to the school and asked her to leave me alone." Years later, Elaine got revenge of a sort. She and a friend went to a Hallowe'en party dressed as pregnant nuns.

Our every meal began with "Grace" and was a family affair. Unless you count when one of us was sick or sent to our room without food because we'd refused to eat what was put in front of us, everyone was at the table at the appointed hour and stayed until the meal was finished. You did not start eating until Mom sat down. You ate everything on your plate. And if you didn't, that same dish of cold, uneaten dinner food was likely to be in front of you at breakfast the next morning.

And you were admonished to "save room for dessert."

Mom had some pretty finicky eaters to cater to, something Dad disapproved of. Ronald insisted on putting ketchup on everything. I wanted mustard. We each seemed to have a few things we'd refuse to eat. I hated Boston baked beans, unless allowed to lather them with mustard. With Elaine it was ham. Mom would fix her a hamburger if the rest of us were eating ham — until Dad put a stop to that and sent Elaine to her room when she refused to eat the ham.

Ice cream was relatively easy. Elaine wanted strawberry, Ronald wanted chocolate, I wanted vanilla. So Mom bought those three-flavored boxes of "Neapolitan" ice cream that had a slab of each, and we each got the flavor we wanted. A tiny bit of our flavor accidentally ending up on someone else's plate, of course, was grounds for sibling warfare.

During Advent and Lent, every evening before bed, we all five went down on our knees and recited the rosary, in French. Conveniently, the rosary has five decades, so we each got to lead one decade. "Leading" meant you said the first half of the decade's *Our Father*, 10 *Hail, Marys* and final *Glory Be* and the rest of the family said the response half. Heaven forbid if you knelt in a slouch. And Dad would make an issue of it if we were "reciting" instead of "saying" the rosary. "Reciting" meant rote repetition of sounds, not even words, clearly indicated by a droning monotone. "Saying" meant meaning the words we said. I confess I did much more reciting than saying, albeit in a well practiced reverential murmur.

St. Louis de France was not only our Catholic school but our Catholic church, side by side, and French. Well, French and English, but mostly French. The Portuguese were Catholics, too, but they had their own church, St. John of God. Our nuns spoke French. The Portuguese didn't have any nuns that I ever saw, and they attended public schools.

We were made to memorize the catechism, in French. Sometimes, Dad would question me from the catechism, speaking out the questions and asking me for the responses.

"Who made you?"

"God made me."

"Why did God make you?"

"God made me to love comma honor comma and obey Him."

And so on. When I spoke the answers, I insisted on getting every single word right, even speaking out the punctuation. That made Dad furious. He'd demand to know if I understood the answers I was giving, to tell him the answers in my own words. I told him the nuns didn't want us to give answers in our own words. They wanted us to be able to write it down precisely as it was written in the catechism book, punctuation and all. His temper would explode out of frustration, but he couldn't argue with the near-perfect grades I was bringing home with my memorized answers.

Most importantly, the church was Dad's anchorage in the storms of life. Any problem he faced, he took to the priests at the church, the aging pastor, Msgr. Prevost, or his assistant, Father Boivin, the way other people today might consult a psychologist or family counselor.

It wasn't long before I was enrolled as an altar boy. I rather enjoyed the special attention I received for that. It was I who got to walk out and around the altar lighting candles for all the congregation to see, and I who brought the water and wine to the priest. It was a rather honorable role to play, I thought. But it did mean being early to Mass every Sunday (altar boys' duties included helping the priest put on his vestments back in the sacristy) and even serving early Mass most weekday mornings, sometimes at dawn. It also meant you got wax on your cassock, that big black floor-length dress they made us wear, which in turn meant bringing it home so Mom could suck the wax out of the fabric with a brown paper bag and a flatiron (steam irons weren't invented yet).

One Sunday after Mass, during my fourth-grade year, we were gathered on the front steps of the church and, as adults are wont to do, someone tousled my hair (I was still a curly blond then) and asked something like, "Young man, what do you want to be when you grow up?"

"A priest," I said, without having given it a whole lot of thought.

I looked up to see how my father was taking the news and found the biggest, brightest all-consuming smile on his face I think I'd ever seen on him, before or since. I had discovered how to please him! More important for me, the great ding-dong of destiny had sounded somewhere in the distance and my own fate was sealed for at least a decade to come. Birthday and Christmas gifts became miniature altars and chalices and monstrances and all the other paraphernalia of Mass. The communion hosts, in order to fit into the miniature chalice, were holes punched out of white paper. They tasted awful.

There was no longer any escape. I was branded. At least that is how I remember it. If someone else has a better version, I'm willing to consider it. Not that I sought escape from my fate. As I said, I rather liked the special attention I received. Altar boy. God's chosen acolyte. Anointed.

None of which stopped me from joining in, even provoking, schoolyard fights. I learned fairly early that big boys try to dominate little boys. They were bullies, by and large. I also learned that, little as I was, the smallest in my class, and skinny to the point of emaciation, I could outrun most of the others. Then I discovered I could pick a fight with a bigger boy just to prove I wasn't afraid of him, then run like hell before he could get a good swing at me. More than once I jumped on a big boy's back when he wasn't looking, pummeled him as rapidly as I could, then leaped off and ran for safety.

Those episodes usually ended with a nun grabbing my arm or ear and dispatching me to find Father Boivin at the rectory next door to confess my sin immediately. Those nuns didn't mess around. Often enough there was a detention period tacked on to my school day, too, but as punishment, that didn't compare to the mortification of having to knock on the rectory door and tell the priest you had to confess something, immediately, no waiting, because otherwise you were absolutely positive that if you didn't make it back to school alive, you were going to Hell.

I especially remember overhearing an adult conversation at our house. I'm pretty sure my mother and father were there, plus a few relatives. They were discussing some mutual relative who didn't believe in God and were wondering aloud how that had come to pass. Apparently he had been brought up with the same rigid rules and doctrines as the rest of us. I have no idea who they were talking about, but it was clearly a "he." Someone remarked, "He reads too much." Someone else said something about "thinking too much about what he reads." Reading and thinking, apparently, could destroy your soul.

That didn't make much sense to me at the time, but it wasn't long before a perceptive adult might have noticed my wandering down that same path to perdition. Because it was at about this same time that I discovered words. Not just that they existed; I'd been saying and reading and studying words for years. But I'd discovered their *power*, especially their power over me. I was reading a novel. It was *Bomba the Jungle Boy Among the Pygmies*, one of a series of 20 titles for young boys written by Roy Rockwood during the 1930s. Around page 50, I think — for some reason page 57 sticks in my mind — I ran into a word way too long for me to recognize or pronounce and brought it to my father. His English was still fairly rudimentary. He handed me a dictionary and said, "Look it up."

That word was "enthusiastic." I fell in love with that word. I think I went around being enthusiastic about everything, from my breakfast of bread lathered with marshmallow fluff and strawberry preserves to the fireflies at night, for days, maybe weeks. But mostly, I'd fallen in love with all words. And here, in this one book, the dictionary, were all the words you could possibly imagine. That dictionary opened up a whole new world for me. You could weave pictures and dreams and wondrous stories just by manipulating words. You could play with them and make rhymes; whether nonsense or not, rhymes had value. At least it seemed so to me. I decided that whatever else I would do in life,

I'd write words. I'd make up stories and write whole books full of words. They became my magic carpet.

From then on, joining the child-sized altar paraphernalia at birthdays and under the Christmas tree, along with the obligatory cowboy pistols and cowboy hats and Erector Set and other necessities of youth, came the books. Asked what I wanted for Christmas, I invariably said, "Books." They came in stacks of four and five and six at a time. One Christmas, perhaps when I was 10 or 11 and in my horse-and-boy phase, one of the books that showed up under the Christmas tree was something called *Laddie*. Dad had bought it for me. He figured Laddie must be a dog, sort of a male version of Lassie. Maybe that would get me off my fixation on horses. About 10 pages or so in, I found no mention of a dog, but an awful lot of kissing and hugging between this Scottish girl and her boyfriend, whom she called Laddie. I asked my father if he'd bothered to read any of it before giving it to me. Of course he hadn't.

I told him I wasn't interested in it, and I really wasn't; girls weren't on my radar screen — yet.

Life was good, but not quite that good — yet.

Seven: Tiny

We almost always had a pet. I remember a pet turtle – one of those little box turtles you put in a dish. It died young, I think. And I used to like to catch fireflies in a bottle. We generously poked holes in the lids so they could breathe while they lit up our nights. Ants were also fun. You could trap a whole bunch of red ants in one bottle, and a whole bunch of black ants in another bottle, and put them together. They would go to war. Literally. Were we learning about racism? I suppose so, in some subconscious way. We just thought it strange how they'd do that. (It would take a lot more years before I'd become conscious of real racism – and then it would hit me like a bomb going off in my heart.)

Mostly, I remember Tiny.

To get to the story of Tiny, that bravest and most foolhardy of little dogs (we called him Tiny for a reason), you have to meet his precursors.

First there was the cat. I have no idea what it's gender or name was. I have no personal recollection of this beast other than what I was told later, still in childhood and impressionable. It appears that as a toddler I liked to play with the cat. It took exception to my playful tugging on its tail, mistaking it for torment, and attacked me. In the face. Considering this a major hazard to the future of their first son, my parents had the beast "put to sleep," as they used to say. I've believed ever since that that feline mauling was the keystone of my belief that cats are not to be trusted, that they only pretend to be domesticated, that in their hearts they are all tigers and panthers, jungle beasts just waiting for the right moment to show their true colors and strike at their human captors. Since then, cats have had great difficulty winning my tolerance, much less my affection. Goldie, of course, was the exception. She, at least, was benign. She had the added benefit of being owned by my daughter and her family.

Dogs are a different matter entirely. You can trust a dog. The first was Fluffy. She followed Elaine home from school one day. As Elaine tells it, she hid Fluffy in the cellar until she could get up the nerve to tell Dad. After that act of courage, Fluffy was clearly hers. We determined (don't ask me how) that she was part Spitz and part Pomeranian. I, of course, had no idea what any of that meant.

Elaine loved dogs before any of the rest of us did, and still does. The older and more sickly, it seems, the more determined she is to have her love for them make the difference in their lives. Fluffy was Elaine's. It was understood. Even Fluffy seemed to understand it. She tagged around behind Elaine wherever she went. She had fun with the rest of us, but a special bond existed with Elaine. When we walked through the forest to the Bark Street School for those summer movies, Fluffy was sure to be trotting along with us. She was especially appreciated on the walk back, when that forest turned into a deep primeval jungle.

Then, one night, as Fluffy tagged along beside us, she simply disappeared into the woods. We never saw her again.

"Dogs know," Dad explained. "She didn't want to trouble you. She knew it was her time to go, and so she went off to do it alone."

We all took it hard, but Elaine clearly hardest of all.

So that winter, Dad bought Queenie, a mere pup, and put her under the Christmas tree for Elaine. Queenie was Elaine's until many years later, when she married and her husband, Bill Lhota, refused to take the dog. He suggested she give Queenie to Mom. Queenie became Mom's constant companion for the rest of her long life.

When Queenie came of age, Dad had her bred with another terrier. But Queenie was a fox terrier, and her mate for the day was a toy terrier. We, of course, were too young and innocent to be allowed to view this act of nature that every farm child sees routinely. In due course, out came five puppies. They were all white with black faces and a black spot at their tales, like their mother. Four chubby, healthy puppies and one sickly teenie one, who had a lopsided black saddle on his back as well, no doubt inherited from his father along with his miniature size.

We sold the chubby pups easily, but no one wanted the little one. With parental permission, I declared him mine and named him Tiny. (I wasn't very original back then, I know. At least I didn't call him Spot!) Tiny was sickly, and I felt that it was my love for him that made him healthy. He didn't exactly grow up to be a dog-sized dog; his little skinny legs just grew a little longer. I don't think he ever weighed more than 3 or 4 pounds, if that. But that little doggie had heart. As the smallest kid in my class year after year, I guess it's easy in hindsight to see why I identified with that little thing. Nobody wanted him but me. That made him extra special.

Unfortunately, Tiny thought he was perhaps a German Shepherd or Collie, a breed used to herding beasts far bigger than himself. The only beasts around were the cars that occasionally drove down our street. He decided to herd those. Off he'd go at the approach of anything on wheels, running like hell and yapping at its wheels.

The inevitable happened one summer day, while I was away in Boston at a Braves game (yes, they played in Boston back then) with my Little League team, called the Swansea Braves. No one else went to Braves games back then, all fans preferring Ted Williams' Red Sox, which goes a long way to explaining why the Braves decamped for Milwaukee in the mid-1950s.

(For those who care about such things, I played first base for the Swansea Braves and actually made the all-star team a few times. I could catch and run, but my skinny arms could never throw the ball all the way to the infield from any outfield position, and even had trouble throwing across the infield. Think about it: the only player seldom called upon the throw the ball any distance with accuracy is the first baseman. That was for me.)

When I returned home from our field trip to Boston, I received the news: Tiny was at the vet's. He had chased a car and been hit. All his ribs were broken on one side.

Queenie and four of her pups. Tiny is the outcast at the left.

The vet had said if he made it through the night, he'd probably live, but the odds were against him. Altar boy that I was, with my direct pipeline to the Almighty, I stayed up all night praying for Tiny. And it worked. He made it!

Tiny was in a full-body cast for months. A few weeks after the cast came off, he chased another car down Hinsdale Street and was killed instantly. I vowed then and there that I would never have a pet again. I've kept that vow. The rules of life and death are that simple: Death, not good. Life, good.

Eight:
My Kingdom for a Horse!

One room in our house on Hinsdale Street was almost never used. It was called the "parlor." It had a set of plush chairs and sofa and a carpet of Persian design. The room was used when "polite company" was coming, a visit by a few aunts and uncles that wasn't sufficient to constitute a "party," which would require the rumpus room or, weather permitting, the back yard.

The parlor's only other purpose, as far as I could tell, was to serve as the path from our downstairs quarters (kitchen, den, parents' bedroom) to the kids' upstairs quarters, our two attic bedrooms. It also had the front door that opened onto the veranda, but absolutely no one ever came in that door that I can remember.

Behind the sofa was a glass-fronted rarity in our house: a book case. Its glass doors were always locked, the books behind the glass enticing but, as far as I could tell, unread. I managed to find the little key that opened the lock. "Find" suggests I was searching for it; the truth is I probably stumbled on it and surmised its purpose.

It fit the lock. Hidden behind the sofa, I pulled out one of the books and read. Not doing so had never been explained to me as one of the rules. Dad found me back there with the book in my lap and took it away abruptly. "You're not old enough for this," he told me. "Someday you will be, but not now."

He put it back in its glass case, re-locked the doors, and hid the key somewhere else that I never found.

That book was *The Wayward Bus*, by John Steinbeck. Not his best, but I didn't know that then. I vowed I would definitely read it to find out what was forbidden to an 11-year-old. I kept that vow, too, sometime in my 20s. It was my first Steinbeck novel, but certainly not my last. Since then, I've devoured every book Steinbeck ever wrote — the great and the not-so-great and the really awful. The author became my favorite for life. I've wondered at times whether I would have found Steinbeck so spellbinding had he not been declared forbidden fruit when I was 11.

I must say here, the movie of that novel, starring Jayne Mansfield, certainly moved me a lot more as a hormonally-driven younger man than it did when I saw it again much later in life. I'm sure that was due to her superlative bosom. It was only later that I learned she had an IQ to match, something she used on me the one time we met. But that was still years ahead.

Back to Hinsdale Street and the forbidden zone of the parlor. There was only one other important event that I know of that took place there. My father sat me down on its huge plush sofa one afternoon and positioned himself importantly in front of me to ask if I knew how babies were made. I shook my head, No. Which was true. I guess I was about 12 at the time, a very innocent 12.

He hemmed and hawed, circling the subject, until the telephone rang and he was called into the kitchen to take the call. "We'll talk about this later," he said as he retreated. We never did resume the conversation, if indeed it was a conversation. I guess I eventually found out on my own using the tried and true method of trial and error.

Innocent I may have been, but everyone kept telling me I was smart. I'd overhear adults talking about my grades, how easy my lessons came to me, how easy it was for me to get A's. At times I wanted to scream at them, "I study hard for those grades!" But mostly I just sat there lapping up the praise like whipped cream, as though it was something I truly deserved.

So I added "smart" to my assumed identity. My grades were good enough, at least starting in the 4th grade, with Sister Roberts and my discovery of the dictionary's wealth of words. I really liked Sister Roberts. For one thing she was small, like me. So I worked to please her, and I guess I succeeded.

I was entering my horse-and-boy reading phase around age 9, having left *Bomba the Jungle Boy* to gather dust. Now I was into the *Black Stallion* series of novels by Walter Farley. And, naturally, I wanted a horse.

Thus began the bait-and-switch game of horsemanship my father played with me. Yes, he was impressed by my grades in fourth grade, but 96 percent wasn't good enough. If I got 97 percent next year, he'd buy me a horse. So I got the 97 percent in fifth grade and he upped the ante to 98 percent. And so it went, year by year.

He did try to explain that we had no place to keep a horse. I suggested we convert the old chicken coop that was now my personal gym, albeit almost never used, into a stall for my horse, and he could always graze in what was our ball field out back. He didn't think that would work, especially in winter. Besides, how could I find time to take care of a horse?

It was an easy step from the *Black Stallion* to trying my own hand at writing a story about a boy and his dream horse. Mine was *The Winning Blood Bay Colt*. Not because I had any fixed notion of what a blood bay was, I just liked the sound of the words together. I wrote my boyish, convoluted tale, about novella length, in longhand on school paper.

Dad brought home an old typewriter from the mill and introduced me to it. It was an Underwood, and you really had to pound hard on the keys to make the letters reach the page on the roller. The machine had been retired from active duty. He told me that if I was going to write books, I had to learn how to type them. So I tried, first with two fingers, then with three or four. (I still do it that way. I never learned The Method. And I still pound the keys as though I'm still on that old Underwood, or one of its immediate successors.) He showed me how to type in folios, front and back, each folio eight sheets folded in half. Then he took my work product to a bookbinder and the next time I saw it, it was a book. An actual book of my words, with my name on it! The cover was, appropriately enough, red. Red leather, or something reasonably close. I was now an official writer. It didn't matter that only one copy was ever printed. It was a book, and my name was on it. I wonder whatever happened to it?

Perhaps as a consolation prize for not getting a horse, I was sent to summer camp a few of those years. I remember swimming in an ice cold lake, the "bug juice" (Kool-Aid) they served at every meal, the bugle blowing *Reveille, Taps,* and a military trumpet summons to meals that we called *Come and Get Your Chow, Boys*. I have no idea what its real name is. But mostly, I remember three things about that camp, especially my last summer there, the one after sixth grade.

The first memory is the horse. This was the first and only time I got to ride a full-sized horse in the woods, not one of those gentle little ponies they put little children on and lead around in circles on dirt tracks. I insisted on getting on the biggest horse I could find. He didn't like me on his back, apparently, because when I'd try to slow him down or turn him he'd pick up speed, then try to brush me off his back by running close to a tree. But I was a stubborn little thing. I refused to be brushed off, although after a short while one of the counselors swapped horses with me, putting me on a far less cantankerous animal.

(If you happened to have come across an oral history version of this event, I think I may have embellished it a little for several people and said the counselor swapped horses with me only after I was thrown off mine. As I said at the outset, I'm trying to be truthful here. And the truth is I'm not entirely sure which version is the truth, so I offer both. Take your pick. The real truth is that Tiny and I had a lot in common.)

The second memorable thing about that summer camp is a baseball game. Only a few innings into the game, as I went up to bat, the coach signaled me to let the first pitch go by. He wanted the kid already on first base to steal second. But that pitch was *so juicy ripe*, I just had to swing at it. I did, and it sailed. It wasn't quite a home run, but the kid on first scored and I made it to third base. The coach immediately benched me and put a substitute on base in my place. I had to sit out the rest of the game for my disobedience. I still say I was right, unless you factor in the notion that as coach, he was boss.

The third and most vivid memory is the trip home with Dad, when he informed me he had had a talk with the nuns and priests at St. Louis de France. They'd all agreed I should skip the seventh grade and go directly into eighth. Needless to say, I swelled with pride. It went a long way toward dissolving the stings of the horse and baseball miscues.

What I didn't appreciate then, but soon recognized, is that the seventh and eighth grades were taught in the same room, just as all the earlier grades were paired at St. Louis. That meant I was sitting on one side of the classroom with eighth graders while my former classmates were relegated to the seventh-grade side. Not a situation designed to breed good fellowship.

The ensuing catcalls, jeers and snubs came to a head during the winter's first big snowfall. As I've said, Jeanine Babin was my chief competition for top grades. I think my grades had come in at 99 percent in sixth grade and hers at perhaps 98.6 percent. Somewhere in that range, anyway. Yet, here I was in eighth grade and she was across the room still stuck in seventh. She didn't like that one bit, and most of my neighborhood friends agreed with her that an injustice of cosmic proportions had been done.

It was a Saturday, I remember, because Dad was home. Hinsdale Street was newly blanketed in well-packed snow and the neighborhood kids were up the hill with their sleds, taunting me to come out and play. I knew what they really wanted was a target, because Jeanine was with them. I refused to go. Dad insisted I not back down. I needed to show them I wasn't afraid of them, he said. He was determined to make a man out of me.

Wrapped in leggings and winter coat and snow mask and mittens, I reluctantly made my way uphill. I guess I was about 25 feet away when the pelting started. Snowballs and, much more painful, ice balls. I'm pretty sure it was Jeanine who hit me on the back of the head with a perfectly thrown ice ball. I went home in tears, my pride hurt far more than my skull, and refused to go back out.

The only good thing I recall about skipping a grade was that, although I was the youngest in class, I was no longer the smallest. The eighth grade had a kid named Wilfred who was even shorter than I. We quickly became friends. He lived on a chicken farm. He explained procreation to me by describing how chickens "did it." The rooster, he said, pecked the hen on the neck repeatedly. That's how sex worked! As I said, trial and error.

I don't know how I managed to make it through that year with my brain, soul and self-respect intact, but I did. Somehow the animosity died down, if not my humiliation, because I had yet one more trial to get through, this one a revelation of my own fallibility.

The seventh and eighth grades were taught by Sister Claire, a massive woman and my sister's favorite nun. I wasn't so sure she was up to the caliber of Sister Roberts, although on one specific day she surely was. She was teaching us how to do averages. She passed out our grades for all our subjects and asked us to calculate our own averages for that segment of the year — I'm not sure if it was a monthly report card or the semi-annual report. I totaled up my grades, counted how many there were and did the division, as instructed. Shockingly, I came out with something in the low 70s. This was impossible! Not the smartest kid in the class, the one who had been allowed to skip a year!

I was hunched over my desk silently crying over this horrible thing that had happened to me. Sister Claire noticed — maybe I was visibly shaking — and came to my side. She quietly asked what the matter was and all I could do in my choked-up state was point to the answer on my piece of paper. She picked it up, did her swift re-calculation and found my mistake: I'd divided by too high a number, miscounting how many grades I was averaging by including the total line as well as the individual items in the added list. She patted me on the head like a little dog and moved on. Mortified again!

But my average had held up just fine. Life was good again. And at the end of the year, I graduated, right there in the front row with the smallest kids.

St. Louis de France graduating class of 1953, with Father Boivin. I'm in front, second from the right. Wilfred is at my left.

Nine: No More Nuns

So it was that I arrived in high school prematurely. We didn't have "middle school" and "junior high school" back then. Just "elementary" followed by the leap into "high" school after the eighth grade. St. Louis de France was a mere bike ride from home. Msgr. Prevost High was two bus rides away, on the far outskirts of Fall River. I was reaching out into the "real" world. The bus carried me past Lafayette Park every day. I was told the young French general, the Marquis de Lafayette, who came to George Washington's rescue during the American Revolution, had camped there once. (I should note here that the Marquis and I share a birthday, albeit almost two centuries apart.) My companion on those long bus rides through Fall River was — Wilfred.

I discovered that I much preferred being taught by men in robes than women in robes. Somehow, the Christian Brothers at Prevost High seemed to have a greater respect for an individual's cerebral activity. Not that they were free-thinkers or anything approximating that. As doctrinaire about matters as nuns, the brothers were at least willing to discuss matters with you. To a point.

I was entered into the school's freshman year oratorical contest. There was some discussion, as I recall, whether I should enter in the French-speaking competition or the English. I had to write a speech in each language. Although born into a French-speaking family, by now my English had overtaken French. My English draft was apparently superior to my French so I was enrolled in the English competition. The speech was about a 1928 fire that had destroyed much of Fall River. It was good enough to land me in the regional competition, where I had to write a speech on a different topic.

This was 1954. The newspapers were full of headlines trumpeting the word "communism" and the name of Sen. Joe McCarthy. *I Led Three Lives* was among the most popular TV series, about a double-agent FBI guy posing as a Communist to infiltrate and expose treasonous cells right here in the U.S. of A. At 13, I wasn't yet ready to tackle national political controversy, but I sure wondered what this communism stuff was all about. I decided to research it and do my speech about it. My "research" amounted to looking up the word in the Encyclopedia Britannica my father had bought us. From that, I deduced that early Christians, hiding in the catacombs under Rome, were communists, that many social movements had been started by communes, and that as a principle it sounded pretty good to me that those who had much should share it with those who had little.

The good brothers took one look at what I turned in and brought me in for, shall we say, friendly consultation. In essence, they instructed me to rewrite the speech to discuss how the Soviet Union had twisted the concept and that modern communism was anti-God, anti-American, anti-free enterprise, just about anti-everything-noble-and-good anybody in his or her right mind could believe in. Communists were going to roast in hell, no question. I thought enough of this event to save both versions of the speech. They exist today, buried somewhere among my scrapbooks. They don't read that dramatically dissimilar today, but back then, I felt the sharp sting of censorship, even if I didn't yet know what to call it.

This was also the first time that my name appeared in a newspaper, unless some scribe thought to record my birth, which I sincerely doubt. There was a photo of the regional winners (not including me), and a list of the also-rans, which did. It was a start.

Shakespeare asked, What's in a name? Not much, I decided. Until now I'd been called by my full first name, Richard. When New Englanders pronounced it, especially members of my family calling me for dinner or to berate me about some misbehavior, it came out sounding like "Rich—*id*!" I didn't like the sound. I knew I'd been named after my Uncle Dick, my mom's brother. I also knew that all my friends had nice, simple, single-syllable names — Joe and John and Frank and Bob. I wanted one, too. I declared that henceforth I wanted to be called Dick.

It was not the last time I would opt for a name change.

Dad went to Miami during my first year in high school. He had had excruciating back pains. They'd diagnosed spinal arthritis and put him in a full-torso cast. I was among those he asked to poke a back-scratcher down inside his cast at the neck to ease the itching. Nothing seemed to help. The doctors finally advised him to go rest in a warmer climate. His older brother, Adelard, now lived in Miami, so Dad went to visit him.

He wrote back that he was feeling wonderful again and doing gardening, his first love. He blamed his pain on office work, sitting behind his desk at the mill, taking responsibility for everyone and everything there. He said in Florida, all you had to do was poke a stick in the ground, any old stick, and it would grow and flower and multiply. He'd decided to move us there.

I didn't know much about Florida, but I knew one thing: it didn't snow there. I knew if we moved there I would never again have to put up with gray slush, shoveling snow, or dealing with the dank frigid wetness of winter. No more snow plows and sand trucks and ice balls. I was thrilled.

Life was good.

Our last family reunion before moving to Florida in June, 1954

Ronald (l) and I are kneeling. Queenie, in front of me, has her backside to the camera. Dad, Mom and Elaine are directly behind us. Marthe is looking over Elaine's shoulder, and Gary is in back, second from the right.

Ten: *Heading South*

We couldn't leave New England without one last family reunion. The Hébert clan gathered in Swansea in June 1954. Cousin Gary and his folks came from New York. So did Aunt Marianne and Charley Blais. Most of the others came from Québec. It was a double ceremony, not only to see us off to Florida, but also to celebrate the Silver Wedding Anniversary of Dad's sister, Gerardine, and Albert Labrie, who lived in Montreal. They came with our cousins, Marthe and Ivar. The Cloutiers (Antoinette and Albert who had inherited the family hotel) came from Thetford Mines.

The anniversary was celebrated with a feast at a nearby private club, or maybe it was a restaurant. We took over a banquet hall, as I recall. The next day, everyone gathered at our home on Hinsdale Street.

One of the cousins, Yvon Cloutier, made a home movie of the event that I still have. We all danced ring-around-the-rosy-style around the big "Welcome" rock at the front corner of our yard. Later, we posed for a group photo in front of the other street-side boulder. Ronald and I are kneeling on the ground. I'm in front of Elaine, and looking over her shoulder is Marthe. Little did I know then that in a few short years, Marthe would begin to figure prominently in my life. In front of me, butt to the camera, is Queenie.

Then, our old Hudson drove off towing Dad's trailer with all our belongings. Only Dad, Ronald and I were in the car. Elaine and Mom were flying; we'd meet them in Miami.

I remember only one thing about that long drive to the southern tip of the country. At some point during the night, I awoke from a deep sleep on the back seat to hear my father shouting:

"*Levez-vous! Débarquez-vous. Vite! Vite!*" When excited, he always lapsed into French. "Get up! Get out! Hurry! Hurry!"

He had smelled smoke. We leaped out and he rummaged through the luggage in the trunk until he found a smoldering cloth that apparently had been tucked up against the wiring of the taillights. Disaster averted, we continued on our way.

Miami Beach was all I had hoped for and more. Palm trees and flowers, hot sand and hotter summer sidewalks. That first summer we rented a home at 1228 Euclid Avenue, in the section now famous worldwide as South Beach. Back then it was a weathered neighborhood of retired old folks, the women mostly with white hair tinted blue or pink, the men in brightly checkered Bermuda shorts. A block behind us was the municipal swimming pool in Meridian Park. About a half dozen blocks in the other direction was the widest, longest beach I had ever seen, and the ever-rolling ocean.

Dad worked as the gardener at Joe Hart's bay-front estate, a walled and gated palatial home. Joe Hart (I don't think anyone dared call him Joseph Hart, for obvious reason) owned the Castaways Motel and a string of restaurants called Pickin' Chicken. We kids were put to work on weekends going through parking lots putting Pickin' Chicken flyers on car windshields. Elaine had an even more formal job. She was dressed in red-and-white shorts and top and handed out Pickin' Chicken flyers along Lincoln Road and Collins Avenue. College boys loved teasing her. One day she passed out from too much sun. The man who brought her home was a bartender at a local strip joint and wanted to take her out. She was 17. Dad said no.

Joe Hart's place had a dock on Biscayne Bay. Dad suggested I go with him one day and fish from the dock while he did his work. All the fishing I'd done before this was in a pond in Swansea, catching 4- and 5-inch perch and pickerel, plus those few times going for eel in the creek with Norman Caron.

Something took my bait. Something *really* big. I pulled and reeled but it didn't want to budge. I thought I might have snagged a tire, as I'd seen in cartoons. Slowly the "tire" came toward me, my fishing rod bent almost in two. Then I saw it: it was the most evil-looking creature I'd ever seen. It was waving its big antennae angrily at me. The creature from the Black Lagoon, perhaps? It seemed to weigh a ton and was huge, sitting there on the dock, still brandishing those antennae back and forth at me.

I shouted for my father. He informed me that what I'd caught was a Florida lobster. I had eaten lobster in Massachusetts. I knew a lobster's sweet briny taste, knew its claws and tender underbelly. This monster was nothing like that. And I had to extract my hook from that thing's mouth? Without warning, I kicked the lobster and my fishing rod overboard. I swore I would never fish those waters again!

I kept that promise, too. Even to the point of turning down a free deep sea fishing trip I won. The *Miami Beach Sun* was running a contest in which, each week, it published an aerial photograph of a city. If you were among the first few to send in the name of the city, you won a day's deep sea fishing charter. The photo a week or so before the lobster-catching episode matched the outlines of the coast at St. Augustine in our family atlas, so I sent that in. Soon after I'd sworn off fishing those waters, I was notified I'd won. I never went to collect my prize.

There's one thing about life in New England: not only didn't we know any Blacks, we hardly ever even thought about racism or racial matters. I think I must have been vaguely aware of the issues involved, the way I was aware that Mars was the red planet. It had little to do with us. What did have to do with us were the other "others" — foreigners. Mom readily talked about how the "dirty" Portuguese weren't like us. She even told me years later that when she first met Dad, she thought he had "just gotten off the boat." His English was poor, and he wore shirts with the sleeves simply torn off at the elbow when they wore through. She wrinkled her nose when she spoke of it, as at something vaguely odorous, her universal signal of disapproval. But Blacks? I don't know that we ever even met any. We saw them on the streets of Boston on our rare visits there, and of course saw the parodies on television, like Jack Benny's Rochester and Amos 'n' Andy. But that was it.

In Miami Beach, that all started to change.

That first summer, Dad's car broke down and he had to walk the several miles home from Joe Hart's place after a full day's work. He told us the "Whites only" city bus refused to pick him up because he was so darkly tanned, the driver thought he was "Negro," and the driver of the "Negro" bus refused to pick him up because he clearly wasn't Black.

We also learned that Blacks (the proper term for them back then was "Negro," although I was to start hearing its nastier variations before long) were unwelcome on Miami Beach after nightfall. They certainly didn't live there, even if they held menial jobs there during the daytime. The seed was planted that summer, but full awareness of the awfulness of racism was to bloom in me only later, when I was introduced to what's called the "Deep South."

Over time, the "dirty" Portuguese would morph into "dirty" Cubans, "dirty" Jews, and "dirty" everything else that wasn't "our kind." I never heard Dad talk like that, and I don't believe Mom was a racist or hated anyone, she was far too religious for that. But she had that streak of intolerance deeply ingrained in her and it showed every time she became upset about something that was "other."

    I think it was also that first summer, or not long afterward, that Dad took us to St. Augustine and I fell in love with the place. I loved the Castillo San Marco and the old cobbled streets, the nation's oldest schoolhouse and oldest jail. The whole city seemed like a fantasy world to my young eyes. By now, I'd seen Québec City with its parapets and cannons and the castle-like Chateau Frontenac, but this was something different, history on a livable scale. I thought I'd like to live there someday.

    We were still on Euclid Avenue, I think, when Ronald and I got new boxing gloves. Dad bought them because we were fighting all the time. One afternoon when we were getting into it yet again, he produced the gloves and ordered us to put them on. Then he said, "Okay, now start fighting." So we did as told, but that grew stale pretty quickly. When we stopped swinging wildly at each other, he ordered us to keep at it, no stopping. By the time he let us stop, we were both in tears, not from physical pain but from the humiliation of it, the needless swinging of tiny fists, the heavy gloves, the dead weight of our own arms and the pointlessness settling in.

    I think our sibling rivalry subsided considerably after that. Life was still getting better.

Eleven: Normandy Isle

Like most of the islands in Biscayne Bay, Normandy Isle is manmade. When they needed more land on which to put houses, they simply dredged up some bay bottom and dumped it behind a retaining wall. To give it class they called it Normandy and gave many of its streets French names. We didn't live on one of those streets. We were at 1355 Bay Drive, a white stucco house with two coconut palms in front, heavy with nuts. We could eat coconut whenever we had the tools and patience to open one. During hurricane season, the town came around and cut down all the coconuts. They could turn into deadly missiles in a storm.

Our island was on 79th Street Causeway, so named because it left Miami from 79th Street, although it was 71st Street at the Miami Beach end. When you crossed the last bridge of the causeway onto Normandy Isle, a large sign welcomed you to "Miami Beach, America's Playground." The next thing you saw on the right were side-by-side motels, the Sir Richard and the Sir Herbert. I felt honored, if misspelled.

Dad met the neighborhood kids first. He usually did. He loved kids and always reached out to them. He introduced us to our next door neighbors, Bobby and Sarah Mendelsohn. Bobby was about my age, Sarah was Ronald's. Now and then you'd hear opera seeping out of their house, across a vacant lot from ours, therefore they were "educated," in the way upper class people were. It didn't matter that Bobby's dad, Lou Mendelsohn, made his living selling eyeglass frames. If they listened to opera, they were upper crust. You never heard opera in our home.

What our house did have was a sun roof — an area where you could bake in the sun. We thought that kind of special until we realized that it was much too hot up on the roof to soak up rays. You didn't tan or even bake. You fried.

We moved in shortly before the school year began, and a big decision had to be made. Ronald, still in elementary school, would be attending St. Patrick's on 41st Street on Miami Beach. Elaine went to Notre Dame Academy, on Northeast Second Avenue in Miami. When I heard that nuns taught at St. Patrick's, I put my little foot down. Having tasted male instruction from the brothers at Prevost High, I asked if there wasn't a male-taught Catholic school around. Dad found two: Gesu, a Jesuit school in downtown Miami, and Archbishop Curley High, an all-boys' school on Northeast Second Avenue in Miami, taught by priests from various parishes, including ours, just a dozen blocks down the road from Elaine's school. Curley was two bus rides away. Gesu was considerably farther away and definitely more academically challenging. Curley it was, but I'd have to work to help pay the tuition.

Slowly, inexorably, life became stressful. It wasn't child's play anymore. At the dinner table, Dad would start barking at Mom. She'd sit there taking it, silently weeping, which made him angrier. He'd order her to stop crying, and she'd cry some more. Often it seemed to be about money. He wanted to spend it, she wanted to save it, and we never seemed to have enough of it.

We all worked to contribute to the family coffers. What we earned went into the common pot, from which we were doled out our allowances, a dollar or so a week as I remember. Dad was branching out now. He started his own landscape gardening business with several customers on the causeway islands, including Dr. Bowers across the street from us, who drove a huge Packard, one of those cars you never see anymore. We'd see Dad pacing back and forth behind his lawn mower, a lit cigarette in his mouth, humming music to himself that only he understood. He always hummed while he worked, a smallish man with boundless energy, an indefatigable life force.

Once, while I was helping him in Dr. Bowers' yard, sweeping the driveway of grass cuttings or clearing debris from under a hedge, he called me to the back yard and asked me to envision two bushes set just so, there and there. What did I think of the idea? I told him I couldn't picture them, he'd have to go ahead and plant them and then I'd be able to tell him if I thought they looked okay. Wise-ass teenager alert! He sent me back to sweeping or pulling dead stuff from behind the hedges, clearly disappointed in his son.

Another thing I remember about Dr. Bowers' house: it was on the water, and from his sea wall you could watch fish, great schools of them, scurrying back and forth, especially when a barracuda came to feed. I thought that old barracuda was just about the most ferocious animal I'd ever seen, or at least a close second to that monster Florida lobster I'd hauled onto Joe Hart's dock.

Mr. Traub, next door to Dr. Bowers, was also one of Dad's customers. He had two cars — an El Dorado Cadillac and a Jaguar, both white. For a while I had the job of wiping them down each morning at daybreak, before heading to school, so old Mr. Traub would have a sparkling clean, unspotted-by-dew choice of cars to climb into. On Saturdays, I washed and waxed both cars.

Dad also took care of the yard at our parish church, St. Joseph's, drove its schoolbus, sang in its choir, and enrolled Ronald and me in its altar boy corps. We served Mass for Msgr. Rocket, a raging bull of a man with a big voice and a reputation for imbibing a bit too much alcohol, and not just the altar wine. What I remember most about him are the veins in his forehead, two of them popping out and branching up his brow like subcutaneous antlers.

Mom felt she should go to work, too. Dad would hear nothing of it. Elaine went to work running the elevator at the Empress Hotel on the Beach. Ronald sold newspapers each evening at a busy street corner. He also eventually got a job as a cabana boy at a local beachfront hotel. I delivered newspapers by bicycle in the morning before school, and worked weekends with Dad mowing lawns, weeding flower beds, cleaning the deck of the yacht of yet another of his customers, and washing Mr. Traub's El Dorado and Jaguar. It was also my job and Ronald's to empty out Dad's trailer of each day's mowings, weedings and prunings onto a compost pile next to the sea-grape tree behind our house.

At Curley High, I stayed a half hour after school each day to clean the cafeteria, my contribution to help pay tuition in order to avoid being taught by nuns. One year, during Christmas break, I stripped and re-varnished desks in one classroom. That's when I discovered the amazing properties of warm Coca-Cola. I'd left a bottle of it standing open while I worked on the desktops with varnish remover. I forgot about it until I accidentally knocked it over. By the time I found rags to wipe up the mess, it had done a better, faster job of removing old varnish than I was doing with professional solvent. I stopped drinking Cokes and started using it on the desks. Later, Gary told me that's what they used to clean acid deposits from jeep batteries in the Army. I don't think I've drunk a Coke since.

One afternoon, I rode my bike to the country club on the island adjoining ours and asked some men in bright shirts and checkered pants if I could have a job caddying. They laughed at me. They said the golf bags were bigger than me; how could I possibly hope to carry them around the golf course? They thought I was cute to ask, though.

I left with their laughter ringing in my head, vowing never to play golf, ever. That's another vow I've kept.

Instead, Dad got me an after-school job making deliveries for Home Mart, a mom-and-pop hardware store where he was a regular customer. By then I was 15 and had my learner's driving permit — daytime only, and only if a licensed adult driver was in the car with me. The owners of the store had their housemaid meet me at the store each afternoon after school to ride around in their 1956 Chevrolet station wagon as I made the rounds of warehouses to pick up buckets of paint, bags of cement, kegs of nails and other materials. Then I did the deliveries to customers, often carrying on my puny little shoulder stuff that clearly outweighed a silly old bag of golf clubs.

Dad also organized a baby-sitting enterprise. He had flyers printed up and Elaine distributed them from her elevator at the Empress Hotel. Our targets were families who brought their small children with them on vacations. Dad babysat, Elaine babysat, and even I served as backup babysitter on occasion – but never with infants still in diapers, thank goodness. One night, walking home from babysitting after midnight when the city buses no longer ran, I was stopped about five blocks from home by a policeman. He wanted to know what I was doing out so late, so I told him. I don't think he believed me. Instead, he put me in the back seat of his patrol car like a prisoner and took me home. Dad answered the door and verified my story. I don't think I was asked to babysit at night again, ever.

After a year or so, I swapped the job at Home Mart for that of bagboy at the Food Fair supermarket across the street, where Mom had finally convinced Dad to let her work as a cashier. We had a great system going there for a while. Dad drove the schoolbus and knew all the children's mothers. They all shopped at Food Fair, so he told them to look for me: they would go to Mom's register and ask that I bag their groceries and help them out to the parking lot. They tipped me lavishly. The other bag boys got wind of what we were doing and complained. I was taken off that job and assigned to stocking shelves. No tips for that work, of course, although it did represent a salary increase – maybe 50 cents an hour.

Normandy Isle life was not all work and no play. Bobby Mendelsohn came up with a scheme to build a raft and go fishing for sand dollars. We pooled resources one summer and turned it into quite an enterprise, diving for sand dollars from the raft. These we bleached in the sun and Bobby stuck little palm-tree decals on them. Then we walked the beach selling "Sand Dollars" to tourists for a dollar apiece.

He called the raft the *Deep-Sea-Doodle*. It shipwrecked in a storm a few years later, while anchored at Baker's Haulover.

Gary and his family came to visit. He and I went to the then new Fontainebleau Hotel, the ritziest place on the beach. I wanted to show it off. In blue jeans and tee shirts, we sauntered through the front doors and through the main lobby. I was looking for the Boom Boom Room when a guard stopped us in a hallway and told us to "leave the way you came in." We about-faced and started back toward the main lobby and front door. The guard thought we were being typically contrary teenagers and marched us to a back door instead. It's not everyone who can say they were kicked out of the Fontainebleau for minding their own business.

On the beach with Gary, now a GI

At some point I started visiting the Mendelsohns next door on Sunday mornings after we arrived home from Mass. I think Bobby invited me the first time, and I simply started inviting myself after that, not because of Bobby but because of his father, Lou. For one thing, I discovered I liked bagels with cream cheese and lox and big slabs of onion and tomato. But even more, I was fascinated by the conversation at their table. There was no shouting or crying, but instead a great deal of discussion about serious matters – world affairs, war and peace, political fortunes made and broken. Lou Mendelsohn talked about these things with me as though I were an adult. Bobby was bored silly by such matters, but I couldn't wait for each Sunday's fresh installment.

Bobby's father also taught me another lesson of value. It had to do with hustling pool. I'd gotten into the habit of stopping off a few times a week at a pool room in Little River for a half hour or so between school and reporting for work at the hardware store. I was not proficient at shooting pool by any means, but reasonably good for my age, I guess. Peewee, the proprietor, pulled me aside one day and said I was good enough that we could maybe both make a little change. He'd let me run a few racks for free and give me a sign when a likely pigeon came in, somebody he thought I could beat and who'd be willing to place a few bets on the games. We'd split the winnings. I had to make sure to lose a game or two and never blow the guy away, always make the other guy think that but for one unlucky shot he could have won. In a word, Peewee taught me hustling. We played for quarters and yes, I made some pocket change. Mostly it was fun — the challenge, not the profit — that motivated me.

I must have told Bobby about my exploits and he must have passed the information on to his father. One day, Lou Mendelsohn suggested we go shoot some eight-ball. Every rack we shot he won with some lucky shot. I knew if I kept at it I could beat him, but I never did. We started playing for quarters. My pockets gradually emptied of all the money I carried, which wasn't much. Then Lou explained that he had learned to shoot pool in Brooklyn, from professionals. He told me he had hustled me, that no matter how often I tried, I'd never beat him because he'd always manage to be just enough better to win but keep me believing I could. He gave me back my money and said he hoped I'd learned my lesson. I don't think I ever played pool for money again, thanks to Lou Mendelsohn.

My literary life was branching out as well. Now grown out of my horse-and-boy phase, I was into science fiction. Both Ronald and I had been fascinated by stars and planets and rocket ships for several years, dating back to Swansea when we'd had a refractor telescope made from a kit. We had a star map and knew most of the constellations and could track the major planets. One night I had even taken a time-exposure photo of the heavens, rigging up a device to hold the box camera's shutter open for a half hour or so. Dad took the film in to be developed. When it came back, they said they'd thrown it away because nothing came out, just white streaks across a black background. Which was exactly what it was supposed to show — the stars' paths through time!

Out of this fascination with the heavens came another pretty awful novel, this one about a trip to Venus where all manner of beasts rampaged, all oddly terrestrial in eating and breathing habits in what I've since learned is a very toxic environment.

This extra-terrestrial fascination also produced back-to-back regional Science Fair projects. One year I built a planetarium inside a big windowed box. It had no sun, because if done to scale, the sun would have had to be bigger than the box itself for the planets to be even visible. So around the imaginary center, in perfect concentric circles, twirled little balls in unison — clay for smaller planets, various other balls for the larger ones, all relatively sized, more or less, and painted appropriately: Venus was yellow, Earth was blue and green, Mars was red, etc. Saturn had cardboard rings that I'd attached to a rubber ball with toothpicks. There were no asteroids. All planets hung from a disc in the ceiling, being turned by an Erector Set electric motor concealed on the roof of the box. As a true model of the planetary system, it left a lot to be desired.

The following year I built a plastic rocket ship, a three-stage affair. It was made of transparent tubes of plastic with fake fuel cells inside. When you turned the crank to make it rise from its platform, by turns lights went off on a display panel to explain each stage firing and then being jettisoned. I think I won an honorable mention for this educational toy. Rocket science was definitely not destined to be my strong suit. But life was lots of fun; life was good.

Twelve: High School Hi-Jinks

Tony Capodicasa arrived at Curley High as a senior when I entered my junior year. He was unique, to say the least. When I first met him at the bus stop leaving school (he also lived on Miami Beach and took the same buses I did), he was dressed in suit and tie, complete with a fedora. Later, as the cooler winter weather set in, he wore a topcoat! Not a trenchcoat, but an honest-to-goodness fancy wool topcoat. Nobody, but absolutely nobody, dresses like that in high school! Not now, not then. And certainly not in Miami!

He told me his name meant "head of the house" in Italian, that he'd been born and raised in an apartment upstairs from a bar in Buffalo, New York, but that his mother had divorced his father there and they'd moved to Arizona. (I never thought to ask him if he'd happened to run into a kid in Arizona named Billy Cain.) His mother had remarried, to a man named Patti, who was some kind of big shot in the Teamsters Union. The union and its leaders, particularly Dave Beck and Jimmy Hoffa, were being investigated for mafia connections by a Senate "rackets committee" in Washington, D.C., and Mr. Patti's pension and other assets had been frozen. Before he was caught up in the investigation, however, he'd had the foresight to transfer title to his car and some other assets to Tony's name. So the big gray Buick Tony drove was technically his. That made him practically an adult in my eyes.

Tony took great pride in all of this, in his Sicilian roots and mafia connections, however tenuous. He was a revolutionary at heart, his favorite expression for all eventualities simply, "Come the revolution...."

My friendship with Tony approached the level of blood kinship, a level I don't think I ever achieved with other friends. We were inseparable. A year older, he had a car and could drive unsupervised. Dad met and trusted him, probably because Tony dressed impeccably and had the manners to go with his attire. Dad approved whenever we went out together, alone or on double dates. We often hung out at an A&W drive-in drinking root beer floats, where our car hop was usually Fannie. Tony dubbed her "Short Fat Fanny" after a then popular Little Richard song. She was short, but in no way was she fat. She was actually quite cute in a petite sort of way.

Tony was dating a redhead named Ruth, and I was dating Mary Ellen Mueller, my first "steady." Dates amounted to little more than school dances supervised by nuns at the all-girls Notre Dame High, an occasional movie, and a little (very little) petting. Tony was a smooth, accomplished dancer. Compared to him I had two left feet. He helped me get over that, showing me steps, teaching me confidence, even bravado. I never did quite master the art of braggadocio, though – something he had in ample supply. I remember one particular dance at which, after the first few bars, he, Ruth, Mary Ellen and I were the only ones on the dance floor, swirling back and forth in an improvised tango (very, very improvised, I must add) as everyone else watched in amazement (or so we believed).

To me, the hardest part of dancing was always walking across that vast empty wasteland of dance floor to ask a girl to dance, risking rejection. Why did all the girls always stay on the other side of the room, I wondered? Did they find safety in numbers there? Perhaps I started going steady with Mary Ellen so I'd have somebody to dance with and not have to make that public display of being rejected, crossing back to my small cluster of male friends alone, certain everyone else was watching my every humiliated step.

With Tony & Dad's 1955 Buick

Mary Ellen was nice if a little chubby, but the one I really pined for was Tim Baker's sister, Patsy. Unfortunately, she was dating a guy named Terry Andros. Tim's father, a house painter, took a liking to me for some reason, and he didn't like the idea of his daughter going steady with this Terry guy. He ordered her to date someone else between dates with Terry, and I became the default. Just once. It was a less than romantic occasion. That's all I recall of that date. I don't think I even got a goodnight kiss.

The only other girl I "dated" during high school was Mary Lou, with whom I went late in my senior year after breaking up with Mary Ellen, reminded all too often that I'd soon be heading for the seminary. I relapsed into dating with Mary Lou mostly because she had very large breasts. The only other girl I remember was a steamy, torrid, one-night escapade with the daughter of some Fall River friends who had come to visit my parents. By then I had a full driver's license and told everyone we were going to a party at Tim Baker's house, then alerted Tim to the deceit. We wound up parking at a well-known "lover's lane" on the causeway, a good vantage point for "watching submarine races," it was said. But it seemed that every car that pulled in to jockey for a parking place was a two-toned Pontiac that looked an awful lot like her parents'. We were so nervous we soon left and found a secluded lot behind some apartment construction. That's where the police car interrupted our teenage explorations and sent us home. I'm not sure I even remember her name. It may also have been Ruth.

Dad's disciplinary hand, so swift and certain in Swansea, became compassionate as I made my way through high school.

There was the "stolen car" incident, for example. It was Frenchy's car, and he'd given me permission, so it wasn't really car theft. He was renting the back room of our house on Bay Drive and also worked at Food Fair. He told me if I needed it I could use his car to go to school, for example if I missed my ride. The car was a 1950 Ford, stripped of all handles and fixtures on the outside — a fad back then meant to make the car look suped-up. He showed me how to open the trunk by pulling a cable beside the driver's seat, and how to hot-wire the car if I needed it and didn't have the key.

I took the car to school only once. After school, Tim Baker, who had a similarly customized 1949 Ford, challenged me to a drag race up Second Avenue. Away we went on squealing tires. I had to slow down behind a truck and Tim zoomed on past, just before the squad car stopped me, at the bus stop in front of Notre Dame Academy, of all places, where both Mary Ellen and Patsy and all the other Academy girls were waiting for their bus. Thus it was that practically all the girls I knew watched as the police frisked and handcuffed me and put me in the back seat of their cruiser, then searched Frenchy's car, figuring out how to open the trunk themselves. They found I had hot-wired the car, therefore it must be stolen. In the trunk they found a considerable amount of radio and hi-fi equipment, also presumed stolen.

I sat in juvenile detention for hours until Dad could come to claim me and tell the police the truth, with Frenchy's backing. There were no remonstrations, no penalties. I guess Dad understood I had learned my lesson without his having to say anything. I was, again, appropriately mortified.

The geometry class confrontation happened my junior year. Father Dolan, our teacher, was explaining on the chalkboard a problem that we'd had in our previous night's homework. I raised my hand to ask a question about his seemingly circuitous route to the answer just as a visiting priest entered the room. The visitor insisted that we not interrupt the class, he only wanted to observe, so why didn't we proceed with the problem on the chalkboard. He suggested that the student who had had his hand up — me — take over answering the problem.

"Do you want me to do it the right way," I asked, "or the way Father Dolan was doing it?"

My next stop was the principal's office, where I had to wait, again, for Dad to come and take me home. Yet again, I wasn't lectured. I was simply informed that I would not be allowed back in school until I apologized to Father Dolan and the whole class. I did, and learned that apologizing isn't so hard once you get the hang of it. Ever since, I've wondered why so many people in public (and private) life find apology so difficult.

One temptation I did manage to resist (to my occasional regret) happened while waiting for my usual ride to school my senior year. That year, Father Segar from our parish was teaching at Curley, and Dad had arranged for me to ride to school with him each day, saving two bus fares. I was at the usual corner with my schoolbag waiting for Father Segar when a fairly well developed woman of indeterminate age came out of a nearby house, walking a bit unsteadily in high heels, carrying a drink and wearing little more than a see-through babydoll nightie. She came right up to me.

"I bet those guys back there that I could get you to come into the house with me," she slurred.

Desperately yearning for the courage to take her up on the offer, I stammered something about waiting for a priest to pick me up. She just giggled and sashayed back to the "guys" watching and laughing from her front door. I've often wondered whether my life would have taken a different course had I chosen the road not taken that morning.

Not that I yet knew what was what. Far from it. At Food Fair with Elaine around this time, I pointed to a box of Kotex on the checkout conveyor belt and asked, "What's that?" She didn't tell me, but she says she did ask Dad if he'd ever explained the birds and bees to me. He hadn't, except that feeble try in the parlor in Swansea years before. I didn't even know why, once a month, Elaine stayed shut up in her bedroom for a few days. And when I asked what was wrong with her, I was usually told it was "female trouble." I had no idea what that was until well *after* high school.

I was still trying to figure out who I was, let alone figure out women. I think it was the summer between my junior and senior years that I tried camp counseling. I was dispatched to a summer camp in central Florida for a few weeks. All I remember is sending daily love letters to Mary Ellen telling her how much I missed her and hated being at the camp. I had reason enough to hate it. As the runt of the litter again, the other guys all took to calling me "Crud." I decided camp counseling was not for me.

I also started smoking about this time, and for that I can thank the church. Okay, that's not fair. Let's say I can thank having been an altar boy. Not just any altar boy, but a member of the Pope's Crew. The Pope's Crew is a select group of altar boys recruited to serve at Masses and other ceremonies for the archbishop when he visited from St. Augustine, at that time the seat of the all-Florida archdiocese. (The archdiocese has since been split in two, with the other seat in Miami.)

When I was 15 and a high school junior, Archbishop Joseph Hurley went to Barry College in North Miami to dedicate a new building. Tom Seeman and I were outside in our cassocks, waiting for the archbishop's arrival. Tom, two years older, a senior and a good foot taller than I, puffed on a cigarette.

"Try one," he suggested, offering me a Marlboro.

"I don't smoke." In fact, I had been vocally critical of my father for his chain smoking.

"Go ahead. You'll like it."

So I did. The first puff made me cough and gag.

"Inhale it," he said. "Suck in down into your lungs."

I did, and became nauseous.

"Don't stop. You'll see. It grows on you. You'll love it."

I did, and he was right. By the time we'd left Barry College, I must have smoked at least half his pack of Marlboros. I was to be a heavy smoker another 26 years. Such is the power of peer pressure.

I was also a cheerleader in high school. As an all-boys school, Curley had no girls to rally our student body, and since I was decidedly not of varsity quality at any sport, except perhaps sprints at track and field, I joined the cheerleading squad. I have this experience and a priest to thank for my introduction to dirty jokes.

Father McDermott, the English teacher, was driving the cheerleading squad to Key West for our annual football game there.

"It's okay to kiss a nun," he told us on the way, "as long as you don't get into the habit."

And this gem that I really didn't comprehend, but the other guys seemed to: "When you're married, the only thing that is not allowed is going in through the back door."

And those from a priest!

Then there was Mr. Kutz, our science teacher — all sciences. A short, redheaded bulldog of a man and a World War II drill sergeant, he acted the part, pacing back and forth across the front of the classroom as he lectured and gestured, flailing his pudgy freckled arms with vehemence.

He lampooned Freud's theory that we demonstrate sexual behavior from the beginning. "Sure," he told us, "but we are also all alcoholics by nature, according to him, because what are the first words out of a baby's mouth?" After a dramatic pause, "M-m-m-m-m, exactly the sound of booze coming out of a bottle. And, 'Pop!' The sound of the cork coming out."

As for Darwin, forget it. He'd do his mock monkey routine, hands scratching his own armpits as he'd bend into a chimp-like crouch and pace the front of the classroom. It's a wonder I got an education at all.

One more morsel of memory from those years had to do, again, with Dad. Every day he came home from work covered in flecks of dirt and grass, tired and sweaty. How often I must have said, intentionally within his hearing, that I was going to make my living with my brain, not my brawn. It is one of the things I am ashamed of.

When I graduated from high school at age 16, in June 1957, I was salutatorian, second fiddle to the valedictorian. That honor went to an Italian guy with a photographic memory whose name completely eludes me now. I still had some growing up to do.

In retrospect, I think that's how we become who we become, by eliminating, one at a time, all the things we won't become: astronomer, rocket scientist, race car driver, geometrician, pool hustler, golfer, camp counselor... My list was growing.

Life was still good, and looking up.

Thirteen: The Seminary

In September 1957, I headed off to St. Andrew's Seminary in Rochester, New York, but not before one final fling at a decidedly unholy life: I went back to New England for a few weeks, staying at my Uncle Dick's with Aunt Fay and cousin Beverly. Bev was a year or so younger than I, long-limbed and cute. That was the summer we were caught necking on the sofa in the basement den when we thought her parents were out.

I only recall one other event from that trip: a blind date. I don't even remember her name or what she looked like. She was in Swansea, I remember, a friend of some of our former neighbors, I think. Mostly what I remember was how disastrously the date turned out: my mouth was in agony. A wisdom tooth had become infected and had to be extracted that day, but I went on the date anyway, bloody mouth and all. I don't remember where we went or what we did, just that we had a most unpleasant time. It was a fitting way to send me off to learn how to become a priest.

The seminary was a single large building in a vast expanse of flat land beside what was known as "the Buffalo highway" outside Rochester, within a short walk of the Erie Canal in one direction and a Shoney's Big Boy in the other. These two marked the boundaries of the world we were allowed to navigate on our own. Anything beyond those limits, we needed permission and accompaniment by one or more other seminarians.

This was my period of most intense religious devotion. I truly gave it everything I had. I threw myself into my vocation like a starving man searching for food. I believed in my bones that I had been "called" to the priesthood. After all, my entire life to this point had drilled that into me, prepared me for this, taught me it was my sole reason for being. Even my literary endeavors dove headlong into my faith.

In high school, Tony "Cap" had read to me once a meditative essay he'd written, a depiction of the agony of Christ in the Garden of Gethsemane, before the crucifixion, from Christ's point of view as a mortal human. It was beautifully written, even if Tony was somewhat inebriated when he read it to me. It evoked all the sweat, the agony, the tears, the blood, the dread Christ must have felt knowing what was in store for him. His words made the Passion of Christ live for me. Then he finished off a bottle of vodka and tossed the empty from his second story porch into the back yard, already littered with emptied bottles and cans.

His reading had stayed with me. In my first semester at the seminary, head over heels in love with God, with godliness, in love with the mere thought of being in love with God, I decided to try my hand at something similar. I wrote a small book of meditations on the Passion of Christ. I must admit now that it was pretty saccharine. I even peppered it with illustrations, some crudely drawn by me, others photographs or prayer cards of Christ in various states of agony. It positively dripped of blood. If anyone is curious, I still have it. I don't have it in me to discard anything I ever wrote that found publication, however limited — in this case again, a single copy.

I called it *"Crux Amoris...et ego sum homo,"* Latin for "Cross of Love...and I am man." It opened with an attempt at poetry:

> *Why such agonizing torments smart*
> *So humble a Heart?*
> *Why brutalities so savagely meet*
> *My Lord, so sweet?* ...

It was self-flagellation at its best. One picture was a photo I took of a thorny-crowned Christ behind jail-like bars in the basement of a church in Syracuse, New York. There were thorns and crucifixes a-plenty. In 11 chapters, 71 short pages, I took Christ from the Garden through betrayal to his death, casting myself as the crucifier. Oh, how I wallowed in my guilt. The booklet ends with another poem:

> *The winds that dash, the waves that crash,*
> *Toss ship and board so weak;*
> *The fishers afright see ought but night*
> *As the planks beneath them creak,*
> *There sleeps a One, the only God's Son,*
> *Full Power and yet full meek...*

Needless to say, this 17-year-old did not have much of a future as a poet, either.

Or a musical future, for that matter. We discovered during our first year that a small group of us had musical talent of sorts. We brought our instruments with us from the next break, Christmas 1957. I brought my guitar. Another fellow had drums, another a fiddle. A fourth played the piano, but the seminary had one of those already. We did some rehearsing. During one of our daily after-class coffee sessions at Shoney's, we discovered that one of the waitresses was an aspiring torch singer. We asked if she knew the words to *Blue Moon* (the original, sultry torch song, not the latter-day rock version). She did. So we made arrangements to sneak her in through the seminary auditorium's back door for our grand opening concert.

We opened with the Kingston Trio classic, then very popular, *Hang Down Your Head, Tom Dooley*. Then another few numbers. Then we asked that the lights be dimmed to blue and struck up *Blue Moon*. She came out in a slinky sequined gown and started singing, unrehearsed. She set the tempo, we merely tagged along. Let's just say she did not shrink from the sensuality of the tune. There was no smoke, but you could almost feel it rising out of the stage. Less than half way into the song the lights went up blindingly. The rector's voice boomed over the intercom: "This concert is over. The members of the band will immediately report to my office."

We were ordered to take our instruments home and leave them there.

During my first semester at the seminary, Dad suffered a violent ulcer attack. He came out of the bathroom one morning coughing up blood. Elaine, who was working at a local bank, was still living at home. My mother asked her to take Dad to the hospital.

What they had thought was arthritis aggravating his spine, and for which they'd encased him in a cast from his neck to his waist and then suggested moving to Florida, turned out to be an ulcer. It had become dormant during the first few years in Florida, when he was again doing the gardening work he loved, but now it was awake again, and with a vengeance. It had perforated his stomach lining. They had to remove almost three quarters of his stomach and much of his intestines.

He was never again the same. He lost a great deal of weight. He gave up smoking but continued to dangle an unlit cigarette from his lips as he worked, humming tunes only he knew. He could eat only pureed baby food and tapioca pudding, and in small quantities — six or more times a day. The man who once could easily down an entire apple pie in one sitting was no more. The father I found when I came home for Christmas wasn't the one I'd left a few months before. It shook me, the way seeing the body of my grandfather in the funeral home had shaken me at age seven.

That was also the semester I went to visit Gary's family — my Aunt Florence and Uncle Len in Wappingers Falls, New York — for Thanksgiving. Gary was in the Army then. Uncle Len took me hunting, a most unpleasant experience sitting still in the damp dark woods at dawn with an unused rifle across my lap as we waited for some luckless buck or doe to wander by. I think my uncle took a shot at one or two, just to see me jump. He didn't hit anything, though. He just scared them away. During that weekend, Aunt Florence gave me a pair of Gary's blue jeans that she said he'd never wear again. This is the event Gary never tires of griping about: how I "stole" his favorite blue jeans. I gave them back, by the way.

The following summer, I got a "job" helping out at the rectory of our parish. Monsignor Rocket loaned me a copy of Dante's *Divine Comedy*. On the left page it had the stanzas in the original medieval Italian, on the right an English translation. I was surprised to see that I could pick out some of the Italian because of all the Latin courses I'd taken in high school and now in the seminary.

I also got a job washing dishes in a local Italian pizza joint, a job I walked out of. The cook was teaching me how to make pizzas one evening when the owner came in and told him, in Italian, to stop talking to me, that he was paying me good money. Thanks to Latin and Dante, I understood clearly what he'd said, took off my apron and walked out the door.

More transformational for me that summer than either of these, however, was Marthe. My cousin from Montreal was 10 years older than I. I think she'd been jilted at the altar — at least she was devastated by something gone wrong in her love life, so she had moved to Miami Beach. She and Elaine were sharing an apartment. I thought she was the cutest human I'd even rested eyes on. I loved her dimpled smile, her sparkly eyes, her very tiny-ness, everything about her. I found excuses to spend time with her every chance I could.

We'd spend free afternoons on the beach, evenings sitting on a sea wall watching the moon rise out of the ocean. I kept telling myself I was a seminarian, to stop this foolishness, but my-self wasn't interested in all that. I simply wanted to be with her.

Let me be clear: as far as I know, we were both still virgins. This was something deeper and more pervasive than sexual attraction. I resolved to give the seminary one more year of trial, but I think Marthe planted a seed that was going to take me down a very different path.

Marthe & Charles Atlas Wannabe

Marthe and I rode out of Miami on the same Greyhound bus that fall, she heading back to Montreal, I back to the seminary. I was wearing a white shirt, I know, because when I reached the seminary I discovered it had a rather copious amount of lipstick and makeup smeared on its collar and shoulder. I rolled it in a tight ball and hid it, unwashed, in my locker to remember her by.

I did see her soon again, because at Thanksgiving I went to visit her and her family in Montreal. I remember being astounded by the loud, rapid-fire French conversations at the dinner table, remember seeing *Cat on a Hot Tin Roof* with French subtitles and, as the second feature, a Billy the Kid movie in which they had excised all the killing scenes. You saw the hero draw his gun but you never saw it being fired, never saw the bad guy fall. All you saw was the gun being re-holstered and the bad guy already dead on the ground. The raw language of *Cat* was okay in Canada, but not the violence of *Billy*. I remember thinking Canada seemed to have its censorship priorities about right.

We were snowed in that long weekend and I was a few days late getting back to the seminary, but with all that family around, Marthe and I did not get any private time together. It was as though Miami Beach had never happened.

The nuns, brothers and priests of elementary and high school had taught me how to memorize and regurgitate what I'd memorized when it was time for exams. It was only in the seminary that I was introduced to critical thinking, a process I now consider crucial to intelligent survival in the modern world.

I took to critical thinking like iron filings to a magnet. I learned that doubt and questions were not bad, they were good. They were the things that exercised the most important organ in our body: the brain, the only thing that sets us apart from the rest of the animal kingdom, and I'm more than a little unsure about that. I learned to question almost everything I was being told, whether in science or religion, art or history. I learned to go in search of answers. And my reading became serious, very serious indeed. An important course was Apologetics, the study that marshals evidence for God's existence. Essentially, what it proves is that God's existence cannot be proven, it can only be surmised. I was no longer sure surmising was good enough.

Into this maelstrom of mental activity waded a man I've never met, Alfred North Whitehead. I'd gone into Rochester one weekend — accompanied by another seminarian, as required — but slipped away into a book store on my own. There I discovered a little paperback that I still keep and cherish: Whitehead's *Adventures of Ideas*. The title alone captured my imagination. The book simply traces the development of human philosophies, showing how common threads run through the great religions and systems of human thought, each building upon the previous one, starting back in deepest antiquity and tracing the evolution of ideas — what we think about our world, our universe, our simply being here — into the mid-Twentieth Century. By now I'd fully appreciated the evolution of life forms (Sgt. Kutz's monkeyshines notwithstanding), but the notion that ideas, too, evolved was new and mind-blowing. It carried cosmic implications.

Not long after that, I caught the Asian flu, a particularly virulent influenza that was all the rage that autumn. I fainted on the altar steps while serving Mass. I awoke hearing an ambulance wailing as I was being rushed to a hospital. After a day or so, I was sent back to the seminary but confined to my bed several more days.

As was customary, Father Louis Hohman made the rounds after saying Mass each morning to distribute communion to those of us unable to attend. He entered my room, placed the wafer on my tongue and, I could see, glanced at the table beside my bed, where Whitehead's book lay. He left but was back a half hour or so later and asked me about the book.

"Do you know that writer is an atheist?" he asked me.

"No, but it's not about God or religion or anything like that," I said.

He asked if he could borrow the book after I finished it and then perhaps we could discuss it. I thank that man for his wisdom almost every day of my life. Remember, I was accustomed to being told *not* to read certain books, that reading too much could turn you into an atheist, that you shouldn't spend your life with your nose in a book.

Thus began a lengthy colloquy. Every evening after dinner, Father Hohman, who was our spiritual director, was in his room available to any seminarian who wanted to discuss anything with him. You stood in line outside his door and waited your turn, each student limited to around 20 minutes. After I'd recovered from the flu and finished reading it myself, I'd loaned him the book, and now I took my place in line outside his door many evenings to discuss it. After a while, I started letting others get in front of me because I'd discovered the 20-minute rule didn't apply if you were the last in line.

We talked of many things, not just the book. We talked of God and philosophy, of why we are alive, of the meaning of the universe and why it needs a creator even if the Creator Himself didn't need one. It was all pretty heady stuff for an 18-year-old. My brain, exploding with questions and discovery, didn't want the fireworks to stop. And so it went, night after night, week upon week, through the late fall and into winter. I was beginning to have difficulty envisioning myself one day standing in a pulpit preaching doctrines I no longer was quite certain had much validity.

In due time, this was interrupted by my trip home for Christmas. My brother Ronald had received an Indian Apache motorcycle for his sixteenth birthday earlier that December. He spent all his time lavishing his attention on it. We were happy for him. None of us realized the tragedy that lay ahead.

A few days after Christmas, Dad took me aside and told me, in a very matter-of-fact voice: "I may not be here next Christmas. I want you to promise me you'll take care of your mother."

I was floored. I didn't know what to make of it, didn't understand what he was trying to tell me. I guess I mumbled some vague assurance, but I don't really know. I was simply dazed.

In that confused condition I returned to Rochester and Saint Andrew's Seminary. On January 13, 1959, as I left a classroom after completing my first end-of-semester exam, I was told to report to the rector's office. I went in and was told to sit down. The priest informed me that my 16-year-old brother had just been killed on his motorcycle while going home from school.

In a state of shock, I went home immediately. I don't know who arranged the flight. I remember seeing my father and sister at the Miami airport, my father in tears. At some point he said to me, "Why him? This was supposed to be my year."

The story was on the front page of *The Miami Herald*, with photos. There were no indications that Ronald was driving recklessly. My brother had had a passenger riding behind him on his motorcycle, a friend from school. The friend had been thrown clear and survived with a broken leg. They were going up NE Second Avenue, around 62nd Street, where the girls' high school, Notre Dame, was located and where I'd been stopped in Frenchy's car. It's four-laned. A Maule Company cement mixer was in the left lane, slowing down as if to turn left. Ronald was in the right lane. The truck turned right instead, directly across my brother's path. The truck had no working turn signal on that side. The rear wheel passed right over the motorcycle and my brother.

It is especially difficult to explain my personal reaction to Ronald's death. It was so sudden, so inexplicable, so outrageous. And yet I did not feel a personal sense of loss. It is humbling now to admit it, because I still don't know why. Over the years since then, and still to this day, I'll see a slender teenage boy in the distance, on a city sidewalk in Rome, in a museum in Athens, browsing through a souk in Morocco or in the shops on St. George's Street in St. Augustine or on a beach somewhere. He'll be kind of lanky, have dark hair, the hint of a ducktail in back, and olive skin and a sweet heart-shaped face, that certain way of bearing himself, lightly, almost cat-like. In my mind I know it is not my brother but in my heart I want to rush up to him and welcome him back, to tell him I am so deeply sorry for not feeling the sharp pain of personal loss way back then, when he was 16 and suddenly gone. I'd never fight with him again. And never have the chance to take back all those meaningless fights.

Life seemed to move in crazy fits and starts. The wake with a closed casket because his head had been crushed under the wheels of the truck...the funeral...the incessant asking why, why, why. Life was cruel. Nothing made sense. That gigantic *Why* hung over us all like a silent sword. And I had to go back to the seminary?

I did go back, of course, after all the others had finished their exams and their mid-year break. They were returning to start their spring semester; I had not yet officially completed my fall semester.

It's far too simple to say I left the seminary because of my brother's death. That almighty question — *Why?* — still hung over my head, but that wasn't the deciding factor. It was much more complex than that. Looking for answers, I resumed my nightly vigils outside Father Hohman's door. We talked, and talked, and talked.

After several nights of this, sometime after midnight, he steepled his fingers in front of his face and said through them, looking me squarely in the eye: "You are waiting for me to tell you that you don't belong here. But that is not for me to tell you. It is for you to decide, and to tell me."

I took a long breath, met his eyes, and made the first momentous decision of my life: "You are right. I don't belong here. I want to go home."

"Are you sure?"

"Yes."

"You haven't taken last semester's exams yet. What do you want to do about them?"

"I want to take them. I want to continue college, so I want those credits."

"When?"

"Tomorrow."

"Which ones tomorrow?"

"All of them." I didn't want to look back. The decision made, I wanted to plow forward and put it all behind me. "Can someone arrange a flight for me to go home tomorrow night? I'll get one of my roommates to pack my things."

He nodded. "*You* will have to tell your parents," he said.

The next morning, I was at Mass at 6 a.m., as usual, had a quick breakfast, and was given a classroom alone with a stack of exams. I flew through them, feeling a giddy sense of liberation I'd never known before. The world was lifted off my shoulders. I aced every exam.

I think it was during the lunch break that I went to the rector's office and telephoned home. I spoke with my father.

"I'm coming home."

"What? Did they kick you out?"

"No. I want to come home."

"Oh, no." The words sounded like a single note, a dull thud, a body falling limply to the floor. I don't remember anything else about the conversation. There must have been information exchanged about what flight I'd be on, but I don't remember. All I remember is the dead sound of that "oh no."

I wasn't going to be a priest, either.

Many years later, in 2000, two years after my mother died, I found a handwritten letter she and my father had received from the priest that I had had so many conversations with. It is dated February 4, 1959. She had saved it among all my letters to her chronicling my travels during the 1970s.

Dear Mr. and Mrs. Hebert,

May I first express to you my deepest sympathy on the sudden death of your son. My prayers are with you as well as with him. Now as regards Dick. He has been coming to me off and on for over six months in a state of indecision as to his vocation.

It is extremely important that one be happy in the life of the priesthood and that is often indicated by one's happiness in the seminary. Dick was not happy. I put him to several tests to make sure he was not just escaping the rigid discipline of the seminary and foolishly feeling that he would be happier outside because it might be easier.

We discussed the situation at great length and concluded that he would be much happier in the world.

I am sure that his happiness is your principal concern, and despite the fact that you must be disappointed in his decision to leave, I sincerely hope you will accept it as the will of God. It is not a sudden one but was well thought out.

Dick is a very intelligent and mature boy and will do well in whatever field he chooses. I am sure you would not want to have him run the risk of being very unhappy in the priestly life, if he were staying merely to avoid disappointing you.

I know you will help Dick make the adjustment just as he will be a help and consolation to you.

If I can be of any help to you at any time, I am at your service.

God bless you.

I believe Father Hohman's letter was in reply to something my father had asked him, either by phone or in an earlier letter, about the wisdom of my decision. When I read the letter some 40 years later, it devastated me. All my life I had believed this singular decision made at age 18 had been my first mature — and correct — decision, and now I was discovering that my father had doubted me. This is not an easy thing to learn. Life was good, but it was hard to believe that day.

Fourteen:
Reaping the Whirlwind

Nineteen-fifty-nine was the hardest year of all. It has been that way ever since it happened, as fresh and painful today, more than 50 years later, as it was then, a scar on my memory that won't go away.

The year was a whirlwind, a tumult. For me, it lasted a mere eight months, but those months encompassed a tornado of deaths and life-changing events. At the start I was 18, a seminarian, one of five members of a closely knit religious family with a permanent address, 1355 Bay Drive on Miami Beach's Normandy Isle. I declared 1959 over and done just before my nineteenth birthday, at the start of September. That night I'd slept in my car in a parking lot at the University of Florida with no idea where I would live, with no money, and no real sense of family: my brother and father were dead; my mother had sold our home on Miami Beach and moved into a small apartment in Little River, a not-so-nice part of Miami, behind St. Mary's Cathedral; my sister was on her own; I had wrecked two cars, and I had fallen in love and been scorned. I was through with 1959. In my private world, 1960 started on September 1, 1959.

After I came home from the seminary, I got a job again at the local Food Fair supermarket and enrolled as a part-time student at the then all-women's Barry College, the same Catholic campus where I'd learned to smoke while waiting for the archbishop. I was one of only a handful of males at the college, fewer than a dozen. Planning to go to the University of Florida the following September, but with no idea what my major would be, I was told I needed a handful of credits in certain subjects to qualify as a junior. I focused on three of those, figuring to add the few others during the summer.

Two of my three choices were disasters. I thought I might want to be a teacher, so I enrolled in a beginning pedagogy course. It was so stupifyingly boring, I bowed out after a few classes. I was definitely not going to be a teacher.

I'd thought I was pretty good in science and had entertained the idea of teaching science. I'd done well enough in inorganic chemistry at the seminary for a semester, so I enrolled in organic chemistry. Starting a week or two after the semester had begun, I was hopelessly behind the others. I stayed up all night poring through the textbook, trying to make sense of it. I think it was in my second class that the nun called on me to answer a question. I stood up and said I not only did not know the answer, I didn't even understand the question. I was hopelessly in the dark, in way over my head. I apologized, picked up my books, and walked out of the classroom, feeling again like the rejected boy who had to cross the desolate dance-floor away from where all the girls stood watching and, probably, trying not to laugh.

One of my second-choice classes was American History, and I wound up "teaching" that course for several weeks while the regular professor was out sick. That meant reading the material the night before and then talking about it with the other students (all women, of course) the next day. That, I admit, I enjoyed.

The second was a writing course. This was something I thought I knew a little about. The whole course was centered on how to research and write a thesis, something I'd never done before. On my first day, unbeknownst to me, the others had been told to come to class prepared to select a topic for their paper. When I was asked to say what my subject matter would be, I stabbed in the dark. Sputnik, Russia's first orbiting satellite, had been launched into space in October 1957, about 17 months earlier, shattering America's notions of scientific supremacy built largely on its nuclear arsenal. I knew precious little about Sputnik but had a sense that it had altered something fundamental in the world. Besides, hadn't I done all those Science Fair exhibits about rockets and the solar system, and hadn't I spent hours watching and photographing stars? How hard could it be? On the spur of the moment, on impulse rather than reason, I said I was going to write about the meaning of Sputnik.

For three months I researched Sputnik, guided by the nun's step-by-step assignments. I learned how to search periodical indices for relevant material (this was long before Google or even personal computers) and how to track down obscure articles and statistics. I read everything I could find about Russia's space program and what the analysts were saying about it. Most important, I learned how to sort information into a coherent storyline and how to think my way through constructing and then demonstrating a thesis. At the end of the semester, the nun in charge handed out our graded papers, but all I received was an otherwise blank slip of paper with a big red "A" on it. After class I asked why she hadn't given me back my paper. She smiled and said she had submitted it to a national magazine for publication, she had been so impressed by it. I was in heaven.

If she told me what magazine she had sent it to, I don't recall. I think it was *Newsweek*, but I can't be sure. I did receive the paper back some time later with a polite rejection letter, which may be why I think it was *Newsweek*, although I have no idea where that letter is now. That didn't matter. I knew now, without any doubt, what I was going to do with the rest of my life.

My Aunt Lorraine sealed that choice for me not long after that. She or my Uncle Roland, I don't remember which, asked me what I was going to major in at the University of Florida. I said I still didn't know, which was true. She had been a switchboard operator for the *St. Petersburg Times*, and he had been a machinist there and was now a machinist in the pressroom of the *Miami Daily News*. "You like to write. Why not journalism?" she asked.

I had no good answer for that, so I applied to the School of Journalism at the University of Florida. By then, of course, my world was in turmoil over much more upsetting issues than what my major would be.

Enter Angela Moffa. She was a student at Barry College and a member with me in our choir at St. Joseph's. Her parents owned a dry cleaning shop a few miles from where we lived, but they lived in Miami. We dated. I recall one double date, I think with my sister and whomever she was dating then. We were in darkness in the back seat. I was still an innocent, recently released from the seminary. Angela took my hand and planted it firmly on her breast under her blouse. Astonished, I did not resist. I was convinced from that moment on that we were meant for each other for life.

At some point during the spring, my father told me he and my mother were going to visit relatives in Québec and asked if I would like to come along, to help him drive. (My mother did not drive and never did learn to.) I knew I already needed at least two more course credits to get into my junior year at Florida, so I told him I needed to stay home to take those classes. One would be an advanced algebra course at the University of Miami, the other a summer course in logic at Barry. I knew he was again disappointed in me, but as visible as the message was on his face, he said nothing. He just nodded sadly. His nod said, "You are being selfish, but I understand."

Elaine has since told me he asked her as well. "He came to Chase Federal Savings and Loan, where I worked as a bookkeeper, and begged me to go with him and mom to Canada," she said. "I could not leave my job at that time. I remember him holding me and crying, saying goodbye."

They left in May. He had stopped smoking after his ulcer operation, but "Mom said he smoked a lot on the trip to Canada," Elaine told me. "Dad did not want to live. He used to cry in the bathroom for hours – blamed himself for Ronald's death. After Ronald's death he lost the will to live. He is the one I wanted to be with when we lost our brother. I would sit in Dad's lap and cry."

Three times on the drive north, my mother told me, he had pulled off the road and taken a nap, usually on the grassy shoulder. (This is still well before there was a national interstate system.) His first was in North Carolina. As I remember it, she prevailed on him to see a doctor when they reached Baltimore. He saw the doctor, but insisted on continuing the trip, against the doctor's advice.

We have very few photos from that trip. One is of my mother beside her bed, on her knees, her head in her hand, praying.

We think they both knew it was the end. Was he planning to remain in Canada with his brothers and sisters and send Mom home alone? Was he making this trip to say goodbye to his brothers and sisters? We will never know. We know the marriage was not a happy one.

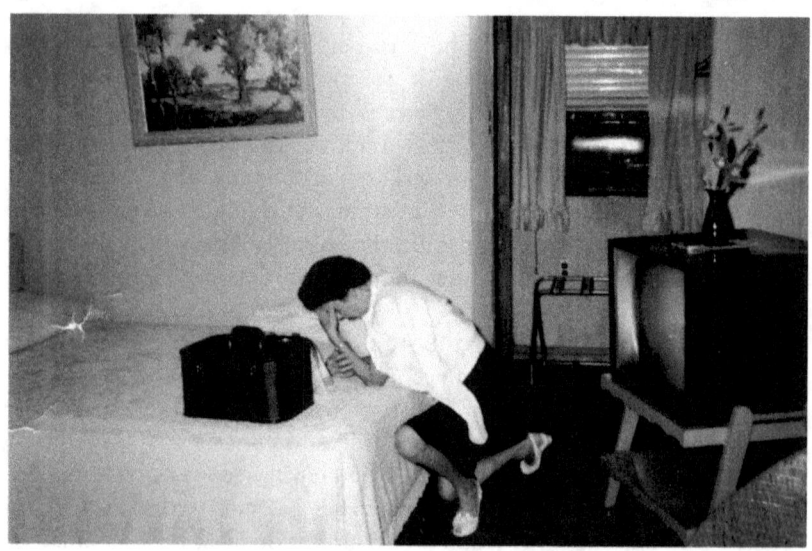

We also know he missed his family. And that he did not expect to see us again.

He saw every one of his still living siblings on that trip. Every cousin and aunt or uncle in Canada that I have talked to remembers that trip vividly, how he was so full of life and yet seemed already so saddened by age, even though he was not yet quite 50. The last stop was the Manoir Hébert, the family hotel his father built in Thetford Mines, now owned and run by Aunt Antoinette and Uncle Albert. I have a photo of him at Uncle Albert's desk in the hotel, on the phone, I think pretending to be running the business. It is the last photo we have of him.

He had one more brother to see, the so-called "black sheep" of the family, Rosaire, the second son by that name. His parents' fifth child also had been named Rosaire but had died as an infant, of pneumonia I think. They named their fifteenth and last child Rosaire as well, but his mind was not quite right. When I met him years later, it was like talking to a child.

Albert and my father went to find Rosaire in my father's car, the 1955 Buick. After visiting a while, as they prepared to return to the hotel, my father said he was tired and asked Albert to take the wheel. He climbed into the back seat and lay down. Albert said he heard my father take a last deep, rattling breath just as he turned into the parking lot at the Manoir, his ancestral home.

I was driving home from my advanced algebra class at the University of Miami that afternoon, having stopped at a friend's house to retrieve a pair of shoes I had forgotten there after a party the night before (I have no idea how or why). I could see a storm brewing in my rear view mirror as I headed north on Biscayne Boulevard. It grew ominously dark as I headed east on 79th Street toward the causeway to Miami Beach. And then I saw the twister, black and angry. I saw a car lifted into the sky, spun like a toy and dropped into a field. The funnel was heading toward me and would cross my path. I picked up speed, judging that I could outrun it.

I reached the causeway bridge barely in time, because my car, a very lightweight Anglia, a Ford product made in England that resembled nothing so much as a sardine tin on wheels, lifted off the ground as I crested the bridge and crossed its draw span. I have no idea how high I was lifted. I don't think it was by much, perhaps a foot or so, but my wheels certainly left the bridge surface. The car landed smoothly on the down side of the drawbridge. Was it my imagination? Perhaps. But in my memory, the fringe of that tornado lifted me across the grate-floored span of the bridge and sent me on my way home. There were photos in the *Miami Herald* the next day of the damage done by the tornado, including a piece of straw driven into a utility pole like a spike, next to the foot of that bridge.

By the time I reached home the rain was torrential. I waited a few minutes, hoping it would subside, but it didn't and as I got out of my car Elaine opened the front door of the house and shouted that Monsignor Rocket wanted to see me at the rectory. I angrily got back in the car. He probably wanted me to substitute for my father to sing a requiem Mass in the morning, or something like that, as I'd promised my father I'd do if needed. (The regular organist and choir leader, Mr. Morell, was also on vacation.) What could be so important that the priest couldn't just tell me by phone?

When I arrived at the rectory, it was still raining furiously. I took off my shoes and ran barefoot across the yard. I remember stubbing my toe on a sprinkler head and hopping on one foot to the front door. The housekeeper opened the door. The first words out of her mouth: "I am so sorry about your fodder."

Then the dark presence of Monsignor Rocket loomed up behind her. He was not that big a man, but at that moment he seemed so to me. His voice growled out of the darkness: "He doesn't know."

That's how I learned I no longer had a father. The priest said something about going into the church with me to pray. I turned and ran to my car. I could only think of one thing at that moment: How was I going to tell Elaine? I decided to go to my Aunt Marianne's, who now had an apartment a few blocks from the church. She was my father's oldest sister and had lived with us a while, although she and my mother didn't get along very well. She would know what to do.

Marianne absorbed the news with her quiet, stoic dignity. She sat me down, wet and shivering, and gave me a cup of hot chocolate, then hurried about gathering clothing and toiletries to take to our house. She instinctively knew not to leave us not-quite-adults alone.

Elaine was at the ironing board across the living room when I opened the front door. She looked up and her face went white. "Daddy's dead!" I didn't have to say a word. She knew.

Life blurred after that. I remember many people in the house, all bringing food, spread out on our dining room table like a feast or set for a party. It felt completely inappropriate, like some inexplicable blasphemy.

It was several days before Mom came home with him. There had to be an autopsy before the body could be released from Canada, and then they flew it to Rhode Island for a wake with the relatives there, before flying on to Miami.

I knew Mr. Morell was vacationing somewhere around St. Petersburg. I felt strongly that he would want to be there to sing my father's funeral. I insisted on driving to St. Petersburg or wherever to find him and bring him back. I had a tantrum over it. All the adults around said I was crazy and I wasn't going anywhere, how did I expect to find him? I yelled, "Leave me alone!" and ran to my bedroom and fell on my bed crying. Angela came to sit beside me and tried to console me. I heard her mother in the hallway telling her it was time to leave, and "that boy needs to grow up."

I sleep-walked through the rest of that time. I know that a week or so after we buried Dad, I had to go to New York to fetch his Buick. Gary's father, Uncle Leonard, had gone to Thetford Mines and driven it to their home in Wappinger's Falls, New York. I flew up on a Friday after classes and my part-time job at Food Fair. I washed the car on Saturday, and left early Sunday morning, before dawn, to drive back to Miami. I tried to make the trip without stopping, driving through Sunday night, because I was scheduled to be at work at the supermarket at 7 a.m.

In the middle of the night, on U.S. 301 somewhere in rural southern Georgia, I fell asleep at the wheel. I awoke just before barreling into the back end of an old Hudson that had paused to make a left turn. Luckily, I had just enough time to slam on the brakes to slow the collision, but still the Hudson leaped away and came to rest on the side of the road. No one was hurt, thank God. I assured the guys in the Hudson that I was sorry, asked them how much they thought their car was worth. They figured around a hundred dollars. I was wearing a wristwatch that had been my father's. I told them it was worth much more than that to me, and gave it to them as surety that when I got home I would send them the $100. They seemed fine with that. I did send them the $100 and they did return the watch. I have it still; although it no longer works, I can't bear to part with it. After that I joked to friends for years that I owned a pile of jalopy junk somewhere alongside U.S. 301 in South Georgia.

The Buick's front grille was smashed in by the collision but otherwise the car was not obviously damaged. It was far sturdier and heavier than what I'd run into. I pulled over at the next convenient spot and napped for an hour or so before continuing my trip home.

I think it was in late July that Angela informed me her mother had ordered her to end our relationship. Her mother believed I was only trying to cash in on an inheritance Angela would collect when she turned 21 in a few months. (Yes, she was a few years older than I.) I told her I didn't know or care about any inheritance, but that seemed to have no impact whatsoever. Her mother ruled with an iron hand.

Frank Sinatra had recently issued a new album, *Songs for Only the Lonely*. Both the name and a few songs I'd heard from it suited my mood. I bought the album, drove to Angela's house, left it in a paper bag leaning against the front door, and sped off. I drove for miles trying to mend my wounded heart. Somewhere on Collins Avenue in South Beach, cruising along and paying more attention to my wounds than the road, I smashed my little Anglia into the rear end of a double-parked car. This time the other car got the best of it by far. My little sardine can was totaled. Luckily (again), I escaped without injury. My guardian angel must have been riding shotgun.

Undeserving as I was, I had one final gift from my father. He had co-signed when I'd bought the Anglia, and the payments were fully covered by his insurance. I owed nothing on the car that no longer was. My mother helped me buy another car, a used 1958 Chevrolet, to get to and from the University of Florida.

I arrived in Gainesville in the middle of the night at the start of September, with no place to stay. That is when I officially declared, as the gray haze of dawn slowly rose around me in the parking lot, that 1959 was over: 1960 was getting a head start.

The family had atomized. We had been five at New Year's, only three not quite six months later. Ronald and Dad died five months apart. Mom had not had the heart to pursue the lawsuit against Maule and settled it for a mere $10,000. That was the price they put on a young, promising life, suddenly snuffed out by a cement truck without a turn signal. Elaine was going off to be married. Mom was living in a small apartment in Little River. I had wrecked two cars, lost my girlfriend, and was on my own. I was 18.

The tumult of those eight months of 1959 left me angry and confused. It took years for the anger to subside, and I only exorcised the worst of it by writing the novel that it sparked in me. Even then, the writing didn't begin until a dozen years after my brother's and father's deaths.

But the scars remained, and painfully so. The scars are twin regrets carved inside me. They remain with me today, bringing tears to my eyes as I write about that time, even when I hear certain songs — *Danny Boy*, or Eric Clapton's *Tears in Heaven*, or Lucy Blue Tremblay's *Oh, Daddy*. One scar is the knowledge that I would never get another chance to tell my father how sorry I am for all the mean, selfish, smart-ass things I had said to or about him over the years. The other is that he would never be there to see what I had made of my life, for good or ill — my education, my children and grandchildren and great-grandchild, my career, what I took from the world and what I tried to give back. He would not be there to applaud, to advise, to disapprove or to smile at me, ever again.

In 1959, I did not think life was at all good.

Fifteen: Campus Life

Tony "Cap" had leapt back into my life out of the night, literally. It happened while Dad and Mom were in Canada. We had a party in the house that night. The place was filled with young people, dancing and laughing. I was in the kitchen opening a bottle of beer when the back door burst open and Tony "Cap" leaped in, landing on one knee with an index finger out like a pistol.

"This is a holdup!"

I spun around, the bottle cap came off and the beer bottle went jetting around the kitchen. Beer foam gushed everywhere. Tony erupted in laughter.

A year ahead of me in high school, upon graduation he had entered the Army. After boot camp, he'd been stationed in Nevada and assigned as assistant to the base chaplain. A sergeant and he had taken a disliking to each other, the way Tony told it, and Tony got tired of the needling. He took a shot at the sergeant once, missed, and was sent to a brig in San Francisco. After serving his term, he'd been given a dishonorable discharge. Typical Tony.

Now he was enrolling at the University of Florida. We'd be together again.

This is how it came to pass that I slept my first night at the University in my Chevy, in a parking lot across the street from the Newman Catholic Student Center. Tony had written he had a room in the Center, but I had arrived after midnight, when the Center was in darkness.

When the sun came up and I'd jump-started 1960, I went inside and found him. Not only did I find Tony, but an old friend, Father Segar, the priest who had been at St. Joseph's and had taught at Curley High, the priest who was my daily ride to school, the one whose imminent arrival had kept me from following that babydoll-nightied blonde's swinging behind back to her house that morning. He now was chaplain of the Center.

The priest and Tony agreed I could sleep on the floor of Tony's room for a night or two until I found other lodging, something that turned out to be far easier than expected. The Center owned a run-down shanty just behind it, a white clapboard structure with a sagging screened porch in front, a tin roof, stacks of bricks at each corner to keep it a couple feet off the ground, and live oaks hovering over it heavily laden with curtains of Spanish moss. Father Segar agreed to rent it to me for $20 a month. I only needed one side of it, so I found other students to sublet the two rooms on the other side, also for $20 a month, thus securing my own shelter free. They had the front door and screened porch, but my side had the kitchen, an alcove with a sink, a hot plate and an unreliable relic of a refrigerator.

My 'home' in Gainesville

The year started inauspiciously. I needed another semester of Physical Education to fulfill degree requirements, so after registering for all my journalism and other required courses, the only thing that fit what remained of my schedule was handball. I signed up. A week or so into the semester, a handball rocketed off the back wall at me and I didn't duck fast enough. It popped me in the eye. I wound up in the infirmary, then the hospital. They saved the eye, but I quickly dropped out of handball. It was too career-threatening.

I had to wait until the following semester to fulfill my physical education requirement, at which point I signed up for something that seemed a bit safer, Social Dancing. That course was at 7:40 a.m. By then I was working at the student newspaper, the twice-a-week *Alligator*, working at night for the most part. On those nights, if I went to bed after work — more often than not around 1 or 2 a.m. — I would usually oversleep and miss dancing class. The only other option was to stay up all night drinking coffee and getting to class in a semi-somnolent state, stepping on my dancing partner's toes and mumbling apologies, something I did often enough. Needless to say, I almost flunked Social Dancing. Only the instructor's benevolence landed me a C.

Journalism became my new passion. I credit H.G. (for Hortense Greely) "Buddy" Davis, my Journalism 101 professor. He suggested I join the staff of the student newspaper, the *Alligator*. Buddy's class was a newswriting lab that mimicked a daily newspaper, complete with deadlines. He was a human dynamo, now playing at being a reporter at a train wreck calling in facts and opinions to the class as we pecked away on typewriters separating the one from the other and assembled them into story form on deadline; now scrawling "MY GAWD!" in red ink across our less than perfect papers or just "GAWD!" if he thought it was really good. He'd project our handiwork on the front wall and critique each submission mercilessly. I can honestly say he was one of the two best teachers I ever had in life (and no, although well up the ladder, Sister Roberts isn't the other). Buddy even took me into his home for the few — and only — home-cooked meals I had while in Gainesville.

During spring of my first year, I was elected managing editor of the *Alligator* by the Publications Board, made up of both journalism professors and students. I was riding high, excited by the brave new world I had found, a calling that had awakened in me every sleeping bone and blood vessel of idealism. I decided to remain at the University the summer after my first year to pick up some extra credits, so I ran for managing editor of the weekly *Summer Alligator* as well, and won. The paper was all mine for those few months. (Okay, the editor, Joe Thomas, had a big hand in it, too.)

Before us, the newspaper wasn't considered much of a threat to the powers that be. Mostly it excelled in sports and Greek coverage, social stuff for the most part. Jim Moorhead, my editor during the regular semesters, and I were from the Gamma Delta Iota fraternity — God Damn Independents – and proud of it. We ran almost no Greek news, unless it was truly "news."

We shook the place up. We dove into investigative journalism, exposing a professor in University College (freshman and sophomore years) for widespread plagiarism of other textbooks in authoring his own syllabus for his course, and requiring his students to buy his book. He was removed. We led a major anti-book-burning campaign when the Florida Board of Regents tried to censor certain books from some courses and from the campus library. Our sports department was the first in the state to expose a list of courses that varsity football players were urged to take because they would be assured of getting high enough grades to remain on the team. That one rapidly swelled into a statewide scandal.

I soon enough also became personally embroiled in controversy. I had a regular column that ran opposite the editorial page. In one of these I lamented the way history was taught, from textbooks that broke it down into isolated chapters — this war, that king, that period — without ever connecting the dots. I urged instead a huge wall chart illustrating the course of history as the starting point, instead of the traditional textbook, because that would spur conversation, inquiry, curiosity about what was happening simultaneously in various parts of the world and how certain events impacted concurrent and succeeding events — connecting dots. History professors (and some students) heaped scorn on me in letters to the editor, in essence accusing me of wanting to "spoon-feed" history to students instead of making them work by reading a textbook. I still maintain I was right. But then, I had never authored a history textbook, and I suspect some of my fiercest critics had.

I also received my first taste of politics. The two guys running for student body president that year were named Bob Park and Bob Parks. Jim and I endorsed Park. I wrote heavily about the race. The next thing I knew, Parks was circulating around campus, in every venue he could think of, a cartoon he had drawn of me, crouched over my desk, pen in hand, with three inkwells in front of me knocked over and spilling contents, labeled "bilge," "bile" and "bigotry." Our guy won. Parks later told me he'd had the large original version of the cartoon framed and mounted over his bed.

Not content with campus politics, I also jumped into the U.S. presidential race between John Kennedy and Richard Nixon. All my friends at the Newman Center were for Kennedy. They said I should support him because I was a Catholic. I thought that a pretty dumb way to choose a candidate. It was enough to make me campaign for (drum roll, please) Nixon.

I argued that Kennedy was too young and untested, that Nixon had the experience. He had debated Nikita Khrushchev, hadn't he? I even helped organize and lead a cavalcade of students from Gainesville to Jacksonville to demonstrate for Nixon at a rally where Lyndon Johnson was speaking. (Kennedy knew he wouldn't win many votes in the South so he sent LBJ instead. After all, that's why he'd chosen Johnson to be his vice president.) We held up our signs respectfully, and after it was over I went up and shook LBJ's hand along the rope line, wearing my huge Nixon button. He just smiled benevolently at me, like an uncle. (Florida, incidentally, voted for Nixon that year.)

The election was pivotal for me in another way. I was taking a course in political science. The professor was William "Wild Bill" Carlton, the other "best teacher" in my life. Years before, he had been a key figure on a commission that had rewritten the Florida State Constitution. He was considered the sage of political science at the University. An aging bachelor, he seldom changed shirts, so they were all yellow around the collar. He scowled and laughed and paced and gesticulated and was just a genuine fountain of luminosity and energy. He was Sgt. Kutz with brains and humor. He chose as his subject for most of that semester the Kennedy-Nixon campaign, analyzing its course, the strategies, the debates, the demographics of voters state by state. As he went, he predicted which states would vote for whom, even which parts of which states, and why.

I was in awe of him. One day, just before class ended, I raised my hand to ask a question about something that puzzled me, something he had said a few days before that seemed contradicted by what he'd just said that day. A few students started calling for me to shut up, class was almost over. And sure enough, the bell did ring. But "Wild Bill" kept them there, upbraiding them, and answering my question. I'm going to have to paraphrase, because I confess I do not remember his exact words, but he commended my question, and then said, "This man is a journalist's journalist." I was in seventh heaven.

Alligator Managing Editor

Those two years in Gainesville were not all politics and newspapering, of course. There was Tony and his circle of friends, especially Ron Draco, who had a huge Plymouth he called the "Galloping Gray Ghost." Weekends we would sometimes pile into it and head for Crescent Beach, just south of St. Augustine. We'd load up on beer, steaks, potatoes, and chips, and camp out overnight on the deserted beach, building a campfire of driftwood, which was plentiful then. No girls, just a bunch of guys. Such days are, of course, long gone.

I also developed a pretty good strategy for feeding and entertaining myself without much cash. I'd garnered a few small scholarships for tuition and books (remarkably less expensive back then), but how was I to eat? I hired myself out as food taster for the university's four on-campus cafeterias. Each week I received a book of meal coupons, used them to eat in the cafeterias, then at week's end wrote a report on the quality of the food, the help, cleanliness, and anything else that caught my attention. For entertainment, as the managing editor of the newspaper I could get free tickets to movies, plays, concerts and such. Yeah, payola. Except that it didn't win anyone favorable reviews; we didn't review movies, plays, etc.

The show I best remember was when Shelley Berman, the stand-up comic, came to campus. I was dating a waitress from an all-night restaurant we frequented, Martha Box, but she had to work until 9 that night. So, in the middle of Berman's monologue, I tried to sneak out. He stopped his shtick and just stared at me, saying something to the effect that he was waiting until he could resume his work. When I returned a short while later with Martha, he stopped in mid-sentence again: "I'm so glad you could rejoin us!" I'd been mortified by one of the best in the business.

And then there was the night I faked a collapse, hoping someone would find me and know how tirelessly I worked, how wonderful I was. I was working at my desk in the *Alligator* office, in the basement of the Student Union. It must have been around 2 a.m. I simply let myself crumble off my chair onto the floor. No one came in to find me. After perhaps half an hour, I got back up and resumed my work. (I've never said I was proud of *everything* I've done!)

My most troubling time at the University involved Tony. He was no longer living in the Newman Center. He had rented a pair of rooms in a decrepit row of shacks across a vacant dirt lot from me, behind the Hillel Jewish Student Center. His shack was even more dilapidated than mine. He had stopped going to class and had been expelled, but his parents didn't know it. He was becoming more and more isolated from the rest of us. I may have been his last true friend.

The sound system "went missing" from the Newman Center chapel. Father Segar had determined that Tony probably had it. He and another student, John Hardman, went to Tony's shack but were afraid to go in. They came across the lot to my place and told me Tony was holed up inside and had a gun. They didn't want to call police unless they had to. Could I talk to him? (I should point out here that John Hardman was at least a foot taller and a hundred pounds bigger than I, the kind of guy I would have jumped on from behind and pummeled like hell back in grade school before running like crazy. And *he* was afraid to go in and face Tony?)

I walked across the lot slowly, calling out Tony's name, John and the priest several yards behind me. "Tony, it's me. I'm your friend. I'm not going to hurt you. Let me come in."

I could see his screen door was closed but the inner door was open. He called back telling me to stay out, not to come closer, he had a gun. This went on for several minutes as I inched my way forward.

"Tony, you aren't going to shoot me. Not after all we've been through."

"Stay away, Dick. Please, please, stay away."

But I could hear he was sobbing now. I reached the door, slowly pulled it open and stepped out of sunlight into darkness.

It was like a dungeon. Everything was black. The walls were covered with bolts of black satin. On the floor was a mattress, covered with black cloth. On it lay Tony, dressed all in black, on his back, his feet toward me. He held a Luger in his hands, both hands. It was pointed in my general direction, but wavered back and forth. He was drunk.

"Tony, don't."

Blam! The first shot hit the wall a few feet to my right. The gun was moving back my way. I leaped to my left and raced around the mattress. A few more bullets slammed wildly into the walls. I pounced on him from behind, yanked the gun from his hand and threw it toward the door. He crumbled in tears.

Father Segar and John rushed in when the shooting stopped. We half carried, half walked Tony across the lot to my place, stood him in my shower and let cold water run over him for several minutes. He was just blubbering now. We dried and put him on my bed. When we went back to his place, we found the speakers and other sound system equipment from the chapel. About a month or so later Tony finally went home.

The Graduate Moves On

As graduation approached, recruiters came to campus from various newspapers. I interviewed with *The Miami Herald, Orlando Sentinel,* and, at Buddy Davis's urging, *The Atlanta Constitution*. All three offered me a job. Miami offered $85 a week, Orlando $70 a week, Atlanta $65. Buddy had worked at the *Constitution* several summers and knew the editors. Without my knowing it, he had sent them clippings from the *Alligator* investigative reporting I'd done.

He urged me to take the Atlanta position, even though it paid least. It was where the 1960s were going to "happen," he said. The city was bursting at the seams, having just crossed the million-population mark. Martin Luther King, Jr. had just moved back there from Alabama, so it was going to be the eye of the civil rights storm. The paper won Pulitzers every year. Its former editor and now editor emeritus, Ralph McGill, was an icon of southern liberal journalism.

I chose Atlanta for all the right reasons. They even upped my salary $5 a week for agreeing to work nights.

The School of Journalism honored me as its Outstanding Graduate of the Year. I'm told the trophy with each year's honoree etched into its plate still sits in a trophy case there, although I've never seen it.

The ultimate prize eluded me, however. The summer courses I'd taken the year before had been intended to lighten my senior-year load so I could juggle newspaper duties and classes. They did that, but it turned out to be a double-edged sword. By reducing my senior year load to

12 credits a semester (I'd been taking 18 to 22 a semester both in the seminary and in my junior year), I was now considered a "part-time" student. That meant I was ineligible for the highest student honor, the University's Florida Blue Key society — the university's version of Phi Beta Kappa, which Florida back then declined to participate in because it required admitting African-American students. In 1959-61, Florida was still very much the segregated South. Perhaps as a consolation prize, upon graduation I was named to the Student Hall of Fame instead.

And for that, I was invited to the University President's reception on commencement day. My mother came up from Miami and attended the reception with me, meeting the university president in his home. I felt a pride in her and in my accomplishment that I cannot hope to describe. I wanted my Dad to be there, too, but at least she was there. Mom was there for me. Life was good again.

Sixteen: 'Stormy'

I have to backtrack in time now. Gail deserves a chapter unto herself, if only because of the lasting effects our relationship had on each of us and on the lives of our daughters and grandchildren.

Her part in the story began early in my first year at the University of Florida, when I came home during my first break, probably in October. Elaine suggested I go with her to the CYO dance – a weekly thing the Catholic Youth Organization had in a hall at St. Mary's Cathedral in Miami. That's where and when I first saw Gail.

She was still in high school, at Notre Dame Academy, where friends called her "Stormy." I kind of liked that. She certainly had a strong and electric personality. That, I also liked. And we danced well together. I especially liked the sound of her laughter. She was fresh and lively and spirited. She was a tonic for my orphaned heart.

We dated again when I came home for Thanksgiving and the Christmas-New Year break. On New Year's Eve we went to a movie – *Ben-Hur*. Not very romantic, I know, but that's what we did. The rule was to have her home before midnight.

The pivotal event was two-staged. The first occurred during Spring Break. Home again, one Saturday evening we were parked outside Food Fair in Little River, waiting for my mother to get off work. Gail said she thought we should break off our relationship because it didn't seem to be going anywhere. Caught off guard, I didn't know what to say. I started chuckling.

"What's so funny?"

"I was just thinking of asking you to marry me."

Gulp. Followed by silence. On both our parts. I think she broke the silence with, "Let me think about it."

She was all of 17. I was 19. Why did I say that? To this day I don't know. Reaching out for something, someone, anything, anyone to hold on to? Perhaps, but that seems too simple to me now. It sounds too much like an excuse. Was there love? Certainly something that I took to be love, but what does a callow 19-year-old fresh out of seminary know about such things?

The only valid answer I can think of to the question of why I said what I did in that parking lot is, I don't really know. Maybe it was simply self-conscious awkwardness at being told I was superfluous, at needing somehow to keep myself relevant. As I said, even for a 19-year-old, I was immature.

I returned to Gainesville and stayed through the summer term, accumulating credits and running the student newspaper. Gail came to visit at the end of the summer. That's when the second stage occurred. We were in my shanty, sitting on the bed.

"Yes," she said.

"Yes, what?"

"Yes, I'll marry you."

That is how it happened. We drove back to Miami to tell our families. No one tried to dissuade us. We went to dinner at the finest restaurant I knew in Miami, the Top o' the Columbus. If I'm not mistaken, we were double-dating with my sister and her future husband, Bill Lhota, that night. That's when I gave Gail an engagement diamond. Yes, I got down on one knee and made all the right moves. I even asked the band to play *Autumn Leaves*. It was September, after all.

We decided to marry the following September, after I would receive my degree. To say I was — that we were — emotionally immature would be stating the all too obvious. I now know this is not the way to plan a future. Back then, I was a ship without a rudder, caught in stormy emotional waters I had no idea how to navigate. I am not making excuses. That is simply the way it was.

After a few weeks, I headed back to Gainesville for the fall semester of my senior year. I soon began casually dating the sister of one of my friends as though nothing had changed. I think her name was Jane, or maybe Judy. Or Julie. Or June. We went on a couple dates of no consequence, a movie or two I think. She was a "good Catholic girl" saving herself for marriage so she had rather hard and fast rules. When I was back in Miami again, snuggling with Gail on her front porch, I said, "I love you, J" —and stopped short.

Gail froze. Of course. She didn't say a word. She took off the diamond and flung it into the bushes, then stormed into the house. I went home. Mortified. Again. I anguished all night. At dawn, I went back to her house, crawled on my hands and knees in the shrubbery, searching until I found the ring. I knocked on her door, apologized, groveled, told her about Judy or Julie or whatever her name was — there wasn't much to tell, really. I did everything I could to win her confidence back.

She accepted me back and I was whole again, and chastened. Judy/Julie was out of my life for good.

I spent the summer after receiving my degree living in a rented room on Tenth Street near downtown Atlanta, in the heart of what in a few years would become the hippy-center of the South. I roomed with Stanley Jackson, a younger Florida journalism student who was interning at *The Constitution* that summer. He taught me to appreciate Frank Sinatra's talent. At the end of August, I found a suitable apartment up a hill off Piedmont Road and moved my few belongings there before heading for Miami and the wedding.

We were married September 9, 1961, three days after my 21**st** birthday. She had turned 18 in March. The night before the wedding, her father, Bill Thomas, took me out for a beer. We sat at a roadside bar near downtown Miami and tried to have a conversation. He was the quiet type. I knew he had been a shell-shock victim in World War II; today we would probably diagnose it as PTSD. I thought him henpecked. Gail's mother was definitely the dominant force in the house.

Bill wanted to know if I loved his daughter. I said I did. Enough to help her through her wild mood swings between ecstatic elation and the pits of depression? He explained it was a common trait among persons with rheumatoid arthritis, which she had had since age 6. I had known, and yes, I loved her and would try my best to accommodate her many moods.

It was awkward talking with him. We were of two widely separated generations. This man was nothing like the father I had lost. This father had experienced it all, the world, the war, the coming home, the building of a family. I had only one central experience: a tempestuous father and family lost. There was little we could say to each other.

Our honeymoon lasted one night, a Saturday night in a Holiday Inn on Miami Beach. Then we hitched a rented trailer to my '58 Chevy, loaded the furniture her mother was giving us — Gail's bedroom set — and drove back to Atlanta. I had to be back at work Monday to help cover Atlanta's city elections. By the time we reached Atlanta, the brakes on my Chevy had burned out. I think I'd loaded the trailer unevenly.

What I remember most about our first apartment was a weekend afternoon soon after we moved in, trying to hang drapes in our bedroom. I'd never done anything like that before. I botched the job awfully, cursing each time I hit my thumb with a hammer or gouged my hand with a screwdriver. The drapes refused to stay up. I don't think Gail laughed, I don't think she cried, I don't think she cursed. I think she was just dismayed.

For five months we fumbled through learning how to consummate the marriage. Her virginity was stubborn, my attempts feeble. And then she was pregnant. Shortly before Renée was born, we moved farther out Piedmont Road to a larger apartment on Cheshire Bridge Road. Gail was in labor for hours, late into the night. Back then, fathers weren't allowed in the delivery room. I paced the hall outside, nervous and angry at not knowing anything, until the doctor came out and told me the news. We had a daughter. And she was a beauty. Red-faced and squalling, but beautiful.

A month after Renée was born, Gail took her to Miami to show her off to her folks, their first grandchild. She stayed through Christmas and New Year's. Soon after she came home in January, she announced she was pregnant again. No one had ever mentioned to us that a woman is at her most fertile immediately after giving birth.

Renée was a ray of hope, a sure sign of stability, the nucleus that was going to turn us into a family. We were turning ourselves into adults, with a few pratfalls along the way, to be sure. Like the Sunday we went to Mass and forgot to turn the stove off under a pan of water sterilizing Renée's milk bottles. When we reached home, the kitchen was black with burnt, exploded milk and sprayed with fragments of glass.

Not long after that, we found a home in Cobb County, the home Gail would live in for the rest of her life, on Long Drive outside Smyrna, Georgia. It had all the prerequisites of a suburban home suitable for Ozzie and Harriet Nelson: red brick, single-story suburban architecture, a carport with roses climbing trellises, a front yard with pine trees, a vacant lot in back overrun with kudzu that kept trying to invade our yard, spreading like a disease no amount of cutting back could contain, and neighbors in similar houses on similar lots in every other direction.

We had three bedrooms. I turned the third into an "office" where I could write, pecking away on my portable manual typewriter, trying to craft a style of my own, attempting poetry, short stories, a novel idea or two. In retrospect, I see now that I was both a miner and the mine, drilling down inside myself in search of the illusive vein of an idea, trying to understand my core and inside it, the great novel I just *knew* I would someday write. And then Gail would come in. Could she get me anything? A cup of coffee? It was lunchtime; would I like a sandwich?

No, no, a hundred times *NO!* I just needed my aloneness, solitude in which to keep on drilling. Ultimately, I asked her never to interrupt when she saw the door to the "office" closed unless it was a true emergency. Not one of my better moves, I agree. My immature selfishness was clearly still dominant.

Somewhere deep inside the mine of my mind, I think I knew what that great novel was going to be; it was going to be linked to my father and his untimely death, the central event of my life. But that event was still too near, too painful to take head-on. It hid deep inside me awaiting its time, like some slowly ripening fruit. No way was I ready to open that idea and let loose its demons, expose the wound to the sunlight of analysis. It would wait almost 10 more years.

We were living in that Cobb County house when Teri was born. She came a few weeks earlier than we'd expected. I was at work, covering yet another inconsequential ribbon-cutting, this one for a new Marriott in downtown Atlanta. The ribbon cutter was Sam Massell, then vice mayor. After the ceremonies, he and I stepped into the bar to have a drink or two and talk politics. My deadline was safely a few hours away. When I returned to the newsroom, I was intercepted and told to go to Crawford Long Hospital immediately. Gail was in labor and already on her way there. She arrived before I did so I didn't get to see her. Again I paced the hall. A few friends from the newspaper came by to keep me company.

Teri had fair hair. She stared out at the world with silent, almost unblinking bewilderment. I was in love with her instantly.

Our little family was formed. None of the four of us knew how to go about being a family, of course. We just kept putting one foot in front of the other hoping that somehow it would take us someplace we wanted to be, although I don't think any of us — certainly not I — had anything but the vaguest idea about what that someplace might look like.

Renée was thrilled at having a younger sister, someone she could instruct what to do, when to do it, and how to do it. And she seemed always to be giggling. Teri, on the other hand, would sit at a window staring silently out at the world. Was she moody? Was she pondering mighty questions? Was she wondering what was beyond what she could see? Was she imagining getting out from under her "big" almost-twin sister's domination? Whatever was going on inside her mind as she stared out at the world, I knew she was a wonderer. And I loved her for it, as I loved Renée's cheery way of running after life.

Meanwhile, the 1960s rocketed ahead with fits and starts. We all remember where we were and what we were doing that mid-day, November 22, 1963, when John F. Kennedy was assassinated. Teri was an infant, barely two and a half months old. Renée was a toddler, a year old. Gail was outside hanging laundry. I was inside getting ready to drive to work for my usual 2-to-11 p.m. shift. When the news came on the radio shortly after noon, I called Gail in and said I was pretty sure I needed to hurry to work right away. A quick phone call verified that, and within a half hour or so, I was at my desk, fielding calls, getting man-on-the-street reactions, immersed in the event.

That's how life went. More accurately, that's how my *lives* went. Both of them. The charged atmosphere of the newsroom, where I was swept into the maelstrom of events as the '60s lurched ahead, and the almost somnambulant passivity of suburbia when away from all that.

As raises came in and my news reporting assignments became more important (no more ribbon-cuttings, that's for sure), life at home became grayer. I urged Gail to resume her college education, to take courses part-time. She didn't see any reason to. I discovered that if something went wrong during the day while I was at work, it was simply left that way until I came home at midnight, even later on Fridays when I worked until 2 a.m. It was that way when the water heater broke down and leaked all over the place. It was even that way with the kitchen clock that needed to be advanced an hour in the spring. (Gary noticed that when he came to visit and asked why I hadn't changed it. By then I think Gail and I were both waiting to see who would break first and get up on a step stool and move the clock forward. I told Gary it would rectify itself in the fall. He has reminded me of that more than once.)

I would tell Gail about the news of the day and my reactions to it, my assignments, my ideas about issues and politics and political candidates. A week or so later, at some house party or other social event, I would overhear her repeating to someone else what I had said, almost verbatim. I began to wonder if she had any independent thoughts.

I know this doesn't sound generous of me, and it isn't. But it is an accurate reflection of what life was like at the time, at least mine. I know now that it was no picnic for her, either, that she was taking care of two small children, taking care of our home, taking care of me, all while enduring the pains of her rheumatoid arthritis. She was the caregiver and nurturer; I was the worker bee. It may have looked like a partnership, but it didn't feel like one. I know now that was my fault. I was not being appreciative of all she did. I simply wanted something else, something hidden on some invisibly distant shore.

Mostly, my restlessness was taking over, my need for new horizons, new places, new experiences. I couldn't explain it that way then, but I can see it now, from a distance. My life as a newspaper reporter was trying to launch me into something new, and my life in Smyrna was holding me back from all that. I loved my daughters, but I didn't love my life. I was growing angry inside, and afraid that my anger would spill out and ruin everything for everyone.

Then my lung collapsed. It was a Friday night in February, as I recall. I was in the newsroom, around 11:30 p.m. Outside, Atlanta was being pelted with freezing rain. The roads were turning into sheets of ice. I got up from my desk for something. A moment later I was slammed in the back by a sledgehammer. At least that is what it felt like. I couldn't breathe. The pain was sudden, sharp. I thought I had pulled a muscle and tried to stretch, bend over, touch my toes, twist my shoulders back and forth. Nothing worked. The pain only sharpened.

The night city editor told me I could go home, but be careful, the roads were treacherous. Half-way home I had to pull over and put chains on the car, despite the agony in my back. At home, Gail tried ice packs. Then she tried a hot-water bottle. Nothing eased the pain.

Saturday morning I drove her to her regular appointment with an arthritis doctor. She told her doctor about my pain and he took exrays. Then he showed them to me: the left lung was the size of a golf ball, completely collapsed. I was breathing with only one lung.

He had an ambulance summoned and sent me to the hospital. Within a half hour I was on an operating table. After giving me a local anesthetic, the doctor (he was hurrying because he was on his way to some convention in New Orleans) pulled an overhead mirror down close to my face. He'd found out I was a newspaper reporter. "Here, you're a reporter, you'll probably find this interesting."

He wanted me to watch him cut open my chest! As the first gush of red spread out over the towels packed around the incision, I blacked out. When I awoke, there was a tube stuck in my chest, the other end of which was in a jar of water on the floor. A nurse was moving around the room. I asked her if she could bring me my cigarettes from the pocket of my shirt hanging there on the wall.

"You're through smoking these," she said, then crumbled the almost full pack and tossed it into a trash can.

I was in the hospital for a week. Every half hour or so I had to cough to force bubbles of stale air from the lung-sack and out the tube, gradually allowing my lung to expand again. In between, I had a lot of time to think.

Bill Westbrook, a fellow reporter and good friend, came a time or two to play chess. A night nurse would chirp "Okey-dokey!" as she came down the hall whenever someone summoned her. And gradually my breathing restored itself.

It was not long after I returned home that Gail and I discussed the state of our marriage. She saw nothing wrong with it. I was unhappy. She went to talk with our parish priest, then asked me to do the same.

I had to wait in his library quite a few minutes, enough to scan many of the titles on his shelves. I particularly remember books by James Baldwin, *The Fire Next Time* and *Another Country*. When the priest entered, we talked about his books a while and he offered to loan me the Baldwin books if I was interested. I had already read one and would get the other from the library soon afterward.

We discussed the marriage, my restlessness, my frustration. In the end, he suggested a trial separation. Gail took it hard. I think she had counted on the priest telling me it was my responsibility to make the marriage work, that marriage was "'til death do us part."

I moved out. I found a second-floor room in a creaky rooming house overlooking Juniper Street downtown, just a few blocks from Tenth Street where I'd started out in Atlanta. My room was spare. The bathroom was at the other end of the hall. The others in the house were mostly old, alcoholic men. In addition to my clothes, I took some books, the record player and a few records, and an electric coffeepot in which I not only made coffee but warmed cans of soup and cooked cans of beans.

The room cost $10 a week. I sent Gail most of my paycheck each week, keeping only that $10 for my room and perhaps another $10 for food and other essentials. She got the house and the car. She learned how to drive. A few months later, she asked me to meet her for lunch.

Over lunch she asked me to come home so we could try again. She had changed, she said. She wasn't specific about just how she believed she had changed. I wasn't very cooperative. People don't just change overnight, I said. It was clear we were on diverging paths. I asked her to file for divorce. I said she should file on grounds of mental cruelty, that I would not contest it.

Back then, there was no such thing as no-fault divorce. Even "incompatibility" wasn't yet in the common lexicon of grounds for divorce. You had to have a concrete reason for asking that a marriage be dissolved. I told her she would fare much better if she filed as the aggrieved party. I had no intentions of even hiring an attorney. It would be amicable.

Not long after that, I was summoned to her lawyer's office, in a skyscraper only a few blocks from *The Atlanta Journal-Constitution* building. When I walked in the lawyer turned on a tape recorder. He informed me they would be asking for more money in alimony and child support than I was making, and that they could force me to take a second job in order to pay it.

Stunned, I immediately contacted an attorney I knew from covering the local political scene and told him what had happened. He said I had been giving her too much, proving I could afford that much, but he would see what he could do. He took over negotiations, advising me what to give Gail monthly between then and final settlement. We never did have to go to court. It was negotiated by the attorneys. At the time of separation, I was a four-year veteran on the staff and earning $106 a week after taxes. She would receive $90 a week, all of it in child support so she would not have to pay income tax on it. She would also get 50 percent of my next two raises. I would have liberal visitation rights with my daughters. We signed the papers.

Strangely, no one seemed surprised. "I'm just not the marrying kind," I told friends and family. I said the failure of the marriage was my fault, not hers. There was nothing wrong with her, it was I and my driving need to be somewhere else, doing something new. I just wasn't a good husband or father. When I told that to my mother, she said simply, "It takes two to tango."

The dance was over. No one was feeling very good about life just then.

Seventeen: Jailbird

Close to penniless after the divorce, I tried to devise a strategy that would see me across the next few years. I tried to join the Army. The Army could feed me, give me a cot and a roof over my head, even pay my wages to Gail and insure her. I had had deferments from the draft until now — first a student deferment while in college, then soon after that a parental deferment. If you had kids, they didn't draft you. The Vietnam War was rapidly escalating. Surely they needed more cannon fodder.

I took my physical exam: no problem. Then they looked at my medical records: big problem. They spotted the spontaneous pneumothorax — that lung collapse a year earlier — and a phrase my doctor had put in the record attributing the collapse to "temporary emphysema." I'd known nothing about that. No one had even mentioned it to me, but there it was in black and white. The Army didn't want emphysemiacs. It didn't want me. I was to be 4-F, deferred for reasons of health, for life. The only recourse left was to work my butt off to pull myself out of my financial hole.

If you didn't live through the 1960s, it's hard if not impossible to truly understand and appreciate what those years were like. I don't believe there has ever been a period quite like it, before or since. It was generational upheaval. It was exhilarating and revolutionary and disturbing. We truly believed we could change the course of history. I felt it as well, though I was a few years older than the "baby boom" flower children, those born after the Second World War. I didn't "turn on and drop out," didn't go their route of beads and sandals and hallucinogens and communal living, but I did endorse the generation's ideology of peace, love, harmony and distrust of authority.

Of course, the forces of stability pushed back, sometimes violently, because they and the foundations of all they had been raised to believe in were being challenged. As a result, by the time the 1960s were ending, the young idealists had been demonized by a president who came to office vowing to restore "law and order," even if it meant throwing all young people and troublesome Blacks in jail.

In the midst of this maelstrom, I felt the elation of personal freedom again, not unlike the liberation I'd felt when I'd first left the seminary.

My first big break came that summer of 1965, after Gail and I had separated but before the divorce was finalized. My editor asked me to look over some letters they had been receiving from men who had done time in the Atlanta City Prison, a farming prison on the city's outskirts. They complained of bad food, of no health services, of primitive conditions, of drug trafficking. I found and interviewed some of them, typically in dilapidated rooming houses not unlike my own. To a man, they had been arrested and sent to the farm for public drunkenness. Some even received their welfare checks there; it was their most common place of abode. I found their stories sad and compelling, and summarized them in a lengthy memo to my boss, City Editor Calvin Cox.

"Sour grapes," he said. "You write anything based on these and people will say of course they are complaining, they were prisoners. Prison isn't supposed to be a resort."

I wrote another memo, proposing that I would have myself arrested and go to the prison incognito to see conditions for myself. I received back an impersonal memorandum from the newspaper's attorney advising against it and stating that if I pursued this and something happened (he didn't specify what), the newspaper would not be held responsible.

I went anyway. Only my city editor, Calvin Cox, and my friend, Bill Westbrook, knew my plan. I didn't shave for days until I had a fair stubble of beard. Dressed in paint-spattered workpants and a torn shirt, I went to seedy bars, mostly around the Greyhound Station, where I was not known. I drank and drank and drank, but I guess my adrenalin was running so high I couldn't get drunk. I called Bill and he tried to help me get drunk. No luck. Finally, around midnight, I bought a pint bottle of cheap whiskey, poured it over my head, and staggered down the middle of the street toward the police station.

A block or two from the station, a squad car wheeled in front of me, cutting across my path. I got in as ordered, mumbled unintelligibly when asked my name, handed over my empty wallet. The only identification I'd left in it was my Social Security card. It has my full name in all capital letters, the hardest form of typing to read accurately at a glance.

The eye sees what it expects to see. I knew this from typography class in college. The policeman entered my name on the arrest sheet as Richard Leo Herbert. Newspaper readers knew me as Dick Hebert. No one made the connection, as expected,

I was fingerprinted and put in the drunk tank with a dozen or so other sleeping or lolling old men and spent the night trying to sleep on the bare concrete floor. In the morning we were herded before a municipal judge. When Herbert's name was called, I pleaded guilty. "Fifteen dollars or 13 days," said the judge.

My name was again called as the only one who had enough money on him to pay the fine and avoid prison. I kept my mouth shut.

A few hours later, I and the other men were bussed to the farm. I stayed there six days. I discovered it was possible to feel excitement and fear simultaneously, that a raging river of emotions could sweep you through pretty much anything. I was elated and afraid, nervous and yet strangely calm, fearful that almost anything could happen to me and yet counting on the warden and guards to not let anything happen to me.

The stories I'd been told about the prison farm were accurate. Soups and watery stews were meal mainstays, sometimes putrid. There was no infirmary and no doctor, despite that most of the people there had serious chronic health problems. No library, of course. Vegetables as often as not were limited to a raw onion apiece.

All the men were in one large common dormitory, the women in another. I used some of my loose change and traded cigarettes for some pills and capsules one of the prisoners had. Someone else tried to sell me what he said were knock-out drops that would guarantee I could sleep, but I declined. He wanted me to take them there, in front of him. It was chloral hydrate, an illegal hypnotic drug typically used in what was known as a "Mickey Finn."

Every day, we worked long hours chopping kudzu on the shoulders of the Interstate Connector through downtown Atlanta. By evening, my shoulders burned with aching from swinging that scythe at the tough vines.

I had an upper bunk. At night, I'd pull a small, palm-sized notepad out of my shoe and scribble notes to myself about the day's events — the food, the fights, the tired cycling of work and dreary waiting. After the first several days, I stuck my notes in an envelope with the pills and capsules I'd bought and addressed it to Bill. The foreman of our work crew obligingly mailed the "letter" for me. I told him I was trying to contact a friend to come bail me out. I'd also included a note with instructions to Bill to come during visiting hours Sunday with a full box of matches we would surreptitiously exchange.

On Sunday we sat across a dining hall table from each other for our allotted time. I told him we were working on the Downtown Connector, if the paper wanted any photos. I asked him for a light and he handed me his full box of matches. I lit my cigarette (yes, I'd gone back to smoking only months after the lung collapse) and handed him back my own matchbox, which contained only a few matches but several more pills I'd bought. On the way out of the dining hall, as expected, I was searched but he wasn't. No one smuggles stuff *out* of prison, after all. Analysis later showed the pills and capsules to be barbiturates and a related anti-epileptic drug, both prescription-only.

I think it was the next day that another friend from the paper, Jeff Nesmith, showed up at our worksite, a camera hanging from his neck. I saw him over my shoulder as I swung my scythe against the kudzu, even walked right past him at lunchtime pretending not to know him. He'd stood there a good while chatting with our guard, toying absent-mindedly with the camera. What he was getting were shots of me in prison garb. One wound up on the front page.

A small gang of young toughs came in. They'd been arrested for street-fighting. They all had bunks at the far end of the dorm. One night, as I was writing my notes, I saw them swaggering down the aisle toward me. I jammed my notes in a pocket, pulled my feet up onto the bed, and put up my puny fists.

"Okay, which one of you wants a piece of me?"

I must have sounded just as scared as I felt because they all started laughing and shaking their heads — then headed back to their own bunks. The next day I went to the warden's office and asked if I was still entitled to a phone call. He had to look it up to see that I hadn't yet made one. He asked why. I said I hadn't had a phone number to call, being an itinerant painter and all. Now I had the number of a friend.

I called Bill Westbrook at the paper. "Come and get me."

I went to the men's room, retrieved the $20 bill from my shoe, went back to the warden's office, and paid my debt to society.

I asked Bill to take me home so I could change out of my painter's rags but he took me straight to the newsroom instead. While he'd been on his way to collect me the city editor had informed the rest of the newsroom staff about where I'd been for the past week. When I walked in, I was greeted with a standing ovation.

This ran with follow-up stories on the prison

My series of articles ran on the front page: "Six Days in Jail." The series was nominated for a Pulitzer Prize. (I didn't win). I was also nominated and chosen one of about 20 finalists for a Nieman Fellowship, a year of free study at Harvard University. I didn't win that either, but mostly because of a screw-up on my own part. More on that later.

Charles Weltner, Atlanta's congressman at the time and a true Profile in Courage, told me how his own father had done the same thing I'd done as an investigative reporter back in the 1920s, and that I was now in very good company indeed.

Awards flowed in. A state Associated Press newswriting award. An annual award from the Georgia Society for Social Welfare. The Junior Chamber of Commerce named me one of Atlanta's Young Men of the Year.

More investigative series followed — police harassment of gays, police harassment of prostitutes, corruption among city judges. Jack Nelson, our Pulitzer-winning investigative reporter, had left to join the *Los Angeles Times* and his slot was open. Bill Shipp, the State News Editor, was thought to be his likeliest successor. He certainly had considerable seniority over me.

Bill was going to north Georgia to interview the head of the juvenile boys' prison there. I forget what the issue was, but he asked me to go along. It was customary on controversial interviews to have a second set of eyes and ears along to corroborate the story. On the way, he told me he would never have done what I'd done, going to city prison like that. He asked why I had done it.

"I'm going to take your job," I said, trying to be quite matter-of-fact about it. He knew I meant the unofficial title of investigative reporter. He just chuckled. We didn't talk much the rest of the trip, but we got a double by-line on that story out of north Georgia, and soon thereafter I was being referred to as the newspaper's investigative reporter. Life was pretty darn good.

Eighteen: Guy Gone Wild

What follows is not exactly one of the prouder episodes of my life. In a phrase, I went wild. Because I could. I was like a little boy let loose in a toy store and told to play with whatever he wanted. Down every aisle I found a new adventure, a new excitement. I could play for a few minutes with a tricycle, run to the train set, only to have my attention diverted to a chrome-plated cap pistol.

Only these weren't toys I was toying with. I was sowing all the wild oats I didn't get to sow during my teenage years, when I had hurtled from the strict rigors of a Catholic altar-boy upbringing and a Catholic high school, to the austerity of seminary life (albeit with the sweet summer interlude with my cousin Marthe), to the turbulence and losses of 1959 and my focus on succeeding in college and then, with hardly a pause, marriage.

It was easy and it wasn't easy. It was easy because I was suddenly quite popular, thanks to my new front-page status with the newspaper. I was welcomed at any party, among the high-brow and the lowly. Everyone seemed to want to know what I was working on next. They flattered me about my journalistic courage, my writing style. Few knew I was living on $16 a week in a $10-a-week rooming house, dining most nights on a half-dozen 12-cent Krystal hamburgers, walking or bussing to work, depending on the weather.

I was part of a small group of journalists who drank and played together. Bill Westbrook, certainly, and Jim Barsky, and Jim Bentley, who went on to become bureau chief for Cox Newspapers (owner of *The Atlanta Journal and Constitution* among other papers and news outlets) in Washington, D.C., and is now comfortably retired on Jekyll Island, Georgia. There was also a guy whose name I don't recall because we all knew him as "The Chief." He was a concocter of quizzes and games. We'd gather at his place, or Barsky's, and he'd test our wits. How quickly could we identify a classical piece of music from just its first few bars? Could we name the novel given only one character's name? I wasn't much good at it, but it did challenge me mentally. The Chief also liked to go into the downtown Woolworth's and order one jelly bean from the bulk bin at the candy counter, or one peanut.

Barsky, another member of our group, was a gruff-talking New Yorker who was on the editorial staff of *The Atlanta Journal*. I especially liked his mother, who lived in Ansley Park. She loved opera and introduced me to it, and to its beauty, reawakening the bits I'd heard wafting from Bobby Mendelsohn's house so many years before. She also introduced me to Atlanta's literary circle, including a woman who probably never knew how much she influenced my career.

Maggie Davis was a successful author, with several novels on her résumé. She took me under her wing. "Dick," she once told me, "this town isn't big enough for you. You will never be able to write what you want to write unless you leave here and go see the world."

I would understand that wisdom soon enough. But for now, I had my pick of dates and places to take them. I volunteered to write reviews of local drama productions, which gave me free tickets and someplace to take a date. After the play, all she had to do was agree to stand by while I phoned in my review. I also volunteered to write a weekly nightclub column for our weekend entertainment section, which gave me free access to the night scene. I interviewed Little Richard in his hotel room, wearing only his BVDs; he dared me to tug on his hair to prove it was real. I interviewed Roger Miller, Kim Novak, Mickey Spillane (more on him later).

I also interviewed Jayne Mansfield when she brought her nightclub act to town. She was wearing a very tight-fitting dress with what I described in print as an "exclamation point neckline" to accent her considerable bosom. She seemed to almost burst through that peek-a-boo slit. In her lap she held a Chihuahua wearing what looked like a diamond-studded collar. I nodded toward her lap and asked, "Are those real?"

"Darling," she said without missing a beat, "everything I have is real."

Gulp. I had meant the diamonds.

It was only a year or so later that she was beheaded in a gruesome collision with a tractor-trailer.

In most nightclubs, I didn't have to pay for drinks, and certainly didn't have to pay any cover charges. I dated a few strippers, including one at The Nitery, a strip club around the corner from *The Constitution* building that I re-christened "Bed of Roses" in my novel. At an after-hours party, someone from the club took secret photos of me with a stripper, or so Becky, the owner, told me when she tried to warn me it might be used for blackmail purposes, but I reported it to the city's district attorney and that was the end of that. I also dated a slim long-legged Press Club bartender named Sam (for Samantha); a nude model for a sketch artist who worked at the Pigalley Lounge (I asked him to do me a drawing of her posed as Rodin's *Thinker*, but he never did, probably because the relationship didn't last that long); a bartender at the Domino Lounge named Louise; a waitress at the Top o' Peachtree; another at a country-western lounge at Tenth Street; even one of the owners of the country-western place. Lest you get the wrong idea, I also briefly dated a woman from the Unitarian-Universalist church who tried to get me to go to church with her. I went once, for the guitar music.

Most of these were relationships that lasted one night, perhaps two or three, some a week or so. But some lasted considerably longer and left deeper impressions.

Maree, certainly. She was the one upon whom I modeled Tonee in my novel, a waitress at The Nitery. She was a bit wild herself. I won't retell her story because it is told (although with ample exaggeration) in the novel. Suffice to say her husband showed up in town, caught up with us at the police station where I was working one night, and tried to wrestle her out of the company car as I swirled around the parking lot, he hanging on to the door, she hanging on to me, I hanging on to the wheel. Police finally broke it up and told us all to go home, with a wink at me. I hadn't even known she was married!

She also was messing around with a pimp who tried to lure her into prostitution. In turn, I tried to get her to set him up to be arrested for soliciting. The police screwed up: he found out about the sting and gave her gonorrhea, on purpose. Guess who had to go get a penicillin shot.

Then there was the gorgeous blonde who was a local radio celebrity. I don't want to give her name because I want to give her plausible deniability. She and her friend had a weekly call-in show. Both were married, she to a doctor, her friend to a lawyer, but both were messing around with newspaper reporters. I was the doctor's wife's mess-around. Every once in a while I was a mystery guest on their radio show, called "Mister X." I would say something outrageous and let the calls flow in. I remember one especially exciting show in which my opening gambit was to state that monogamy was unnatural. Boy, did that light up the switchboard!

She was drop-dead beautiful. The trouble was she knew it. We found ourselves in Miami in August 1968, she to cover the Republican National Convention for her radio station, I on a forced leave of absence from the newspaper. (More about that later.) We were staying at her mother's vacation condo on Miami Beach. She knew somebody who knew somebody and got us into the swank, members-only Jockey Club. She was wearing the hottest of hot pants, the tightest of tight little shorts, all the rage among the jet set back then. After dinner, she got up to go to the rest room and asked me to count the number of guys who turned to watch her walk across the room. I didn't count, she got peeved, and the relationship ended soon thereafter.

And Clara Vann. I was sent to South Georgia to investigate reports that the teenage son of a Green Beret had been arrested and thrown into a dungeon of a jail. Clara was working at the motel where I stayed. Ever on the lookout for an attractive woman, I struck up a relationship with her that soon blossomed. She had a couple small children but her husband was long gone. She, her kids and her parents lived in a shanty on the edge of the Okefenokee. I returned several times. One time I especially remember because a local nightclub owner loaned me his Cadillac to drive down there. What I remember most was the spicy-hot chow-chow that her mother made and gave me a large jar of every visit. I used to throw a dollop of it into spaghetti sauce to liven it up.

Fran Vaughn was the mother of a go-go dancer, Theresa Green (we called her Trees-are-green), in a club up the street from the flophouse where I lived. Truth be told, I was much more interested in the daughter than the mother, who was slightly cross-eyed, but the daughter wasn't available. The relationship was tempestuous, to say the least. She needed an abortion. I connected her with a doctor I knew who was willing to do it, clean. Back then, that was illegal and the only way the not-rich and not-well-connected could get an abortion was with back-alley hacks, usually wielding nothing more than coat-hangers. Fran's was safe.

Fran was usually to be found in a nightclub. Sometimes she waitressed. We'd meet at a second-floor after-hours club. One night she saw me there with someone else and started a ruckus. The only way into or out of this illegal nightspot was a long, rickety, wooden staircase outside. I kept telling her to get away from me, she didn't own me, or words to that effect. She followed me out onto the landing of the stairs and then pushed. I tumbled most of the way down the stairs before breaking my fall. That ended that. (No, no broken bones.)

And there was Diane. Two Dianes, actually. One was another reporter on the paper, whose father, although retired from the Navy, insisted on being called "Captain." She said he told her he didn't trust me because I had "shifty eyes." The other, the longer-lasting Diane, was the wife of yet another reporter at *The Constitution*. She and Joe invited me to drinks at the Press Club one evening to meet "a friend" of theirs, a young lady named Billie. Except Diane kept playing footsie with me under the table, rubbing my leg and such. I got the impression Joe was doing the same with Billie and that that was the *real* end-game of the evening.

Billie and I never did hit it off, but Diane started coming around after that. She was clearly the aggressor. Not particularly attractive in a physical way, she taught me that looks are definitely not everything — not even close. Let's just say she brought a lot of talent to the relationship. She was also something of an artist. She found a large slab of plywood and turned it into a work of art, rubbing natural colors into the grain of the wood, making abstract images of faceless nude bodies, men and women, emerge from the flow of the grain. I kept that painting for years. It was destroyed in a fire in Montreal in 1973.

Among other things, Diane told me Joe was a sadist who liked to tickle her until she screamed for relief. One day at the office, Joe invited me across the street to a cafeteria we frequented on coffee breaks. He sat across the booth from me and quietly announced, "I know you are sleeping with my wife. I'm going to kill you for that."

I laughed — probably that same uncomfortable laugh I used when Gail had told me she wanted to end our relationship, and when those young toughs had approached me at the city prison. "Joe, you know you're not going to kill me."

He just shrugged. As we now know, he didn't.

And yet another Fran. Fran Smith's story is told in heavily fictionalized form in *The Questing Beast*. She was the model for April, a timid, quiet young woman. Long dark hair, large dark eyes that always seemed on the edge of weeping, perhaps in her early 20s when I first met her. At the time, she was a reporter for the *Atlanta Times*, a newspaper started as part of the South's swing to the Republican Party, an artifact of the Barry Goldwater candidacy for president in 1964. She took to stopping by the press room at the police station on Sunday nights, when I would be on duty relieving our weekday police reporter.

She asked me about my work, how I researched stories, how I approached people for interviews. She was slim and attractive but distant. And fragile. In fact fragility seemed to be her essence. She was fragile both on the outside and on the inside. She made you want to protect her from the world. She didn't talk much. She never talked about herself, never said where she was from, what family she had. I knew almost nothing about her, and yet I think I saw her soul, that fragile, searching, tender soul. I wanted to protect her, but didn't know how or from what.

She started coming by my rooming house at night, sometimes waiting on the steps outside until I came home. Maree, the Nitery waitress, saw her there more than once when we'd arrive, sometimes well after midnight. If Maree was there, Fran never let on she knew me. She simply got up and walked away, but Maree guessed that more was going on than was really going on. If ever I had been in a platonic relationship, Fran was it.

Maree decided that it was Fran who had done that plywood painting above my bed. I came back from the bathroom one night to see Maree scratching a nail file across the painting in a rage. I wrestled the file from her, but damage had already been done. There was an end-to-end diagonal gash across the painting. Diane later tried to fix it so it didn't show, but you could always see the shadow of the scar.

Late one night, I heard a feeble knock on my door. When I opened it, Fran stood there sobbing. Her clothes were torn, she was bleeding from several cuts to her arms and face. I asked her what had happened, but all she could say was that she'd been raped. It turned out to be a gang rape. I took her to Grady Memorial Hospital, helped her talk with police. They were not gentle with her, and I remember getting more than a little angry at them for thinking that somehow she was responsible for it. After all, they wanted to know, what was a young woman doing walking the streets at midnight?

She was never quite the same after that. I'd see her pacing up and down the sidewalk in front, as though debating whether to come in or not. She was unusually silent when with me. Then she moved away. First, she went to Athens to work for the *Banner-Herald*. This was about the time that a Black soldier in uniform was killed in a drive-by shooting by what turned out to be Ku Klux Klansmen. Fran had reported on it, then investigated the local Klan's activities and membership. I don't know how much she learned, but she aroused the KKK's ire (which wasn't hard to do). Soon they were burning crosses in the yard in front of where she lived. I think she was asked to leave. She visited Atlanta and told me about it, then moved to Macon.

It was in Macon that she committed suicide. I was in the newsroom when it came over the teletype, about a young woman who had gone to the local medical examiner's office, opened his desk drawer, took out his pistol and shot herself. She had written most of the story herself, before going there to do it. I was devastated. I knew she had been disturbed, I just didn't know how much.

I put her story in *The Questing Beast*, published some 17 years later. I wove it into a mystery about her origins, that perhaps she was a lost half-sister who had come to find André (I concede, my thinly disguised alter ego).

My mother read the book but never said a word about it to me. Not one. I learned from my sister much later, after my mother died, that sometime around 1990, Mom received a mysterious phone call from a woman asking for my father. She had asked, "Who is this?" The woman had said she was my father's daughter. Elaine says my mother believed I had known some deep dark secret about an illegitimate daughter. I swear on both my father's and mother's graves that is not true.

April may have been modeled on Fran, but their stories are very different. I know, absolutely, that Fran was not related to us, because her real father called me almost a year after her death, waking me around seven in the morning. I remember that conversation as though it were yesterday.

"You knew my daughter."

"Your daughter? Who is this?"

"Fran Smith?"

"Yes?"

"I'm her father."

"Yes?"

"I want to know why you haven't filed a claim for her insurance money."

"What insurance money? What are you talking about?"

"You don't know? She left half of her life insurance to you. Why, I don't know. But they won't give me my half until you claim yours."

"You can have my half."

"They won't do that. And for some reason she wanted you to have it. I don't need it and I don't want it."

"Tell them to send me whatever forms I need to sign."

That was it. I gave him my address, the paperwork came, and soon afterwards a check for $2,500. I used it to buy a car, a 1967 Mustang, direct from the factory, arranged for me by the local Ford publicity guy. I even got to order the color scheme I wanted: candy-apple red with white-parchment leather interior.

Dawn Hester was a cousin of a photo-retouch artist at *The Constitution*. She had a young daughter and was divorced. She was susceptible to weeping fits. We both said we didn't know what "love" was, so instead of

"I love you" we said "I hate you" to each other. You had to be there. The late 1960s was that kind of time.

Her mother had her declared incompetent and committed to the state mental hospital at Milledgeville, then took custody of Dawn's child. I wound up driving Dawn to the hospital. I couldn't believe where she was being sent, watching the truly insane loll about the corridors, hearing the great metal doors clang shut behind her. For several months after that, I went to visit her on Saturdays. She lived behind locked doors, among people who were clearly insane. She didn't belong there. I managed to get permission to take her out of the hospital for a few hours on our Saturday visits. Eventually, she was released to a halfway house. I like to think I offered some solace to her life. Some 20 years later, while I was living in Washington, she found me. She was living in Colorado by then and was happy. That made me feel good, as though I had done at least something right to prove I wasn't a complete cad.

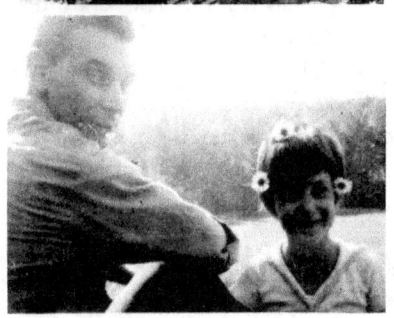

Not everything in those first years after the divorce was wildness. Now with a car, I also could go out to Smyrna to see my daughters. On one outing I remember taking Teri and Renée to Kennesaw Mountain National Battlefield Park and running down through a meadow of wildflowers. Diane (the reporter's wife) was with us and later told me Renée had asked her, "Why is Daddy running?"

"Because he's happy," Diane said. And I was. We were together and the kids were fun to be with.

I still have black-and-white snapshots of them from that day in the park. The photos are seriously deteriorated now, because they lived in my wallet for years, well into the 1980s. I especially like the one Diane caught of Teri, the flower child.

Life was good. Very good.

Nineteen: Goodbye to All That

I also think of the period from the mid-1960s to the start of 1969 as my professional and cultural awakening. The turbulence of the 1960s was at full throttle in Atlanta, with anti-war marches, civil rights marches, Ku Klux Klan rallies, and riots euphemistically called "civil disturbances." I added a bit of my own reportorial excitement to that mix.

On September 7, 1966, all hell broke loose in Buttermilk Bottoms, a slum on the edge of downtown. The city fathers, in their wisdom, had decided simply to bulldoze it down and replace it with Atlanta Stadium, because they had enticed the Milwaukee Braves to move there. They had no plans to relocate the 40,000 or so poor Blacks crammed into that hell-hole. They were simply going to be driven out.

Into this volatile mix stepped the late Stokeley Carmichael, an incendiary Trinidadian activist and leader of the Student Nonviolent Coordinating Committee, who later became known as Kwame Ture. He got the folks riled up over some police action of relatively minor import. They were massing in the streets. I was sent to see what the commotion was all about.

The Mayor, Ivan Allen, came to the heart of Buttermilk Bottoms to demonstrate concern. He climbed atop a police car with a bullhorn and tried to talk to the crowd. (A few years later, the Kerner Commission would conclude this was the absolutely worst strategy: instead of dispersing the crowd, it offered a focal point for the anger.) The crowd became thicker and angrier.

I was standing next to the police car, just behind a policeman, taking rapid notes of what the mayor was saying. Some men in the mob started rocking the car from the other side. The next thing I knew the mayor tumbled off the roof and landed in a heap at my feet. The mob was going berserk. I helped him to his feet and said something like, "Mr. Mayor, I think we'd better get the hell out of here."

We ran through the milling throng, rounded a corner and ducked behind a building just as the canisters of tear gas started flying. I mentioned to the mayor that yesterday had been my birthday. "Happy Birthday."

*Moments before the mayor fell at my feet.
(Associated Press, Sept. 7, 1966)*

We both just shook our heads, stunned to see Atlanta, the self-declared "city too busy to hate," succumbing to all-out violence.

In early summer 1967, I was sent to Jackson County in North Georgia to meet with a Jaycee fellow. He claimed to have inside information about corruption among local government officials, starting with the sheriff. He told me what he knew, which wasn't much, and what he suspected, which was a lot. There was only one man you could trust, he said. That was the local solicitor, Floyd G. "Fuzzy" Hoard, the circuit-riding district attorney for Jackson and two other counties. The sheriff's name was "Snuffy" Perry. Watch out for him, I was warned. Sounded like a comic strip character to me.

I told my editors there seemed very little substance we could hang a story on. Back then, we didn't write news stories about conjectures, rumors and suppositions. (These days that rule seems to have fallen by the wayside.) We decided to wait a bit. We waited too long.

At around 7:30 a.m. on Monday, August 7, 1967, I was jarred awake by the telephone.

"They bummed Fuzzy," a voice shouted at me.

"What?"

"They done bummed the s'listah. They put some dynamite in his car and blowed him up."

I was now enough awake to recognize the voice as that of my Jaycee contact in Jefferson. Fuzzy Hoard had been murdered by a dynamite bomb under the hood of his car, wired to his ignition switch. He was dead, the windows in front of his home were blown out, parts of his car were strewn as far as a hundred yards away.

I spent the better part of the next six months in Jefferson, Georgia, living in the Crawford Long Motel, in a room next to that of agents of the Georgia Bureau of Investigation. I did some investigating of my own and learned about the car theft rings and bootleg whiskey rings that were at war with each other and seemed to dominate the economic life of the region. A 76-year-old man named Cliff Park was the ringleader of the bootleggers, those who brought whiskey and beer into the dry county for retailing out of shacks scattered around the rural foothills.

I got to know quite a few of the bootleggers personally. I also got to know the king of the auto theft rings, A.D. Allen, said to have had a million-dollar-a-year enterprise running statewide. He'd done his time and now lived in a house trailer where he raised fighting cocks. I also got to know quite a few moonshiners, people with names like "Hog-Jowl." And lots of GBI agents. I was their constant companion. At one point, when they had a meeting in their motel room next door to mine, I tried to listen in through a glass held against the wall. I didn't learn much, except for one heated expletive-filled exchange. Soon after I asked them what that was all about they moved to another room.

In the end, they arrested five men for the murder: the two young ones who actually planted the bomb in the car, John Hyman "J.H." Blackwell and Lloyd George Seay; another who helped them acquire the dynamite in South Carolina and then assemble the bomb, George Worley; a fourth who recruited those three for the job, and Cliff Park himself, who had paid $5,000 to have it done.

I covered their trials, which ran several weeks. Blackwell and Seay turned state's evidence in exchange for lesser sentences. Worley and the fourth man, George Pinion, got life. Park was the only one sentenced to death, but he died in prison before they could electrocute him.

Out of all this was revealed the drama of Fuzzy Hoard's illegitimate son by the wife of his preacher, and the widespread trafficking in illegal booze that greased the pockets of the sheriff (who was never tried) and others. There was even a *femme fatale*, Tillie Gayton, a curvaceous redhead who looked like she had stepped right out of a L'il Abner comic strip. When she entered the courtroom in her oh-so-tight miniskirt, all heads turned. It was she who had talked her boyfriend Blackwell into confessing. The GBI had let her visit him in Atlanta's Fulton County Jail after other leads had led them to suspect him. They left her alone with him for an hour in an infirmary holding cell, complete with a cot. When she came out and they went back to him, he confessed.

It was truly a story worthy of the old comic strip, "Snuffy Smith," the moonshine-drinking old coot who presumably lived up in the mountains of Tennessee or Kentucky.

I told Joe Cumming, the *Newsweek* bureau chief in Atlanta, that there was a book in all this. I asked him to collaborate with me on it. I wasn't sure my skills were up to so large an undertaking. We did work on an outline for several weeks but he finally backed out. He said I didn't need him to do "word-smithing." We had too many differences of opinion about how the story should unfold.

By now I was back in Atlanta, investigating rumors of mafia efforts to move into the city and take over restaurants and nightclubs to launder its money, now that major league sports were coming to town. There was also talk of a new spike in drug trafficking. I was nosing around, asking a lot of questions that apparently were making some people nervous. One evening in a lounge not far from my rooming house, a bouncer I knew pulled me aside and said there was a contract out on me. I didn't put much stock in the rumor, but then he said, "That's him." He nodded toward a blond guy in a dark suit at the far end of the bar. "Watch out for him. He uses a knife."

I still don't know whether I should have believed him or not. Was he just playing on the fear of a young reporter for the fun of it? Was he trying to scare me off the story for his own sake? Or was someone else trying to scare me through him and the bouncer was simply the innocent messenger? Whichever was the truth, it was succeeding. I was scared enough that I didn't think it wise to hang around that lounge much longer.

Only a day or so after this, I was summoned into the managing editor's office as soon as I arrived at work. With Tom McRae were a couple guys I also new: city vice squad detectives who themselves had unsavory reputations on the street, if not in their official files. They told me they knew I was investigating drug trafficking and wanted me to lay off, I was messing up their own investigation. My boss said nothing. He just listened, nodding, as the cops said they knew about my work because one of my own sources was also theirs — and he'd blabbed.

I looked at my boss, again asking for help.

One of the detectives said, "If you don't drop the story, we can make you do it."

"How?" I was getting angry.

"We'll find drugs in your car."

"That would be a neat trick," I said. "I don't have a car." (This was before Fran Smith's insurance policy put me into a Mustang.)

My boss finally chimed in, asking if I had made a buy yet. I said no.

The cop insisted. "We can find them in your possession."

The managing editor made a decision: he ordered me to stop my investigation. The police promised that when they finished theirs, I'd get an "exclusive" on the story. I knew they would never "finish." And they never did. There never was a story told, and by all accounts the drug trafficking continued unabated.

I was put on six-month administrative leave, without pay. I was told to go somewhere out of town until things cooled down. I wrote Gail a note with my last check, explaining that I would be incognito for six months and without pay. If she could manage that long, I'd make every penny up to her when I came back.

First, I stayed briefly with some friends on the faculty at the University of Georgia, sleeping in their basement. I spent my days visiting Jefferson, interviewing key people in the Fuzzy Hoard story for the book that would never be written. Prominently among them was his widow, Imogene. We met in the coffee shop across from the Crawford Long Motel. The first words out of her mouth when she sat down were "What's in it for me?"

She wanted the book to portray her husband as a paragon of virtue. Something like Peter Marshall, she said, the inspirational Scottish immigrant preacher who went on to become a revered chaplain of the U.S. Senate, made even more famous by the book, movie and play, "A Man Called Peter."

I told her she would get to tell her side of the story as she knew it and I would let the facts speak for themselves. She walked me through her and Fuzzy's wonderful courtship, his early life as a triple-A baseball player, his move to Jefferson to marry her. It was a beautiful story, unfortunately belied in more than a few respects by what I already knew. He had challenged the corruption in Jackson County, however, and for that deserved great praise. It was widely believed, including by me, that on the morning he was killed, he was on his way to a newly convened grand jury with evidence of corruption in the sheriff's office and possibly other officials. We never knew because he and his evidence never got there. The dynamite bomb that went off virtually in his lap also shredded whatever papers he was carrying with him that morning.

After a few weeks, I moved to a shack higher up in the mountains, a place rented by a moonshiner I'd met. He let me and my portable typewriter stay there rent-free. He even taught me how to run a moonshine still. (Actually, you don't "run" it. It runs itself. You mostly watch, occasionally stirring the mash.) And I proceeded to try to write the book about Fuzzy Hoard, using it as the platform to tell the larger story of Georgia mountain culture clashing with modern civilization, and what happens to those who dare confront that culture. I saw it as a grand tapestry of the Georgia hill country, and a not flattering one. The working title: *Kudzu Castle*. In the end, that tapestry grew so large I was unable to control it. I wrote hundreds of pages but couldn't move the story forward. Ultimately, I surrendered and put it away. The chapters, the copious notes, the photos all live on, consuming most of a drawer in my filing cabinet still. I kept kidding myself that one day I would resurrect it, but I know that I, too, had become entangled in the kudzu.

Fuzzy's son, G. Richard Hoard, did write a book about it, the one Imogene probably wanted written. It's a memoir of his father called, *Alone Among the Living*. I have a copy.

I was at the moonshiner's shack when he returned from a trip into town for groceries and told me he'd received a message for me: call your office. I had told my editor that if they needed to reach me, to call my friends in Athens. I'd told them whom to call, and so on, leaving messages like a trail of jelly beans.

Martin Luther King, Jr. had been killed. My editor wanted me back in town. The white Mustang that police believed the killer had used to flee Memphis had been found abandoned in a Black public housing project in Atlanta. They thought I might have the best contacts to pick up the trail from there.

I came back and pursued the story for a few days, but James Earl Ray had skipped out of the country and was caught in a London airport some while later with no help from me. Instead, I was arrested.

As soon as I entered the newsroom one day, two sheriff's deputies walked up to me, handed me an arrest warrant, read me my Miranda rights, handcuffed me and walked me out again. Gail had sworn out a warrant for my arrest for nonpayment of child support. She had called the sheriff's office that morning to let them know I was in town and where I could be arrested. She knew I was in town because a substitute night city editor had put my byline on a silly rewrite of a news release the night before, a minor story about MARTA, the rapid transit agency, which had been another of my reporting specialties dating back to my first year at *The Constitution*. I had specifically asked that I be given no by-lines during my return. This substitute editor obviously didn't get the memo.

Marion Gaines, our city hall reporter, came to see me in the holding cell at the courthouse. When he had the facts, he talked a judge into releasing me on my own recognizance, my promise to show up for a hearing. I headed back to Jackson County and the office of Wesley Channell, the lawyer who had been named to succeed Fuzzy Hoard as solicitor. Wes and I had become friends. He agreed to negotiate a settlement for me and told me I really was going to have to pay something, that I shouldn't have handled it the clumsy way I had.

Wes negotiated with Gail's attorney, with a judge in Atlanta, and I guess with a bank for a short-term loan. A sum was agreed upon (I honestly don't remember how much, a couple thousand, I would guess). It was transferred to Gail on the promise that when my six months leave was over I'd resume all payments. The arrest warrant was dismissed and I was free to go back to the moonshiner's shack. It was about a year later that I learned that Wes Channell, an admitted alcoholic who had told me about binge drinking and lost weekends in his past, drove to his ex-wife's home in a nearby county, parked in front, and shot himself in the head. Suicide was becoming a morbid shadow following me through life.

During that summer of 1968, I was dating the blonde bombshell from talk radio. When Bobby Kennedy was killed, I was again at the moonshiner's shack. In fact, he delivered the news to me. I was shocked. The world had lost its mind. Bobby had won my heart politically as the last best hope of our generation. Now *they* had killed him, too.

In August, I went with the curvaceous blonde to Miami Beach for the Republican National Convention and her sashay through the Jockey Club in those too-too-short hot pants. We visited the Fountainebleau Hotel and this time I did get into the Boom Boom Room, where we had a few drinks and ended up in a shouting match. We had wonderful nights in her mother's condo on the beach, saw the Republican convention up close, and went to a Nelson Rockefeller rally on the beach itself. Little did I think then that the end of my career in Atlanta was just around the corner.

It was on this trip, incidentally, that I learned from my mother, wrinkled nose and all, that Elaine was pregnant with Lise. I don't think Mom wanted her to keep her baby. I'm glad she did.

By now, I had digested many a lesson about the South and all its charms. I knew it in all its Bible-thumping, twangy-music-stomping, deep-fried, smarminess-coated racism. Civil War obsession was rampant.

People wearing white sheets were taking small children to cross burnings.

I was sent to Macon, Georgia, at the request of Ralph McGill himself, the acknowledged dean of southern journalism, a hero of a man with uncombed steel wool for hair and a raspy voice. As editor of *The Constitution* he'd won every award there was to win. He was the conscience of the South on matters of race, culture, and barbecue. At a distance, he had replaced the father I'd lost. I respected him more than any other person in Atlanta.

McGill said he had a friend in Macon, a minister in an all-white church. Baptist, I think. The congregation was meeting that night to vote on his ouster because he had invited Black people into the church. He wanted me to just sit quietly in the congregation, witness the event, then come back and write the story. He said to take an unmarked car.

The church was packed. I found a seat in the middle and listened. Right at the start a man got up and said he wanted to make sure everyone there was a member of the congregation. He demanded that any non-members identify themselves. I saw the minister nodding at me from up front. I knew he meant for me not to try to lie. I stood up. Where was I from, the man demanded. Atlanta. Who did I work for? *The Atlanta Constitution*.

That was it. Five or six very big men came down the aisle and stood staring at me. I knew enough to leave without a fight. They followed me out the door and to my car, then climbed into pick-up trucks. They stayed in my rear-view mirror all the way to the Macon city limits. And yes, the preacher was ousted. He called me later to give the sordid details.

Earlier in the '60s, I'd sent a trivial attempt at fiction — a few chapters of what was to be a novella about a boarding school in upstate New York, where the janitor committed suicide by giving himself a detergent enema — to a critic and agent who had advertised he was looking for new authors. He'd sent back a nice long letter, the essence of which was that I had promise but I wrote like a "smart-alecky Charles Dickens." He said I seemed to be steeped in classical literature, which I was, and that I needed to read more contemporary fiction. So I put aside my *Ivanhoe* and *Tale of Two Cities* and launched into satiating myself with 20th Century fiction — Hemingway, Steinbeck, John Dos Passos, Sherwood Anderson, John Updike, and John O'Hara, who had lost his own father at age 19.

And I read the southerners, William Faulkner foremost, but also Eudora Welty, Tennessee Williams, Truman Capote, Flannery O'Connor, Thomas Wolfe. I found that so many of the very best were from the South. Perhaps it takes a history of violence and hate to breed great literature? I haven't yet resolved that in my own mind. But I knew the South was equally and simultaneously capable of producing great literature and culture and some of the ugliest, most demeaning forms of human behavior imaginable.

So, when the mud hit the fan in September, I think I could see the finish line. The beginning of the end of my "Atlanta period" was a short editorial written by a just-out-of-college writer, B. J. Phillips. She had been a standout at the University of Georgia School of Journalism. Gene Patterson, our editor-in-chief, had hired her to bring a younger and female perspective to the stodgy old white-guy thinking that had dominated southern journalism, even at our own progressive newspaper. Her column that day was about a meeting of the Georgia Public Service Commission scheduled the next day. It was to hear and vote on a request for a rate increase by Georgia Power Company. She wrote that if ordinary citizens wanted to see how the "big boys played the game," they should go to the hearing.

The Chamber of Commerce, the real arbiter of Atlanta's political and cultural life, didn't like that. Someone called Jack Tarver, then president of Atlanta Newspapers (or maybe Tarver thought it up all by himself, I don't honestly know). Tarver called Patterson after the first edition hit the streets and ordered the editorial removed. Patterson refused. Tarver ordered B.J. fired. Patterson again refused. Then Tarver fired Patterson himself, on the spot, as well as B.J. (The initials stood for Beecher Jamieson, a heck of a name to give your daughter, although apparently not uncommon in the South.)

We got the story the next day. Patterson and B.J. were both gone. (They soon both surfaced at *The Washington Post*.) Remer Tyson, our political editor, and I, as the now acknowledged investigative reporter, were the top staff members, he the top of the beat reporter pyramid, I the top of the general assignment pyramid. We stewed privately about developments all day. Then we heard that Gene Patterson was going to be replaced by Remer's own predecessor as political editor, Reg Murphy, now the managing editor of *Atlanta* magazine, the Chamber of Commerce mouthpiece. Among other things, we also knew Reg was a darling of the Talmadge political machine, which had been running most things in Georgia since the 1930s.

Remer and I met at midnight at the Varsity, a vast hot dog emporium near the Georgia Tech campus. We decided that at 2 p.m. the next day, when all staff, both day and night crews, were in the newsroom, we would stage a walk-out in protest of this business office intrusion on editorial prerogative.

I was scheduled to report in at 2 p.m. but came early. As soon as I arrived, Remer stopped at my desk. "He wants to see you."

I looked up with question marks in my eyes. He nodded in the general direction of McGill's office.

Ralph McGill shut the door behind me. The meeting did not last long. He was sympathetic. But in so many words, he asked me what he had asked Remer: don't do it. He argued it would ruin our careers and hurt the newspaper, and not achieve what we hoped.

I told him we were worried that the business office and the Chamber of Commerce were going to control the newspaper's content. He assured me, "As long as I'm alive, that will not happen. If you ever have any problem in that regard, you come to me."

If those were not his exact words, they're pretty close. We called off the walk-out.

But the die was cast. It was only a few months later that I was invited to address the international convention of the Institute for Rapid Transit in Pittsburgh. Its executive director was Bob Coultas, whom I'd known from covering MARTA, Atlanta's rapid transit agency, because Bob had been a behind-the-scenes lobbyist with General Electric, interested in selling rapid transit motors. Bob explained that they wanted to have a panel of four knowledgeable reporters, one from each of the four jurisdictions that had had ballot referenda that November to authorize funding to build rapid transit systems, two of which had passed (in Washington, D.C. and New Jersey) and two of which had failed (in Atlanta and Southern California). I, of course, said I'd be honored to participate.

The newspaper had other ideas. The Pittsburgh convention was to be in February 1969. That, they said, put it smack in the middle of the Georgia legislative session. They couldn't spare me. But I had never before been assigned to cover the legislature, I said. I would be this year, they said. I offered to use my annual leave. Nope. I'd use compensatory time they owed me for extra hours I'd worked (*The Constitution* did not pay overtime, they paid it in extra time off). Nope.

I called Bob and said I was coming anyway, but to please not tell anybody. He said he needed a text of my speech to put in the proceedings. I agreed to do that.

It's my conviction that the editors and their business office superiors knew I was not going to be complimentary in explaining Atlanta's failure to approve bonds to build MARTA. I'd already made that fairly clear in some of my post-election analysis. Because of the threatened walk-out; because of several appearances in court and before labor arbitrators challenging the newspaper's policies, including not paying women reporters equal pay for equal work; because of my reporting that uncovered police brutality, police harassment of not-so-nice people; for my exposé of the city prison that had embarrassed the power structure, for these and many similar reasons, I believe, I was "branded." I was a troublemaker. I was not good for Atlanta's "image." Maggie Davis was being proven correct.

I should also mention that in 1967 I'd started growing my goatee and mustache, something the newspaper's vice president, Bill Fields (who, incidentally, had recruited me from the University of Florida in 1961), never failed to mention whenever he passed by my desk. "Shave that damn thing off," he'd snarl every chance he got. This, of course, made me firmer in my resolve to keep growing it.

I wrote my speech as a child's parable, a story about a poor girl named MARTA who had five daddies, none of whom wanted to take responsibility for her. Each had distrusted the others, the ones in the outskirts (read Cobb, Gwinnett, and Clayton Counties) thought she would just bring unsavory dark-skinned people to their clean white enclaves, while the daddies in Fulton and DeKalb Counties thought they'd be paying too much to help those who fled the city's taxes to come back and work in the city. I sent the piece to Bob and he had a crew make an interesting set of fairy-tale slides based on my allegory.

Then the bottom fell out of my world, again. Ralph McGill died. It was at his birthday dinner, I believe. He was at home with family and friends and simply pitched forward over the dinner table and was gone. The South lost a great voice for reason. I lost my mentor and protector.

On the Friday before the trip to Pittsburgh, I wrote a memo with multiple copies: one to the city editor, one to the managing editor, one to the president of our union (I was vice president at the time). I sealed them in envelopes and handed them to a copy boy with literary aspirations, Pascall Grubs (what a great name for an author!). I told him that on Sunday he should put them in the addressees' mailboxes. The note simply informed them that if they did not see me in the newsroom on Monday, it would be because I would be in Pittsburgh, addressing the Institute for Rapid Transit. If that meant I was forfeiting my job at *The Constitution*, so be it.

I flew to Pittsburgh. I told Coultas what I'd done, and word quickly spread through the hotel. I was stopped in the lobby, in elevators, at meals. People I didn't know wanted to know how it had happened. I told the truth.

When we sat up there on the dais to give our presentations, we four reporters found the hall jam-packed. I was told there were more than 3,000 people in the room, which would mean pretty much everyone at the convention. The speeches went off without a hitch, followed by standing ovations.

Then the job offers and speaking invitations started. A campaign manager for somebody running for Virginia governor wanted to know if I'd go to Norfolk and meet with his candidate. I didn't. Someone from the National Defense Institute, a Pentagon think tank, invited me to give the same presentation to his group of interns on my way back to Atlanta. I agreed, although what MARTA had to do with national defense I had no idea. Someone from Westinghouse Electric told me they were opening a new public relations office on Long Island and would love to have me work there for $36,000 a year. My Atlanta salary at the time was barely $9,000 a year, but I politely declined. I was not a PR kind of guy, and certainly not for a corporation.

I returned to Atlanta on Wednesday, after making my presentation at the National Defense Institute. In my mailbox I found my memo. Across it the managing editor had scrawled, "So be it." I was told to turn in my building and parking lot passes immediately. I did.

I then paid a visit to the Georgia Senate to say goodbye to friends, both among the press corps and the senators. There on the senate floor, Leroy Johnson, the first Black elected to the Georgia State Senate since Reconstruction, pinned a badge on my lapel. It was just like the name badges senators wore, except this one read, "FAL FAL GGA I FAL."

"What's it mean?" I asked. "Give me a hint?"

"Free...at...last..."

I finished: "...free at last, Great God Almighty, I'm free at last!"

The Senator was grinning ear to ear. Reporters standing around were applauding. Joe Brown, who had threatened to kill me, said, "He may be a sonofabitch, but he's our sonofabitch!"

A month later, I packed my few belongings into my candy-apple red Mustang and headed for Washington, D.C., Maggie Davis's words ringing in my memory: "You will never be able to write what you want to write unless you leave here and go see the world." And on my chest that badge declaring my freedom. I still have it. Life was indeed good.

FAL FAL GGA I FAL

Twenty: Hello, D.C.

My first stay in Washington, D.C., lasted three and a half years. These were, again, transitional years. (I seem to "transition" quite often.) Atlanta had taught me at least one more thing I was not destined to be – a lothario. Those last few years in Atlanta I had bounced from relationship to relationship in an almost dizzying whirl. I discovered that was not me. In Washington, I began seeking more lasting relationships, a more stable social life.

I also transitioned from news reporter to advocate, from a dad with two daughters to a father with none, from an aspiring author to a published one, from a political neophyte to a graduate of the school of political hard knocks. These were the Nixon years.

My first stop was Art Pine's home. Art was the *Constitution's* Washington correspondent. He helped me find a suitable apartment in Adams Morgan, a multi-cultural, night-life-heavy neighborhood where the "lefties" tended to live, but downscale in rents, especially compared to the more trendy Georgetown. I found a furnished first floor studio apartment on a one-way street in the heart of Adams Morgan for $115 a month, utilities included. At the end of the block, on Columbia Road, was a fine — and inexpensive — Cuban restaurant; next to that a grocery store; a short walk up Columbia Road a topless go-go bar; around the corner on 18th Street a bar, Millie & Al's, which became my regular haunt; across from that a basement jazz club that brought in top talent; and a half-block farther up Columbia Road, Avignon Frères, a pastry shop *cum* catering business that also had a large showroom that brought in top national musicians. What more could a young man want for neighbors?

Parking, I guess. Finding a parking place for my Mustang each night became the biggest headache. You could comb the alleys and side streets for hours hoping to see someone vacate a parking slot, sometimes blocks from your own home. I collected parking tickets like kids collect baseball cards. Within a year I sold the car (for almost exactly what I'd paid for it three years earlier) and bought a bicycle.

Now, I needed income to pay for the rent, the groceries, the entertainment, and the parking tickets, not to mention child support. I called Gene Patterson, my former editor, now managing editor of *The Washington Post*. He invited me to his home where, over dinner, he told me he was sorry, he was already under fire for hiring too many of his old Atlanta staff, including his protégé, B.J. Phillips. I wasn't really interested in another newspaper job, I told him. I hoped for something that would engage me in the social movements of the day. He said he'd see what he could do. Gene Patterson knew people.

I went to see Cody Pfanstiehl, the public information officer for the Washington Metropolitan Area Transit Authority (WMATA, D.C.'s version of MARTA), whom I had met in Pittsburgh. Yes, he needed another staff member, but he was under pressure from unions to hire an African American.

I went to the Urban Mass Transit Authority, a branch of the U.S. Department of Transportation, which was looking for a staff writer. I had met some of these people in Pittsburgh, too. After a few days I got my reply, quietly and not in writing. They had sent my application, as was the custom, to the congressman from Atlanta, where I had last lived. His name was Fletcher Thompson, a Republican. A few years earlier, when he had been a member of the Georgia Senate, I had investigated and reported on his links to the John Birch Society, an extremist right wing group. He had used his government office and phone lines to broadcast its racist messages and sell its publications. Now he was using his office to pay me back. He had vetoed my application, I was informed. I could forget about working for the federal government, the city's largest employer by far.

I took my résumé to a "headhunter," a job-finding agency for professionals. The woman behind the desk munched on her lower lip as she read through it. Finally, she put it down. "I'm guessing that your favorite color is pink," she said.

"Pink" was code for "Communist" in Richard Nixon's Washington.

"Actually, it's more like beige," I said. I picked up my résumé and left.

Too liberal, too white, too "pink," an enemy at large in the Congress. I was beginning to think there was no slot in Washington that I might fit into, let alone my Mustang. Had I made a gigantic mistake? It was too late to backtrack now. I had little choice but to continue pushing forward. Only weaklings gave up, I told myself.

Rep. John Conyers from Detroit, Michigan, helped a bit. He was a friend of the partner of the stunning blonde I had left in Atlanta. On her recommendation he hired me to write responses to constituent letters. It wasn't much, and I wasn't much good at it, but it kept me afloat for a few weeks. Conyers has since become one of the most powerful and respected members of Congress. I owe him a debt of gratitude.

I finally hit pay-dirt when Gene Patterson called and suggested I talk to the folks at the Urban Coalition, a foundation-funded organization started by former HEW Secretary John Gardner to try to resolve urban conflicts between haves and have-nots before they erupted into rioting. My job: to go quietly into designated cities with the names and contact information of a few people, investigate local conditions and file a case report. Who were the key players on both sides of the economic and power divide — the key business and political leaders, and the key people in the African-American community? What did each want? What did each fear? What areas of common interest might they share? What strategy might work best to bring them together in meaningful dialog? I was asked to keep a low profile and use my investigative reportorial skills.

I went to Bridgeport, Connecticut; to Niagara Falls, New York; to my old back yard, New Bedford, Massachusetts; to St. Paul, Minnesota. While in Niagara Falls I made a side trip to Buffalo and looked up my old high school and college friend, Tony Capodicasa. He had been married but was now living alone, running an underground newspaper and still using his old refrain for every situation: "Come the revolution!" He had changed little.

(A few years later, in 1973, while living in Montreal, I received the news from Tony's wife, whom I'd never met: Tony had checked into a motel room in Buffalo and stuck a gun in his mouth. He, too, like the revolution he'd awaited so ardently, was dead.)

It was the St. Paul trip that most redirected my life, in more ways than one. I was told to go to the Minnesota Club to meet with a group of people from Washington who were planning a retreat for key players in the city. When I arrived, a strikingly attractive woman was at the front desk, obviously frustrated. They wouldn't let her in. Unfortunately, not only was she a woman, Mary T. Howard was also Black. The Minnesota Club was for "White Males Only."

Mary was getting nowhere trying to convince them she belonged in the meeting. I asked if I could help. It turned out she was also from Washington and going to the same meeting as I. I suggested to the clerk behind the desk that he ask the people in the meeting whether she should be allowed in. After considerable cajoling, he admitted her.

At the meeting, we sat across from each other. I was just an observer; she was a psychologist, a consultant to the firm that was going to run the weekend-long "sensitivity training session" that summer in a seminary outside Minneapolis. When I reported back on the planning session, I was assigned to attend the retreat as an observer. Mary was one of the session trainers. After introductory sessions, in which we were instructed that we were all participants, that there were no "observers" here, we were divided into working groups. Each group had a few people from the African-American community and a few from the power centers of the city, all personally invited.

In my assigned working group, I soon discovered that the Catholic bishop, a key figure in the power circles of St. Paul, had not bothered to come himself but had sent a priest, his secretary. On several occasions, issues brought up by blacks — park space, swimming pools, other amenities for their neighborhoods — received no response from the bishop's delegate. Asked whether the bishop would use his considerable influence on such matters, the priest repeatedly said he couldn't speak for the bishop.

I'd had enough. I asked to speak. I said I found it offensive that the bishop thought so little of his community that he couldn't attend the retreat himself. I said he apparently needed it more than any of the others. Instead, he had sent his lackey, who couldn't make any decisions and was making a mockery of the whole exercise. Couldn't he hear his fellow St. Paul citizens crying out for understanding and a little help? What kind of Christian was he?

I sat down to a spatter of uncomfortable applause. That evening, as dusk gathered, I was walking the grounds and having a cigarette when Mary walked up behind me. "I heard what you did in there today. Everyone is talking about it. That took a lot of guts."

"I don't know about guts. I was just pissed off."

We talked a long while that evening. At some point she said that after this weekend she was flying to New Hampshire for another training program. Her car was already there, and she planned to drive back to D.C. She'd welcome company.

I told her I had to go first to Dayton, Ohio, on another consulting assignment, this one for a "Center City Transportation Study" funded by the President's Commission on Urban Transportation and run by the National League of Cities and the U.S. Conference of Mayors. By then I'd been hired as one of a handful of team leaders to investigate and report on transportation issues in mid-size cities, an ill-disguised attempt to woo congressional support from such communities for funding for mass transit projects (big-city congressmen already supported it). But after Dayton, I was free. What if I changed my flight plans and flew to Boston instead of back to Washington? Could she pick me up there and drive back to D.C. together?

We had different flights from Minneapolis, but oddly enough we both had connections out of Chicago. When I arrived at O'Hare, I found her standing alone in the center of a large open space, fists clenched and trembling at her hips. They had lost her luggage, she cried. I remember thinking, for a psychologist, she did not handle stress very well. I took her to a baggage claim counter, helped her file a claim to have her bags sent to New Hampshire, then bought her a drink.

We fulfilled our respective duties in New Hampshire and Ohio and reconnected in Boston. We were hardly 50 miles from Hyannisport, Massachusetts, on our way to New York City, when we heard on the radio about Ted Kennedy's tragedy at Chappaquiddick two days before. It would prove to be the doom of his presidential ambitions.

I took Mary through Swansea to show her where I had grown up (it had changed remarkably little) and we stopped at Naragansett Pier to have a traditional New England shore dinner.

We arrived in New York City the evening of the historic moon landing, July 20. We'd decided to stay the night and watch the landing on the jumbo TV screens in Central Park. We stopped to get a room at a midtown Howard Johnson's. I forget the exact sequence of events, but while I waited in the car, they refused to accept her credit cards at the front desk. She assumed, probably correctly, that it was because of her skin color. She came out and asked how much cash I had. We pooled our money and went in together. She slammed the money on the counter and said something like, "Is this the right color for you?" We got the room. We insisted on a room with two beds, and I promised we would sleep separately. I kept that promise.

We headed to Central Park to watch the moon landing. It had rained and the park was muddy. Thousands had gathered for that historic "one small step for man, one giant leap for mankind." It was an inspiring moment in a turbulent age. Something bonded between Mary and me that night, something that had started at the Minnesota Club and slowly grown during the weekend retreat.

It was not long after this that I asked Gail to let Teri and Renée come to visit me. As I recall, they spent a week, perhaps two. They slept in a spare bedroom at Mary Howard's house much of the time (my own place had only my single cot). They played in the parks and swam in a public fountain in front of Union Station on a sweltering day wearing only their underpants. They were fun to be with, and then they were gone again.

Mary and I dated for about two years. After I'd traded my Mustang for a three-speed bicycle, I'd peddle my way across town to and from her home. In bad weather I took buses. Adams Morgan is in the northwest sector of the city, she lived in the southeast, perhaps 10 miles away. She was counselor to students at Federal City College, akin to a dean of students.

Once, while I was visiting, her cat, not at all a friendly sort, wandered down the alley behind her home. A large dog leaped out at her and the cat raced back up the alley for home, the dog in hot pursuit. I was on the back porch watching all this. "Catch her! Catch her!" Mary shrieked as the cat bounded up onto the porch and started up a tree. I caught her hind legs. The cat tried to wiggle and climb out of my grip but I held on for dear life. Then the cat let go, spun around, threw herself over my shoulder and raked my back with her claws, drawing blood. As I said, not friendly. Mary has been laughing about this incident ever since.

We (Mary and I, not the cat) got along famously until her friends came to visit, and then I would feel slighted. I'd go to her home at a pre-arranged time, and she wouldn't be there. Sometimes I'd wait, sometimes I'd return home, piqued. When we fought, it was over that. The fighting finally reached the breaking point. One night, a little after midnight, I was leaving on foot, crossing Lincoln Park up the street from her home. She chased after me, yelling something. We stood facing each other, a hundred or so feet apart, screaming obscenities at each other.

It was finished, but it was not over. After we had both left Washington, I to Montreal and she to Rutgers and then New York City and, finally, St. Cloud, Minnesota, our friendship re-blossomed and became more durable and more understanding than ever. She is a truly remarkable person and a "best friend" to this day.

I continued consulting — a fancy Washington way of saying you are paid to do things but you are not on staff and you do not get benefits like annual leave and health insurance or unemployment insurance. You are under contract. When the contracted work is done, you are out of a job.

My most lucrative project was the urban transportation study "team," consisting of myself and a graduate student. In addition to Dayton, we studied Indianapolis, where the then mayor (now U.S. Senator) Richard Lugar treated us to a tour of the city by helicopter, and Flint, Michigan, already a half-deserted former hub of automobile manufacturing, the ancestral home of Buick. Our studies of these three cities, plus what I already knew about Atlanta's and Washington's transportation histories and problems, became my first book, *Highways to Nowhere*, published in 1972. I had no strong yen to write the book, but was pressed to do so by George Smerk, a graduate business school professor at Indiana University who was also a technical advisor to the transportation study.

He urged me to write it, then helped me find a publisher, Bobbs-Merrill. Later, he even assigned it to his graduate students at Indiana, helping it to respectable sales figures. George and I exchange Christmas cards to this day.

I wrote much of the book sitting in a booth at Millie & Al's, sipping beer and playing Frank Sinatra's *My Way* over and over on the jukebox. Millie was long gone, but each evening, Al would sit at his table at the back of the restaurant eating his spaghetti dinner and smoking his cigar, looking for all the world like a *padron* in a gangster movie. Sometimes fighting would break out among the Latinos who gathered there. Beer bottles might get broken for use as weapons, and the woman behind the bar (it seemed Al only hired big burly women bartenders) would come out with a Billy stick, pop a few heads, grab the offenders by the scruffs of their necks and almost lift them off the floor as she headed them out the door. Amid this turmoil, I wrote my chapters in longhand, for retyping later.

At the end of 1969, barely nine months after my arrival in D.C., work opportunities evaporated. The Vietnam War wasn't going well. We'd invaded Cambodia. Nixon went on an austerity drive, canceling all federally funded consultancies in one fell swoop. I returned from my Christmas-New Year trip to Miami to discover I had no more work, no more income. I'd already lost the Urban Coalition consultancy — they didn't like one bit what I'd done at that retreat in Minnesota — but now the funding for the transportation study was gone, too.

I'd also done some editing and writing for documentary films by another long-time friend, Bob Johnson, that was federally funded. Nixon had decided the way to heal society's wounds was through volunteerism. The government presented awards to four volunteers of the year — two domestic, two international. Johnson had the contract to do 10-minute docudramas on each recipient and hired me to help put them together. For the international winners we used stock film footage they had accumulated, but for the domestic winners, we went on site to shoot original footage and interviews.

One site was in Detroit. While there we took a night off and crossed into Windsor, Canada, to see Sammy Davis, Jr. We were lucky and got a table next to the stage. It was one of the most memorable performances I've ever seen. Sammy was on stage for two hours, non-stop, singing, jumping around, dancing, telling jokes, perspiring profusely in a bright pink jumpsuit, a tightly wound bundle of energy. Unforgettable.

The four docudramas were shown at a gala banquet at the U.S. State Department. We of the film crew were invited, of course. But every dish came served with heaps of California grapes. Cesar Chavez had been trying to unionize the migrant workers who picked the grapes in California and had called for a national boycott. I spread the word from table to table not to touch the grapes, they were obviously Nixon's plan to undermine the boycott by having the government buy up grapes. I don't know how effective I was, but it didn't make me any friends that night.

Then came a film Bob Johnson was doing for the Civil Service Commission about low-level federal employees. We called it *Nobody Knows My Name*. We filmed intense round-table discussions with janitors and cleaning ladies, with their union organizers and their supervisors. We did the film in *cinema verité*, using their own voices to tell the story, knitting together pieces from these round-tables and individual interviews with no narrator. The film was severely edited by the agency that had hired us. They wanted fluff, not honesty.

I protested, but Johnson understood that he who pays the piper calls the tune. I wasn't placated. I wrote an angry article about it for *The Nation* magazine, published under the title, *The Federal Job Ghetto*. Bob was furious. He sent me an angry letter about breaking trust, that I had no right to make public what were private conversations with our clients, and that he'd see to it I never worked again in Washington. He certainly never spoke to me again.

I guess I was still the kid swinging at the first good pitch that came along, regardless what the coach said.

With no more work in sight, and with child support payments still due each month, I frantically circulated my résumé again. I did get calls, but most were from entities like the Petroleum Institute and other corporate members of the vast highway lobby. I had to explain to each that I had built my career largely on fighting the highway lobby, why would I go to work for it now?

Then Ben Kelley called. He said he was communications vice president of the Insurance Institute for Highway Safety and that someone had passed him my résumé. He needed a senior writer. Was I interested?

"With all due respect, it sounds like the highway lobby again. And if there's one industry I dislike and distrust more than the highway lobby, it's insurance."

"You don't understand," he said. "You don't know what we do."

"Okay. What do you do?"

"We crash cars."

"Now that sounds like fun."

I went to the Watergate Office Building where the Institute was headquartered just downstairs, as it turned out, from the Democratic National Committee offices that were burglarized a few years later, the burglary that turned Watergate into a household name. We talked, and I became Ben's senior writer.

Ralph Hoar, Dolores Smith, Chuck Wixom and I soon became inseparable. Chuck went on to a normal married life in Detroit, the only "normal" one in the group. Ralph "came out" in a letter, delivered to me in Mexico in 1975 by my good friend Wolsey Semple, informing me he was gay. Dolores "came out" to me even before that, while we were still working at the Institute. After lunch at Howard Johnson's across the street one day, she asked me to join her for a drink in the Watergate Lounge. There she told me she wasn't getting ahead in her career and that she was afraid it was because she was lesbian. Had I heard anything? I hadn't, and I swore I didn't think anyone knew. I certainly hadn't guessed it. I told her, "Listen, this news doesn't bother me, but don't tell Ralph. I don't think he could handle it." It was several years after this that we both discovered he, too, was gay.

Ralph was only recently returned from his tour of army duty in Vietnam where he said he hadn't seen any combat. His function was a "go-fer" for some brass. He was the editor of the Institute's newsletter, innocuously named *Status Report* but feisty. Ralph did great investigative pieces on dirty little secrets in both Detroit and among the supposed regulators of the automotive industry. Dolores was an assistant to everyone. I helped write and edit the newsletter, but my primary function was outreach to the media and writing the films and testimony that exposed how cars crumbled in crashes (those "we crash cars" films), and how cars and roads could both be designed for greater safety. The descendants of those films are still used in car and insurance commercials today.

It should come as no surprise now that I was often at odds with the Institute's president. William Haddon was a renowned epidemiologist who had introduced the concept of studying car crashes as a scientific health problem. He had headed the National Highway Traffic Safety Administration under Lyndon Johnson. That was the agency created in the mid-1960s after Ralph Nader's blockbuster book, *Unsafe at Any Speed*, had exposed the hazards built into cars by Detroit. When LBJ left office, so did his appointees, including Haddon. The Insurance Institute had snatched him up, promising he could change its focus from blaming the driver — "it's the nut behind the wheel" — to scientific examination of all three elements in a crash: the occupants, the vehicle (package) and the roadway (environment). It is that concept that gave us, largely because of the Institute's work, padded dash boards, air bags, and a host of other car safety features.

I felt we were doing important work, and we were. But our in-house attorney, Andy Hricko, too often made us take things out of our films and newsletter articles and other publications because he didn't think he could defend them in court. I told Haddon I thought the attorney's job should be to tell us *how* we could say certain things, not to just not say them when we knew them to be true. I told him the "vibes" weren't right between us. Big mistake.

"So you believe in black magic?"

I should note that years later, Andy and I became good friends.

Gail asked me to allow Teri and Renée to be adopted by her new husband, Junior Dalton, a guy she married just home from Vietnam. Junior loved the kids, she said, and they loved him. They were now in school and didn't know how to answer when they were asked why their mother's last name was different from theirs.

I returned to Georgia to talk with them and meet Junior. His attitude, his tattoos, his "muscle" car — I found it all off-putting. Gail pleaded. I asked the girls what they wanted. They both said they wanted Junior to be their daddy, although I must admit they seemed a little less certain about it than Gail was. Gail made it clear she did not think I had any right to stand in the way of their chance to form a new family and find happiness.

I returned to Washington and thought about it a great deal. I was truly in a quandary. I loved my daughters, but I was hundreds of miles away from them. And, as Gail had said, who was I to stand in their way? In the end, I agreed. I tried to convey to them that the adoption was a piece of paper, a legalism, and that I would always be their father, that they would always know where to find me. It isn't much, I know, but I think I have tried to keep that promise. That single decision is the one thing in my life that I deeply regret, that I wish I could do over, that I could unmake.

Meanwhile, my personal life took another abrupt turn. One evening, as I sat on my stoop sipping a beer, Ann Eyerman walked by. She stopped, we chatted, I probably offered her a beer, and that, as they say in the movies, was the beginning of another beautiful friendship. This one lasted more than 10 years and flourished internationally, from Canada and Mexico to Greece and Spain. To start with, she was attractive, smart, and lived just down the street, not clear across town, as Mary did.

Her home became an extension of mine. We helped organize a block party in the neighborhood. When the Larry King Show (then on radio, from midnight to 2 a.m. or 3 a.m. as I recall) asked me to be on to discuss a cover story I'd done for the *Washingtonian Magazine* (I'd also become a regular contributor by then, starting with minor freelance pieces that eventually evolved into assigned stories featured on the magazine's cover), it was at her apartment down the street that I sat, sipped my Scotch and chatted with Larry and callers from around the country. The article had been titled, "Why Is Everyone in Washington Scared?" and was about the security binge running rampant in and around the city — multiple locks on doors, private police forces, gated communities, all by-products of Nixon's branding Washington the nation's "murder capital." I'd demonstrated that crime was actually worse in the suburbs than in the city, but it was the city that was paralyzed with fear. Needless to say, this brought out all the "Lolitas," as the little-old-ladies-in-tennis-ankle-shoes were known in the parlance of the day.

In January 1972, Ben Kelley asked me to join him for lunch. He took me to a restaurant near Adams Morgan. After a few martinis, he asked, "Have you thought about your future?"

"What do you mean?" I think I knew perfectly well what he meant, but I needed time to think.

"To be honest, I'm tired of being a buffer between you and Haddon. I'm constantly having to explain each of you to the other one."

It occurred to me to ask why he didn't suggest that Haddon quit instead, but this time I had sense enough to keep my thoughts to myself. I ordered another martini so I'd have more time to think.

"I'll make a deal with you," I finally said. "You've been talking for months about how you want to do a documentary about roadside hazards. As far as I can tell, you haven't done much of anything on it. I've helped with film editing. I've helped with film writing. But I want to lead the whole orchestra, just once. Give me that movie. Let me write it, organize it. Put me in charge of the project. When it's over, I'll leave quietly. No fuss."

"You've got a deal."

The movie was *Boobytrap!* It dramatically displayed how highway roadsides were designed to kill anyone who strayed: the sign post made stronger after a car hit it, so the next time it was hit, the car and passengers were damaged even more; the guardrail end that speared right through errant cars instead of being flared and buried to guide them back onto the roadway; the sign strategically placed in a "gore area" at Interstate exit ramps so any straying car would have maximum chance of ramming into it. The film won the Golden Eagle Award from the

Council on International Nontheatrical Events (CINE). It premiered before a congressional committee. And it launched Dolores' film career.

I'd asked to have Dolores assigned to assist me with the film. She and I rode all over the Maryland and Virginia suburbs and exurbs looking for the best locations to film. We went to New York City to work with the production company and its editors. She was on the scene with me when we filmed Ben, as the narrator, talking from the roadside of an Interstate highway near Baltimore.

A while after I left the Institute, so did she, to launch a career as an independent film-maker. She now has numerous successful films to her credit, all highly acclaimed. I believe I have copies of all of them.

Ralph, too, left the Institute not long after me, to try his hand at a variety of lobbying and safety-related investigative tasks. I worked with him on several of them during the 1980s, when I again found myself with no funds, no income, and few prospects. Ralph, now deceased, and Dolores are the definition of true friends.

In addition to freelance writing for *Washingtonian* and working at the Institute and writing *Highways to Nowhere*, I was also writing and editing a monthly news digest for the Institute for Rapid Transit, Bob Coultas's outfit.

All this work was finally bringing in money that I was able to hoard. It also afforded me precious little time for playing around or spending money on anything but necessities. I was too busy to have fun at anything but being too busy. If we went out to a fine restaurant, it was late at night after putting the Institute's newsletter to bed, often to the Watergate's restaurant, but sometimes to La Niçoise, a fabulous French restaurant in Georgetown where the maitre d' and waiters were all on wooden-wheeled roller skates, silently gliding over carpeted flooring. Women customers received a kiss and a flower at the door. After dinner, the staff of the restaurant put on a raucous comedy and music show.

Suddenly, we learned we were unable to get reservations there anymore. It was always "booked" for the whole month. We discovered it had been taken over by Nixon's White House staff, who had ordered all tables for every night. This, of course, did not help endear us to Nixon.

Nor had the author in me disappeared. Each year, the American Booksellers Association held its convention in Washington. I went to it to hang out and to meet agents and authors. I recall one conversation there with a publisher's editor. I told her of the novel I wanted to write about my father, how he had lived, how he had died so abruptly, so prematurely, and as though he had known it beforehand.

She shook her head. "That," she said, "is where your novel starts." She was right.

After *Boobytrap!* was in the can, but still a few weeks before it was to premiere before a Congressional audience, I prepared to exit Washington. I told Ralph and Ann and others that I'd be gone 10 years. If I didn't have a novel published by then, I'd come home and try to re-assemble a "normal" life. The folks at the Insurance Institute gave me the traditional going away lunch, in a Japanese restaurant in Georgetown where we sat on cushions on the floor. Ben Kelley, whose wife was Japanese, especially loved Japanese food. Before lunch, Ralph detained me at the office after the others had left and produced a few joints.

He told me to get high. This was going to be emotional, he said, and he wanted me mellow. He said that regardless what was said, I should keep my cool, pretend everything was really nice, that there was no bitterness, no anger. I assured him I really wasn't feeling any of that but I smoked the weed anyway. Then he drove me to the restaurant, both of us fairly stoned. The ceremony must have gone off without a hitch, because I don't remember much about it except for the going-away gift. Inside a "bon voyage" card was the picture of a bicycle cut from a magazine: they'd bought me a bicycle that would be delivered once I got to Montreal. I needed only to call the bike shop. (My own bicycle had been stolen a few months earlier.)

Ralph and Ann were both at Union Station to wave me off at the end of September 1971, on my way to write my long-delayed novel. Life was good and, I knew, soon to get better.

Twenty-One: Parlez-Vous?

What I remember most about the train ride from Washington to Montreal is the slow, grindingly cautious clickety-clacking, inch-by-inch, across a seemingly endless rickety trestle bridge over a lake, wondering all the while, "What's next?" What was I about to get myself into? Was I embarked on a fool's mission? I was not at all confident about next moves. I wasn't even confident that that train wouldn't fall off that thin wobbly bridge and plunge us all into the lake below. That, of course, didn't happen.

In Montreal, I stayed a few days with Ivar, Marthe's older brother, a lifelong bachelor who had a small apartment in Cartierville on the city's outskirts. Ivar worked in a printshop downtown but seemed to spend most of his free time in a tavern drinking beer. He looked for all the world like a long ago comic strip caveman named Alley Oop — the grim mouth, the squared jaw, the square head. He was short and square all over. We rapidly became friends and he helped me brush up my long rusty French skills. (Marthe and her new family — a husband and two young daughters – were then living in Toronto.)

After perhaps a week, I found an inexpensive room on Boulevard St. Joseph, an easy bike ride from Mount Royal, which became my favorite haunt. The mountain looms over downtown Montreal and the venerable ivy-clad edifices of Victoria Hospital and McGill University.

At the mountaintop stands a huge iron cross, illuminated at night by hundreds of light bulbs.

A short walk from the cross is a "chalet" and a large semicircular overlook, beneath which spreads the city's downtown, the St. Lawrence River beyond, and the flat farmland of lower Québec Province beyond that. The "chalet," which is what everyone calls it, in reality is only a huge dining hall with an exposed-beam roof. Carved wooden squirrels stand in the angles of crossbeams and the slanted roof beams, as though supporting the roof on their heads. A few dozen picnic tables are pretty much the only furniture in the great hall, or were back then. Behind it is a cafeteria and vending machines. It's a perfect place for lavish parties — weddings, graduations, bar mitzvahs — and for the quietude necessary for writing a novel.

I plunged into the work. Each day I bicycled from my room to the mountain and up the snaking gravel roadway to the chalet. I'd choose an out-of-the-way table and start outlining and writing my novel, longhand, on legal pads. I'd spend much of the day up there, lunching on a wedge of *tourtière* (a uniquely French-Canadian meat pie) from the cafeteria and sipping not very good coffee or a hot chocolate. In the afternoon, I might lie in the grass under the cross and look for four-leaf clovers.

I had been gone barely four weeks, but I was lonely. What social life I had revolved around meeting Ivar for beers at his tavern after work. The beers cost 25 cents each and you usually ordered two or four at a time. Back then, taverns were for men only. A recent law requiring all commercial establishments to serve women had grandfathered taverns, primarily because they did not have ladies' room facilities and were mostly small mom-and-pop operations without the finances to remodel. If you wanted a beer with a woman, you went to a "brasserie" instead, much more refined (and better smelling) establishments.

I bored Ivar silly with talk of my writing.

"You want to write a real novel, something different?" he asked me one evening after I don't know how many beers. "Write about failure."

"Failure?" Either his voice or my hearing was blurry, perhaps both.

"Everybody writes about success. That happily-ever-after crap. Write about real failure."

He obviously was self-referring. I didn't know the details, but I knew that as a young man he'd been in love with a woman who had left him. I also knew he had wanted to be an architect, but his father had belittled that plan and told him to be realistic and become a printer, like himself.

I don't think I understood then the depths to which Ivar's own perceived failure had plunged him. It was not failure of achievement. It was, I came to believe, his sense of having failed himself, an abject giving up and being utterly unable to lift himself up again. I didn't see it then because I had never myself experienced that kind of failure. Many years later, Ivar died, virtually homeless, unemployed, a drunk, dependent on his sisters for handouts.

What he'd said that evening lodged in my mind, however. Years later, while I was in Morocco, I did write a novella I titled *Failure*, a pretty ridiculous, avant-garde story with all manner of symbols of failure, real or impending — mirrors shattering into shards, leaps back and forth across time. Absolutely everything the protagonist tried to do ended in failure. Never published, it was pretty awful. Ironically, renamed *MindWarp*, it became the title novella of a book of short fiction published three decades later to considerable acclaim, including being listed among Kirkus Reviews' "Best of 2011" and the novella winning first prize in the Florida Writers' Association competition for the 2011 Royal Palm Literary Awards.

Under the giant cross atop Mount Royal I found a four-leaf clover and sent it to Ann and invited her to visit me. She agreed and stayed about a week. I took her to my mountaintop, and in my best imitation of Satan offering Jesus the world after his 40 days in the desert, I spread my arms out over the city of Montreal and beyond.

"I want to go and see it all. Why don't you come with me? I'm offering you the world."

She didn't say yes, she didn't say no. She said she wanted to think about it. That was October.

In November, at my request, Ivar took me to Thetford Mines to visit our relatives at the Manoir Hébert. It was now being run by a cousin, Yvon Cloutier, son of Aunt Antoinette and Uncle Albert. I visited graves of long dead relatives. I browsed through a used book store and a small book almost leaped off the shelf at me from across the room: the history of Thetford Mines, written in 1926, the 50th anniversary of the discovery of asbestos in the area and the founding of the mining town. It was in that little history that I learned of the rigid autocracy of my grandfather, his leadership in all things having to do with morality, like banning demon rum and driving "foreign entertainments" (like movies) out of town. I think the book burned up in the Montreal fire a few months later. I no longer remember its name or author.

Ivar returned to Montreal and I caught a bus on the highway out of town to the mountain village of Ste. Claire, because that is where

Ivar and Marthe's mother, Aunt Gerardine, had told me our grandfather had come from. It was snowing heavily, and as the bus pulled into town, I saw a sign on a rather shabby building: "Hotel Hébert." I knew where I would stay.

It was a bug-infested flophouse, but I have no doubt it was once a fine place owned by some ancestor of mine. Down the street was the Catholic Church. I went to the rectory and introduced myself to the priest in my halting French. I wanted to look at old baptism and wedding registries. He was grumpy but took me to a library, gave me a desk, and showed me the books — rows of large, leather-bound ledgers, all hand-written, recording all the births, baptisms, marriages and funerals back to the founding of the parish in 1824. I dug back into history, looking for the Héberts.

I don't remember how many hours I pored over those ledgers. I think I spent a couple afternoons at it. I traced my father's lineage back through a succession of great-grandfathers to Jean. I found he had served as godfather at the baptism of a child named Napoleon Blais in 1846, but couldn't sign his name. The priest spelled out the name, Jean Hébert, and said he was the spouse of Marie Turgeon. All Jean could do was sign an "X" at the bottom.

But in 1852, when he served as a witness to the marriage of one Joseph Hébert-Couillard, the priest identified him more fully, as Jean Hébert-Couillard, still the husband of Marie Turgeon, so definitely the same man, but he had now learned to sign his name, if shakily: "Jean Hébert." Apparently by the 1800s the family was commonly called Hébert, "Couillard" a mere encumbrance and possibly even considered pretentious and too difficult to spell. There is only one way to be an Hébert-Couillard: you must be a direct descendant of that marriage between Guillemette Hébert, Louis' daughter, and Guillaume Couillard, who had received the French King's permission to keep the Hébert name and *seigneurie* alive.

The import of this only struck me much later, after more research, but I stared at that entry a long time, trying to comprehend fully its significance. How do you establish a link to the distant past? Imagination fails you. You can't put yourself there. Not really. What was my ancestor like? Was he poor? A farmer? A builder? A leader in his community? A shopkeeper? Was he gentle or gruff? And Marie Turgeon. What was she like? The one thing I knew about Jean now was that he was a striver. Illiterate into adulthood, he had learned how to write in his later years — his own name, at least. He had not been satisfied with his place in life. He'd wanted it better. I felt certain of that.

Imagination might fail you, but you do feel the tug of history drawing you into itself. I dug deeper, trying to find out who Jean's parents had been and whence they had come, but without success. They must have pre-dated the parish, or come to Ste. Claire from elsewhere. I was at a dead-end, with nothing but conjecture to take me further back.

I caught a bus to Québec City and visited the few other siblings of my father who still lived (other than Marthe's mother, of course, then still in Montreal). These were the two nuns, now living in a church retirement home, Soeur St. Jean du Sacré Coeur and Soeur Marthe. Soeur St. Jean, born RoseAnnette, was the elder, and feeble. I had a hard time understanding her French. Soeur Marthe was much the livelier one, with dancing blue eyes and wit. I loved talking with her, but she had a hard time understanding *my* French. She said I kept choosing the wrong gender for my adjectives. If a noun was masculine, I was modifying it with a feminine adjective and *vice versa*. (These things matter in French and other Latin-based languages, if not in English.) She advised me always to do the opposite of my first inclination. That only made matters worse, because then I was second-guessing which instinct was truly my first.

Soeur Marthe told me how to find Rosaire, the "black sheep" youngest brother. He had been going to the nuns for hand-outs whenever he needed food or shelter. They would let him do small chores around the retirement home, and then give him food or money. He was living with a daughter (one of his many offspring scattered over much of French Canada, I was told) and her new infant in downtown Québec.

Soeurs Marthe (l) & St. Jean du Sacré Cœur

I went to see him. The baby squalled endlessly, the daughter stayed busy in the kitchen, and Rosaire, looking very much like an older, skinny version of my father, brought out his scrapbooks, huge compilations of random clippings and photos, trivia that seemed connected to something in his mind, linkage I never did quite fathom. These were trinkets in his life that he believed had big meaning, but he was unable to convey that meaning. I left understanding that he was considerably disconnected from reality. When you open the closets of your past, you must be prepared to find the unheroic.

It was also on that trip that I first visited, and photographed, the monument to Louis Hébert where it originally stood, at ground level outside City Hall. (They later moved it to make way for the entrance to an underground parking garage.) Louis, Guillaume and Louis's wife and children all stood on a platform barely a foot off the ground, a tryptic of my ancestors. Snow had fallen and lay on their heads and arms like shreds of blanket. I photographed them that way, in black and white.

Hébert Monument at original City Hall location, 1972

My photo of Louis, shaking a sheaf of wheat at the heavens, is on the cover of *The Questing Beast*.

By December, Ann said yes, she'd travel the world with me. She quit her job as assistant to the director of the National Folk Festival Association and gave up her apartment. Her father (or maybe it was her mother) asked why she wanted to travel the world, she could find anything she wanted right there in her own back yard. Her parents never did take to me, nor I to them.

I rode a Greyhound back to the States and visited my family in Miami for Christmas. On the way back, I stopped in Washington, D.C., and Ann accompanied me the rest of the way to Montreal. When we arrived, I discovered that the building where I'd had my room had had a small fire and had been vacated for repairs. My things were there, undamaged, but we had to find other quarters, immediately.

We found an apartment in an old stone building on Park Road, even closer to the foot of Mount Royal and next door to a Kentucky

Fried Chicken (KFC), complete with a giant bucket of chicken revolving just outside our window. It was said our building had been a Scottish castle that had been transplanted to Canada stone by stone. Our rooms were in that front part of the building, the "castle" overlooking the street. Behind the stone part were more nondescript red brick apartments clearly added much later.

I resumed my daily climb up the mountain to write. Each day, Ann retyped what I'd written the day before, which I would then re-read and modify for her to type yet again. She also went to the city library to do research I needed. She researched all the flowers that are in the novel, flowers my father planted, their life cycles, where they would thrive and where not. She researched how tornados are formed, how stomach ulcers can creep up on you and finally pierce through the stomach's lining to knock you to the floor. She became very much both writing partner and sounding board.

Ann also found the library book that clinched our lineage. It was a biography of Louis Hébert and the story of his descendants, written around 1910 by a bishop or cardinal named Couillard, himself a descendant. The book was in celebration of the 300th anniversary of Louis' settling in Québec. It informed me how the Couillards had kept the Hébert name alive so that my great-great-grandfather would inherit it, even if he couldn't spell it out, to pass it down to me. The cleric had included the line of ancestors that had led to him, but it was impossible for me to decipher which branch of that tree had finally produced Jean Hébert. Still, there now was no doubt: we were descended from Louis.

During the winter months, when snow was piled high everywhere, my bicycle stayed locked in the basement of our apartment house. As soon as spring peeked through the earth's frozen crust, in early April, I brought it out and locked it to a railing beside the building. That's where the bicycle was when Ivar and a friend of his, a guitar-playing wannabe folk singer, took Ann and me to a cabin in the Laurentian Mountains for a weekend getaway.

The weekend was restful, a truly bucolic event. It was good to get out of the city and see the stars again. But when we returned, as we approached our apartment, we realized something was terribly wrong. Fire trucks and police cars were everywhere. You couldn't drive within a block of our home. We walked instead, then ran. Our building was rubble.

In the Laurentians with (l-r) Ann, a friend and Ivar

Ann came up behind me. "Your manuscript!"

I went berserk. I ran to the nearest police car, shouting that I needed to get inside to see if my manuscript might have somehow survived. The driver had a clipboard on the seat beside him.

"Do you live here?"

I nodded.

"What's your name?"

I told him. He crossed me off the list on his clipboard. "OK, that's one more accounted for," he said to his partner in French. Then in accented English to me, "Mister, there's nothing left in there. No, you can't go in."

It took both Ivar and Ann to calm me down. As I recall, 13 people died in the fire. It came out in court later that it was an insurance fire set by the janitor, Romeo, a rather nice old guy we'd befriended. He'd done it at the behest of the owners, who were defaulting on a mortgage. The newspaper said people had been throwing babies out their second-floor windows. Others were jumping out themselves with no safety nets. A section of roof had collapsed right through where our apartment had been.

Ivar took us to a nightclub. I remember the entertainment was a transvestite. You didn't know he was a guy until the very last moment of his bump-and-grind routine. We talked about anything but the fire, the loss. We kept laughing to keep from crying. Ivar took us home with him. All we had were the clothes on our backs and what few things we had taken to the mountains. Even my new bicycle was gone.

But not for long. It was in the newspaper the next day. On top of page two were three photos: a broken doll, my bicycle and a wheelchair. The caption said: "Three lives disrupted — a child's, an adolescent's, a senior citizen's." I was the presumed adolescent. I called the police department and, sure enough, they had the bike. They had cut through the cable locking it to the fence and "rescued" it to their station. I was free to come and get it.

Clothing, books, records, record player: all gone. I had sent Ralph carbon copies of a few early chapters of the novel to save for me in my filing cabinet, which he was also storing for me. We went back to Washington by Greyhound, with an empty suitcase and temporary passports issued by the U.S. Consulate in Montreal. We had the newspaper front-page article about the fire to support our story, both to the consulate and to Customs and Immigration officers at the border, all of whom were fairly skeptical of it.

Ralph collected clothes, linens, pillows and other household items from friends. He even hosted a party for us at which all our friends came bearing the wherewithal to get us started again. It is at times like this that you reflect deeply on how important it is to have friends, that being alone in this world is a disastrous policy. We are none of us alone. We can make enemies or we can make friends. I vote for family and friends first, in that order. Ralph had proven more than once the depth of his friendship.

Back in Montreal, we located a ground floor apartment in a different part of the city, still reasonably close to downtown, but much farther from Mount Royal, too far for a daily trek to do my writing. A small park down the street, where mothers brought their babies for fresh air and old ladies walked their dogs, would have to do. I resumed my writing there, on a park bench.

My first decision was that the fire had done me a favor. When I re-read the chapters Ralph had saved, I realized they were worthless. I started over, from the beginning. This time, instead of writing the way one might flush a toilet, just letting it all gush out, I painstakingly constructed the novel's ebb and flow, much as it was eventually published. I walked the streets collecting names for my characters. There was a rue St. André, a rue St. Dominique, and many others that helped me name the characters in my story.

I went overboard trying to spread our money thin. We ate kelp and lots of soy beans instead of meat and fish. In May or June, Ann went back to Washington briefly to work for her old employer, the National Folk Festival Association, to help organize its annual summer festival, but she soon came down with double pneumonia and landed in the hospital. I returned to Washington after that and tried to help her. I wrote and organized the brochure for the festival (which was where I met the young and little known songwriter and folk musician John Prine and shared a joint with him and others at a late night jam session). Then we resumed our life in Montreal, albeit with a sturdier diet.

By August, I had a first full draft. Ann and I had sat on our front stoop sipping beers in the evenings, we had explored the island outskirts of Montreal with Ivar on Sunday afternoons, but mostly we had not only worked on the novel, we had lived it. It was a labor of love that consumed our days and nights, dreams during sleep, conversations during meals. We talked about how we felt we knew the characters intimately, as real people.

We rewarded the culmination of our work with an adventure. Ivar proposed taking us to the Gaspé, the fat thumb of Québec that lies south of the St. Lawrence and juts out into the North Atlantic. We hitched our bicycles to the back of his car (she also had one by now). Together we camped out near *Roche Percé*, a huge rock through which the ocean has chewed a tunnel. We ended up in Québec City, where Ivar left us with our bikes, as he had to return to work.

I introduced Ann to Québec and to Soeur Marthe, to Louis and the ramparts and cannons, to all the history and unique culture of that grand old city. Then we bicycled back to Montreal, 160 miles down the road than runs alongside the St. Lawrence. We had no tent, just our backpacks and sleeping bags. A strong wind soon came up off the river and forced us to walk much of the way. Then came the rain, driving against our faces. We spotted a house with a large front porch and went to it, trying to crouch under its roof. A woman came to the door dressed in black.

We asked her permission to stay there until the rain let up. She wouldn't hear of it. She brought us inside, made us get out of our wet clothes, gave us warm bathrobes, and put our own garments in a dryer. She even fixed us hot chocolate and soup. Then she apologized: she was on her way to her brother's funeral and couldn't stay with us, but she wanted us to stay there at least until she came home. When she did return from her brother's funeral, she insisted we eat again.

I wish I knew her name now. She exemplified a level of hospitality I have not seen anywhere else. I hope someone was as kind to her when she was in need as she was to us that day.

We eventually made it back to Montreal, tired but proud of our endurance if not our skills. And, by now, we were researching the next big question: where next?

We went to "Man and His World," the world exposition that had been held in Montreal several years earlier. We collected brochures and information on countries in Europe. We liked what we read about the climate of Yugoslavia (mild winters!), and the historic city of Dubrovnik. We decided to start by heading there.

By now I had found an agent in New York. I don't remember how I happened across his name, but he had agreed to represent me as an author. I sent him my completed manuscript of *The Questing Beast*. Later, after he'd read it, he said it was a good "first draft," but that I should set it aside for a year or so, then re-read it and see what I thought. It proved to be exceptionally good advice.

We didn't want to fly to Europe. That was too swift. One needed to approach an adventure like this slowly, moving from one culture to the other the way they once did, with excitement and anticipation and wonder, with time to absorb the distance the spirit would travel.

The romantic thing to do was book passage on a freighter. Way too expensive, we soon found out. Then Ann put her considerable research skills to work and came up with the Canberra, a Cunard Line luxury ship that was in trouble. They had tried to use her for Caribbean cruises, but her draw was too deep and her drunken captain had grounded her off Martinique. She was just too big and clumsy for what they wanted, so they were going to take her back to Southampton, England, and scuttle her. They were offering a one-price, one-class, one-way passage from New York City to either Cherbourg, France, or Southampton. We opted for Cherbourg, departing in mid-September. (The ship was not scuttled; a few years later, while in Greece, I saw her steaming through the Corinthian Canal.)

Some sadness had to be dealt with first. In May, I had learned that Jim Barsky, my old friend from Atlanta newspaper days, had been diagnosed with bone cancer. By September, he was hospitalized. He had moved to New York City even before I had moved to Washington, and I had visited with him in his West Side brownstone several times. Now his mother was there from Atlanta. She let us stay in the apartment for a few days before our ship left. We went to see Jim in the hospital. His mother left us alone with him.

He was unrecognizable. The cancer had spread everywhere. Always a portly man with a ready grin and a big Brooklyn voice, Jim was now emaciated and quiet as a whisper, lumps of bone cancer visible on his head and over his skimpy body. He had lucid moments, but many more in which he went away to places unknown. He asked me about some leather jacket I had loaned him. (I hadn't.)

He took my hand and said, "Have a good trip."

I squeezed his. "You, too." I said.

What else could I say? It was clear he was leaving us. Pauline, his mother, came in and we said our goodbyes. He died while our ship was in the Atlantic. He was 33 years old.

If it had not been drilled into me enough when my grandfather lay dead, when my dog Tiny died, when my brother was killed, when Dad died, when Fran Smith and Tony Cap and Wes Channell committed suicide, none of which events I was physically present at, I was vividly there now. Death stared me in the face with all its finality. How portentous those polar extremes of living and dying! For Jim, life was over. For me, mine was entering a new beginning.

I knew as never before that life is a limited engagement. Shakespeare said it best:

> *Life's but a walking shadow, a poor player*
> *That struts and frets his hour upon the stage*
> *And then is heard no more...*
>
> (Macbeth, Act V, Scene 5)

While you're strutting your hour upon the stage, you had better make it good.

Twenty-Two:
On the Road Again

Simply too much happened between September 1973, when we embarked for Europe aboard the Canberra, and September 1976, when we settled in Spain, to cover completely. It would take an entire book of its own, one I have thought of writing but wondered who would bother reading it, much less buying it. What might be its central, unifying theme that could turn these events into a compelling narrative? Here, I'll limit myself to a series of verbal video clips, a sort of in-print highlights film of what we did and saw over those three incredible years. It is hard now to believe it all happened in such a brief span of time.

Language, a stumbling block for many travelers, posed little problem. I've always picked up foreign languages fairly easily, perhaps because I heard both English and French as a child, then topped those off with Spanish and Latin in high school in Miami, plus classical Greek in the seminary. And Ann was fairly conversant in German. From those roots, we were able to communicate pretty well everywhere we went.

You'll notice there are no photographs in this chapter. We travelled without a camera, by choice. I felt, and Ann agreed, that too many people go out to see the world and see it only through a camera lens, a picture circumscribed by a frame. They see many trees but never see the forest. I wanted to engrave photos and filmstrips on my memory, not in a scrapbook. The photos resume after we settled in Spain, when we acquired a camera and visiting friends also took pictures.

The Crossing

The Canberra was huge. They fed us five times a day — breakfast, lunch, "tea," dinner and a midnight "snack" that was actually a massive smorgasbord. It was a floating hotel. The ship had a movie theater, a night club, two swimming pools and, if I remember correctly, four dining halls. We ate too much, then tried to burn off the calories jogging around the deck between meals. We did get up one morning early enough to see the sun rise out of the ocean.

We landed in Cherbourg and took a train to Paris where we were met by Marie-Hélène, a friend of one of Ann's brothers. She worked as a simultaneous translator for UNESCO. She gave us a place to stay for a few days and took us on a tour of the city. We vowed to come back.

Germany — 1973

The train from Paris deposited us in Stuttgart. I did my morning exercise routine — a 15-minute workout drawn from the Royal Canadian Air Force exercise program — in a small park beside the train station, then we boarded a bus for the town of Bönnigheim in the south of Germany. Ann had friends there, from a year she had spent there as an exchange student; she had ended that year by hiking across the Black Forest into Switzerland. We stayed with her friends a few days while we looked for longer-term housing.

I didn't feel particularly welcome, not by them, not by the prospective landlady we called in a nearby town in response to an ad for a room to rent (she raised the rent as soon as she learned we were Americans), not by the unhelpful folks at the Tourist Information bureau, not by Germans and Germany in general, and not even by my cousin Gary's wife. Still in the Army, Gary was stationed in Nuremberg but wasn't home when I called. I thought, inasmuch as we were so close, I might stop in to see him. His wife, Cookie, said it wasn't a good time to do that. His parents had been there and had just left the day before. And they had colds. It was only several years later that Gary and I reconnected.

We hopped on a train for Yugoslavia instead. There was still a Yugoslavia then. For those too young to remember, it was a small Communist-ruled country but quite western in its ways, a hodgepodge of ethnicities held together by the force of one man's will, Marshal Tito. When Tito died, all hell broke loose, leaving us with such fragments of the old country as Serbia, Bosnia, and Kosovo.

As our train rolled across the countryside, I saw out the window a strange park bench sitting alone, in the middle of nowhere, facing the tracks. I wondered about that bench and eventually wrote a short story about a lonely war veteran who put it there to watch trains go by each day, waiting to see the engineer who, he discovered, had been sleeping with his wife while he had been at war. The story made it into print decades later, much modified.

Dubrovnik, Yugoslavia — 1973-1974

On the train we shared a compartment with a gray-haired lady who was returning home to Yugoslavia after a tour of teaching in Germany. She spoke English as well as German and Serbo-Croatian, the language of Yugoslavia. By the time we arrived at the end of the line in the ancient Roman city of Split, she had taught me to count to 10 in Serbo-Croatian and to speak useful phrases, such as "Where's the rest room?" and "How much does a pack of cigarettes cost?"

We took a bus the rest of the way to Dubrovnik. Upon arrival, we went straight to the Tourist Information office. It was staffed by a tall, slim young man named Zdravko. He made a phone call, then told us he had found us a room we could have for three months — the duration of our tourist visa — at a reasonable price, complete with kitchen privileges. It turned out to be his own bedroom. The person he'd called was his mother. He spent our three months sleeping on the living room sofa.

He was the only one who spoke any English in the house. His mother, Stanya, mumbled to herself in German a lot when she wanted us to know of her displeasure. Each morning, as she used a whisk broom and dustpan just outside our door, we would waken to the sound of her muttering *"schmutzig, schmutzig, schmutzig"* over and over. Ann explained that it meant "dirty."

I became good friends with Zdravko's father. Using a lot of sign language, my little Serbo-Croatian and his little German, we managed to communicate quite well. He told me about being with the resistance against Hitler's army when he was a child hiding in the mountains; about how he was proud to be a member of the Communist Party because that allowed him to get a job at the bank, where he worked only until 2 p.m.; how, after that, he went fishing every day, returning usually late at night with his catch. He would often eat a whole head of garlic at one sitting, raw, the way I might eat an apple. He said it kept him healthy and strong. He taught me to love garlic, which had never been a staple in our home.

Ann learned to buy live sardines at the waterside fish market and fry them just right. We learned other Yugoslav dishes, and enjoyed walking the old walled Roman city that had been a key link in East-West trade during the days when Venice ruled the seas. No cars were allowed inside the city, except very late at night, and then only to deliver groceries and other goods to the shops and to pick up the day's trash. Everyone was on foot or on bicycles. You had to cross a drawbridge over a moat to enter the city, and all the streets were paved with stones smoothed by centuries of feet. At a sidewalk café, reading a copy of *Newsweek*, we were engaged in conversation by a visiting Russian. He pointed to our magazine: "This is a wonderful country," he said of Yugoslavia. "In Russia you cannot find that magazine."

Stanya took us on a bus to visit her family in the farming village of Konavle. The first stop when we left the bus was a small graveyard. Immediately upon entering it she fell to her knees beside a grave and started wailing, rocking from side to side as we stood by watching, feeling like intruders. Then, as abruptly as she had started, she stopped, got up, dusted off her skirt and led us out of the little cemetery. I based another unpublished short story, "Ana," on her and that visit to Konavle. Years later, "Ana" also made it into my prize-winning short fiction collection, *MindWarp*.

It snowed in December, despite all the information in our brochure about Dubrovnik's mild winters. Our host still went out fishing and sometimes brought home squid, which he cooked at midnight and shared with us. I learned to love squid, and do to this day. One day Zdravko took us out for a few hours in his father's motorboat to fish for squid. We didn't catch anything, but at least I learned how to do it, dangling a baited hook just inches off the sea's bottom and gently tugging the line repeatedly to make it bob up and down to lure the squid. It is boring and tiring work. As a result, I learned to appreciate squid even more.

Christmas and New Year's was a special treat. We went to Midnight Mass with Stanya, in a great vault of a church with no pews. Everyone stood throughout the ceremony. As a registered Communist, her husband didn't go with us. And a neighbor joined us at the small New Year's Eve party our hosts threw. He was the maestro of the Dubrovnik Symphony, just back from a tour in which he had conducted the National Symphony as a guest conductor at the Kennedy Center in Washington, D.C. He and I got quite tipsy on plum brandy – *slivovitsa* – and kept exchanging greetings, "*Sretna nova godina!*" (Happy New Year).

Our visas expired in January and we had to leave. We had hoped to go south to Greece, but there were tanks in the streets of Athens. They were having another revolution. We took a ferry to Italy instead.

Amalfi, Italy — 1974

The town clings to the face of a cliff-like mountainside overlooking the Mediterranean, about midway between Salerno and Sorrento, down the west coast of Italy from Naples. Most of the "streets" are staircases that wind upwards among the houses. We found an apartment near the very top, at the end of one such staircase. Its owners ran a restaurant on the village square below, where we picked up our mail and ate many wonderful meals.

Sophia Loren and Carlo Ponti had a villa just off the cornice highway not far from Amalfi. The closest I ever came to my teenage heart-throb was when we passed by the villa on a bus ride to Naples to see the archaeological wonders of Pompeii and Herculaneum, both destroyed when Mount Vesuvius erupted in 79 A.D. Sophia and Carlo didn't seem to be around.

We visited Rome and Florence. I much preferred Florence. Rome was sooty and noisy. Besides, one can look at only so many statues and paintings of Madonnas and bleeding martyrs, after all. But Florence was classic Renaissance, the city of Michelangelo. It has ever since been one of my favorite places in the world.

One day we returned to our Amalfi apartment and found it occupied by a British woman and her pre-teen son. We had been told we were renting the entire apartment. Our privacy was suddenly shattered. They were taking the other bedroom, which we didn't need or use, but that meant they were also sharing our bathroom and kitchen. When we complained, our relationship with our landlords deteriorated rapidly. They were soon spreading rumors around town that I was having a sexual liaison with this other American woman in town, a rather heavyset friend of ours. As our three-month visa was expiring, we said *arrivederci* and set our sights on France.

Villefranche, France —1974

Our Villefranche is not the famous resort on the French Riviera. This one, Villefranche-sur-Saône, is north of Lyon, deep in Beaujolais country. Ann had another friend of a friend there. A young American school friend of hers living in Sevilla, Spain, had met and, I think, dated briefly the son of a farming family that had cherry orchards outside of town. The son, a much-pampered young man, was an excellent oboist in the village marching band.

The family helped us find a lovely apartment in town. We were delighted to learn that our new landlords were Yugoslavs. We traded stories with them of our time in their homeland, and they took us on tours of the wine country and the best *caveaux* — the wine cellars where the Beaujolais was made and sold by the jug. As I recall, a liter of the local red cost about 25 cents.

At harvest time we went to the farm and helped pick cherries. In return they gave us so many cherries we had to become extremely inventive with them. When we grew tired of eating them straight, Ann made cherry pies, then cherry preserves, then glazed chickens with mashed cherries. I have never since particularly liked cherries.

Wolsey Semple wrote from Washington. He and his girlfriend, Lynn, who had been a neighbor and friend of Ann's, were going to Norway for an international conference. Could we meet afterward in Paris? Our French visas (three months, as with most countries) were drawing to a close so we packed up and left Villefranche. We tried hitchhiking to Paris, but after several hours standing unsuccessfully at the side of the road on the outskirts of town, we surrendered to reality and bought tickets on the next train out.

We had a wonderful few days with Wolsey and Lynn in Paris, visiting all the usual sites and taking in the Latin Quarter's late night club and music scene, all the things we hadn't been able to do on our previous brief stop with Marie-Hélène upon arrival in Europe.

Wolsey and Lynn returned home and we resumed our travels. The plan was to swing through the northern countries of Europe – Amsterdam, Holland; then Copenhagen, Denmark; then across the North Sea to England to stay, believe it or not, with the lady and son who had moved into our apartment in Amalfi (after all, it wasn't *their* fault); and then back to Paris to rejoin Marie-Hélène and ride with her to the south of France, where she was to wed a young doctor. She invited us to her wedding.

Holland, Denmark, England — 1974

Amsterdam, the city of canals, of Anne Frank, and of storefront bordellos where near-naked prostitutes sit in bay windows enticing clients into their lairs. Marijuana was plentiful on the streets, in the parks, wherever hippies gathered. America's backpacking young had taken over one large park and filthied it up with their trash, bathing in the lake and leaving it soapy. And it was expensive. We didn't like Amsterdam very much.

Ann told me that a Dutchman had told her, when she'd visited during her year in Germany, that Holland had once commanded a huge empire and had learned how to be a small country again. America, he'd told her, needed to learn how to be a small country.

We took the "Magic Bus" from Amsterdam to Copenhagen. It was a van with perhaps a dozen or so seats, painted in psychedelic patterns to attract maximum attention from the authorities. All the other passengers were teenagers or barely out of their teens. I believe we were the elders of the group. As soon as we left Amsterdam, out came the marijuana. Joints were passed around. Yes, we inhaled.

To get to Denmark from Amsterdam, you have to go through a small chunk of Germany. Germans do not put up with nonsense. As we approached the German border, the joints were jettisoned out windows, or doused and swallowed whole. The guards made us all get out, then searched the bus thoroughly, but found nothing. All they discovered was that our driver did not have a commercial driver's license: he was not authorized to drive a bus. Luckily, a Dane on board did have such a license, so he was ordered to drive across Germany. A few miles into Germany, the bus pulled over again, we switched back to our original driver, and someone got out, then returned with plastic pouches of pot. They had been stashed in the gas tank.

Copenhagen was beautiful, but the most expensive place we'd yet seen. After considerable searching, we landed in a youth hostel, Ann sleeping in the women's dorm, I with the men. The city was clean, the homes painted in bright colors, apparently to compensate for the long gray winters. The most remarkable thing was seeing the elderly walk around proudly, happily. They rode buses for free, went to movies for free. Their health was tended to, and they were respected by both the citizenry and the government. I was not used to seeing proud, elderly people on the street.

We took a train to Elsinore at the northern tip of Denmark, famed as the setting for Shakespeare's *Hamlet*. We toured its beautiful medieval castle, thought to be the prototype for Hamlet's, and its dungeons. But the best part of that trip was the return train ride. A man with laughing eyes told us to throw our luggage up to him and helped us onto the train, then invited us to sit with him. He was a Danish sea captain, home after 10 years on ships all over the world — off the coasts of Africa, South America and North America. He'd fished for swordfish and caught his share. From the luggage rack above he hauled down and unwrapped about half a dozen swords he said were from the fish he'd caught.

He was a man of many tongues and many accents. He could speak English like a New Yorker and like a southerner, could speak French with the accents of Paris and those of Marseille, Spanish and German as though he were native to those countries as well. He shared his Five O'clock Mints with us. All the while he chattered and laughed and his sparkling blue eyes danced. He'd told us his wife was waiting for him at the station, but he was so into his tales that he missed his stop. He realized it a stop or two later and had to jump off and catch a train back in the other direction. I wish I had written down and saved his name. I'd have liked to resume our conversation.

A ferry took us to England. We stayed in Wimbledon, not far from the world's most famous grass tennis courts. We were there about a week, but I cared little about tennis then. I spent almost every day at the British Museum, devouring the antiquities from places I'd been and places I still dreamed of seeing, especially the famous Elgin marbles from the Parthenon in Athens. There were days when I arrived before the doors opened in the morning and had to be ushered out when they closed in the evening. I remember very little else about London from that trip, other than warm beer and deep fried fish-and-chips.

Pays Basque — 1974

We rode with the bride-to-be, Marie-Hélène, from Paris to Bidart, on France's border with Spain, in the *Pays Basque* (the Basque Country). The wedding was on the beach. I remember there had been an oil spill in the Atlantic off the coast of France and gobs of oil had washed up on the beach. When you walked barefoot, the black goop stuck to your feet. You had to wash it off with gasoline.

It was the wedding party *after* the ceremony that was most memorable. We drove up a Pyrenees mountainside until the road simply ended, then walked up a winding goat trail, higher and higher until we reached a large cave. There waiting for us were trestle tables, a generator-powered record player with a stack of American rock and roll records, and two goats turning on spits over a fire. The feast was on.

We ate and drank and danced well beyond midnight. Ann and I became a hit showing off our American dance steps, twirling in the old rock and roll style, then helping the European youngsters learn the steps. Someone suggested onion soup and said he knew precisely where to get the best, thickest French onion soup around. So, with lit candles we picked our way back down the goat trail, climbed into cars and returned to the town below. Everything was closed and dark. Our local guide knocked heavily and long on the door to a small restaurant until the owner peeked out. A half hour later we were inside eating the best bowl of onion soup I've ever tasted. A few hours after that, around dawn, Ann and I were on another train, heading south to Sevilla, Spain.

Sevilla, Spain — 1974-1975

Our contact in Sevilla was Ann's friend, Cindy, the one who had connected us with the cherry orchard family in Villefranche. Her mother was fearful of another revolution breaking out, like the one that brought dictatorship to Spain in the 1930s. She had rooms full of boxes ready to pack and haul out should trouble erupt. I think each box was marked with its intended contents — books in this one, TV there, etc. These were the final years of the dictator, Francisco Franco. By 1976 he would be dead, a monarchy and elected government restored in a bloodless revolution. She needn't have saved those boxes.

Cindy had found us a wonderful upstairs apartment in the barrio just up the street from the cathedral, in the heart of the city. We fell in with a circle of American expatriate friends, the undisputed fulcrum of which was Muir Weisinger, a millionaire who had made a fortune on Madison Avenue, then written a hugely popular movie making fun of the advertising industry. I don't recall its title, but at the beginning the chairman of the ad agency's board of directors pitches over dead at a board meeting, then the board members, each wanting to be chairman but not allowed to vote for himself, secretly votes for the janitor instead, refusing to vote for the others. The janitor becomes head of the agency and turns the advertising world on its head. The movie is hilarious and made Weisinger a ton of money.

He had been friends with Andy Warhol and regaled us with stories of debauchery at Warhol's home. He'd bought a yacht, which he said he subsequently sold to Aristotle Onassis for Jackie Kennedy's daughter, Caroline. When they'd moved to Spain, he and his wife, a slim, beautiful woman named Merle, had their Mustang shipped to them. She studied Flamenco dancing, Muir watched over his stock portfolio, and we all went partying. Often. I first met Muir at one such party and found a kindred spirit. He loved word play as much as I did and hurled puns about like confetti. Soon the *double entendres* were flying between us as we tried to outdo each other's quips.

Muir taught me about bullfighting and took us to our first *corrida*. Sevilla is perhaps the capital of the bullfighting world, home of most of the famous matadors. Bullfights were always Sunday afternoons. Monday mornings, butchers carved up the bulls and distributed the meat to the poor. Once in a while, parts of the bulls would show up at the huge outdoor market where we shopped for pretty much all our food. Muir had a favorite butcher there whom he asked to save him the testicles from a bull because he had heard they were a delicacy. The man did, and as Muir entered the market, the butcher called out from his stall, "Mr. Muir, Mr. Muir! I have the bull's balls!" That, at least, is the way Muir told the story. And yes, they were quite good.

Muir also introduced us to many new foods. Calf's liver I knew; he fed us calf's heart. It was also with him one evening that we went *tapa*-hopping. We moved from bar to bar, sampling their hors d'oeuvre specialties and having a drink or two at each stop, mostly champagne as I remember. I think Muir was celebrating something, maybe a birthday or a jump in his stock portfolio. I remember eating pickled robins' eggs, then little songbirds, fried and tough but tasty, each bird but a single bite, holding it by its toothpick legs in one hand and head in the other. I got drunk. Drunker than I've ever been. I never could handle champagne. When we got home and I fell on the bed, the room was whirling. I headed for the bathroom, but before I could get there, all those tapas — songbirds and robins eggs and Lord knows what else — came surging up and out, spraying all over the bedroom. We spent most of the next day cleaning up the mess.

The best time by far to be in Sevilla is Easter week. All week long, processions wind through the streets, each church's congregation carrying its Madonna on a platform to the cathedral. Many of the Madonna statues are decked out in gold and jewelry worthy of a monarch. Each procession is led by stevedores bearing the platform on their shoulders, followed by parishioners and penitents, people who promised to bear a cross in the procession to ask forgiveness for some misdeed during the previous year, or to bargain for some special favor from God. Some of the churches have good-natured — or not so good-natured — rivalries. Two in particular always time their processions to cross paths at a certain intersection. As they approach each other, they hurl insults back and forth.

"Your Madonna is a whore!"

"No! Yours is!"

Whoever reaches the corner first gets to pass. The other must wait. During the whole process, great quantities of beer and wine are consumed. And then, at night, when the processions of the day are done, the young men come out with their guitars and serenade their sweethearts on street corners. As Americans, we had six-month visas in Spain and stayed all six months. Happily, those six months extended through the Easter festivities.

Chechouan, Morocco — 1975

While we were in Sevilla, Marie-Hélene and her new husband had visited us en route to Morocco and had invited us to join them there. In France, everyone is required to give two years of public service, either in the military or in some other way. As a young doctor, Marie-Hélene's husband was donating two years of medical help at a hospital in a Moroccan village, Beni Mellal. (I wish I could remember his name; he taught me an excellent French recipe for mussels cooked in peppered white wine with sautéed onions.)

We took a ferry across the straights of Gibraltar from Cadiz, Spain, then a bus to our first stop, Chechouan, a village in the Rif of the Atlas Mountains, the rugged spine of the country. A mountain beckoned outside our bedroom window. I suggested we climb it before resuming our trip.

The going was fairly easy at first, but the mountainside became steeper and steeper the higher we went. Scrub brush was all that grew at this height. Ann decided to sit a spell. I told her I just wanted to see what was beyond that big jutting rock perhaps another hundred feet or so above us. I made it to the rock, then edged around it to see what was beyond. What I saw was breathtaking, a great expanse of nature. I was standing on the edge of a cliff, clinging to the face of the rock. There was nothing but a sheer drop of several hundred feet beneath me, maybe a thousand feet. I tried to inch my way back the way I had come but couldn't. I no longer could find footholds. I began shaking. I tried to inch my way further forward around the rock, hoping to circle back to safety, only to find myself further suspended over seemingly endless space.

Then I saw him. A scraggly, leather-skinned man in a ragged robe, a beard, a long staff, sandals. He looked for all the world like every image of John the Baptist I had ever seen. He was walking easily toward me, loping along the mountain ridge above and to my right. He stopped perhaps 50 feet away and looked down at me. I tried to reach for a fresh handhold, he shook his head, No. I moved my foot to a fresh niche and he nodded, Yes. And so it went, inch by inch. He guided me with his eyes and his nods and head-shaking until I stood again on safe ground. And then he was gone.

He didn't walk away and he didn't disappear. He was there, then after I looked down to watch my steps and looked back up, he was no longer there.

I went down that hillside to Ann on my butt through the thorny brush, shaking too much to stand. The mountainside seemed much steeper going down than it had been coming up. When I reached Ann I asked her if she had seen him.

"Who?"

"That man. He stood up there and watched me."

She had seen nothing. Is it possible I imagined it all? It seemed so vivid to me, then and still.

Beni Mellal, Morocco — 1975

Beni Mellal is surely the strangest place we lived. Beggars with glaucoma lined the major streets. Children dug in mountains of trash, competing with rats for bits of food, rags, a scrap of cardboard. Temperatures reached 130 degrees in the shade in June and July. At least language posed no difficulty. Most Moroccans speak French.

We found a vacant apartment on what the locals called *La Rue d'Amour*, the Street of Love. While we talked with the lady of the house, some young women in very filmy pajamas peeked around the wall to the sitting room and giggled. They looked like characters out of *Scheherazade*. The lady took us upstairs to see the apartment. It was unfurnished but otherwise perfect, large with a rooftop patio. When she left, Ann said, "Did you get the same impression I did?" It was a brothel, one of four that had given the street its name.

Marie-Hélene and her husband wrinkled their noses when we told them we would stay in town with the locals. They warned us that "those people" were known to throw themselves in front of Europeans' cars so they could collect the insurance. No problem: we had no car. Our friends did help us round up a few pieces of furniture, a mattress and a couple straight chairs from the local Catholic Church, plus a few cardboard boxes to convert into a dresser of sorts.

Ann made friends with a Berber woman across the street who taught her how to make bread and take it to the communal oven each morning. You couldn't buy bread, you had to make it yourself, and wrap it in your distinctive dishcloth so the baker knew which was yours when you came back to fetch it. We also befriended a couple of young Peace Corps volunteers. I think they were teaching Moroccan kids how to speak English, but mostly what they did is smoke pot.

Another new friend was a young Moroccan boy who followed us everywhere, begging to be of service. He introduced us to the best place to get mint tea and the best vendors in the souk. All he asked in return was that we translate a song he had on an American record. He said its name sounded like "Ah Shop Sheree." Ann finally discovered it was Bob Marley's "I Shot the Sheriff." She translated it for him. (I couldn't understand the words even in English.)

We bought and wore *djellabas*, the national dress. These were thin, floor-length robes that kept you cool in 100-plus degree weather. Without such wear, you sweat to death.

The town's water came from a huge spring in the mountainside that poured millions of gallons a day down cement troughs through town and to the lush farming valley below. The spring also fed the town's water taps. The water was so heavy with calcium, however, that our joints and bones soon ached. We learned we had to boil the water to rid it of calcium. The pot we used quickly became coated inside with a thick bone-like crust.

We also got a case of worms, we believe from a head of cabbage that wasn't properly washed before we ate it. Worms are bad enough in any circumstances, but when your only bathroom facility is squatting over a hole in the floor, it is doubly disgusting. We had to take these huge pills for a couple weeks to clear it up.

At the end of our block was a *madrassa*, an Islamic school. Each afternoon, we would be serenaded by small children chanting their Koranic verses. I know that since 9/11 we Americans have been indoctrinated to think *madrassas* are evil places where kids are taught to become suicide bombers. Based on my limited exposure — three months or so in Morocco — I think that is typical American over-reaction and over-simplification. Our *madrassa* seemed quite innocent to me, an Arabic variation on Christian children reciting the Ten Commandments.

One day the madam of our brothel came upstairs to ask a favor. She had been tipped off that the police were going to raid the houses on the street that night. She needed to hide her beer and whiskey. The police didn't care about the sex traffic. This was a conservative Islamic area of Morocco, where alcohol was strictly prohibited. As American tourists, we were exempted.

We agreed, and soon her "girls" came up the stairs in their pajamas bearing cases of beer, wine and whiskey. We stashed it all in a closet. The police came, found nothing downstairs, and the next day, the young ladies returned in their pajamas and carried their booze away. An hour or so later they returned yet again, this time bearing platters of food. They had made us a delicious *tagine*.

When the summer heat built up too high, we slept out on the roof, under the stars. That's where we were when we witnessed an amazing Perseid meteor shower that kept us spellbound one night.

We had also been warned about the donkey-man. This, we were told, was a mysterious creature that wandered the town's streets at night, knocking on doors, hoping to find young women he could capture and whisk away to his lair, wherever that was. He was part man and part donkey, we were told in all seriousness.

One night, around 2 a.m., we were awakened by the strangest noise — like the braying of a donkey, but not quite, more like the sound of a man pretending to sound like a donkey, and the unmistakable clip-clop of hooves on the street below. We lay there on our mattress, transfixed. We agreed we both had heard it, but neither of us was willing to go to the shuttered window and open it to see this strange creature. I finally did, but by then he was safely out of sight. You could hear his hoof-beats fading in the distance.

Yes, Morocco was a strange, strange land. But life there was full of wonder, and still good.

Twenty-Three:
South of the Border

I stood with our luggage on the curb just outside the terminal at John F. Kennedy Airport while Ann was inside changing our Moroccan money back into American currency. A Mercedes Benz taxicab idled next to me, spewing noxious exhaust. I was crying, a serious attack of culture shock, my first in all my travels. What in the world was I doing back here, in the land of noise and car fumes and people too busy to care much about anything but what they themselves were doing, where they were going?

This was July 1975. We had planned to hitchhike from Morocco across the Sahara, along one of the caravan trails that truckers still ply, to Tunisia where we'd hoped to catch a ship or ferry to Greece, a long-deferred destination. Then, in rapid succession, we both received letters from home detailing family issues. People seem to be in denial about this now, but I distinctly recall what made us change our plans. Ann's brother was going to marry and wanted her there. Elaine wrote about problems she was having, which seemed pretty soul-shaking to me at the time. The stars were aligned to take us home, it seemed. We booked a flight from Casablanca to New York.

From New York City, we parted ways, Ann to her folks in Columbus, Ohio, I to my family in Miami. Elaine's letter had been full of anguish. I forget the details, but it had to do with harassment from guys following her, a single mom, with sex on their minds, much of it not very gentle. When I saw her, though, she shrugged it off. It was nothing. Certainly nothing that should have brought me back across the ocean. I was confused, to say the least.

Ann and I rejoined at her sister's home in Oklahoma City. I remember four things about that one and only time I've ever been in Oklahoma City: the topless bar down the road from her sister's with its lot always full of pickup trucks and where they played incessantly a tune called *My Ding-a-ling*; the obnoxious oil well on the grounds of the state capitol; doing research on comparative religion (I forget why) at the University of Oklahoma campus library, and helping a newly retired monsignor, a friend of Ann's sister, arrange his considerable library of books, alphabetically, by subject matter.

It was while taking his books out of boxes that I discovered the link between my Hébert heritage and that of the Louisiana Héberts. He had a doctoral thesis by a former student who had found some old papers about the Héberts of Louisiana. There are thousands, if not millions, of Héberts in the former French territory that reached from New Orleans to St. Louis, what came to be known as the Louisiana Purchase. This student had traced the Héberts of Louisiana back to what appear to be kin of my own ancestor, Louis Hébert. They had gone on the long march to Louisiana when the British came and told the French to get the hell out. (Our share of Louis' descendants was among the stubborn few who refused to leave.) The student had dug even deeper than that into our common ancestry — to a fellow named Olaf, an aide-de-camp to William the Conqueror, the Norman who invaded England and defeated King Harold II at the Battle of Hastings in 1066. You can thank William (and I guess Olaf) for the fact that the English language today has so many French-based words and doesn't sound more like German.

Ann and I borrowed a car from Ann's sister, a Volkswagen "beetle," and drove back to Columbus for her brother's wedding. Her parents refused to let us sleep in the same room in their house (German-Americans, they were quite strict about people not sleeping together unless they had a document from the government stating they were legally licensed to do so), so we moved in with another of her brothers. Ann came from a fairly large family; only that one brother ever showed me any courtesy. We left right after the wedding and went back to Oklahoma City, where we caught a Greyhound to Mexico. I felt painfully that my homeland, the United States, no longer felt like home. It was time to resume our travels.

We celebrated Mexico's Independence Day, September 15, with a spectacular fireworks display in the Zócalo, Mexico City's huge central plaza. Gobs of confetti flew at your face every time you opened your mouth to say "Ahhh!" After reaching home, we spent hours digging confetti out of each other's eyes and ears.

We visited the Cathedral of Guadalupe, gradually sinking into the lake-bottom soil of the city. Our Lady of Guadalupe, "The Brown Virgin," has an enigmatic history. She appears to have been imported from Spain, where she was called "The Black Virgin," then morphed into the patron saint of Mexico. Spanish missionaries had a propensity for adapting Indian customs and beliefs into their Catholic mythology as a way to convert the indigenous tribes. The story of her Mexican origin, almost certainly apocryphal, is that Mary appeared to a poor Aztec boy with a Spanish name, Juan Diego, miraculously cured his grandfather and imprinted her image on his cloak. That story, however, was never committed to writing until 1649, some 118 years after it supposedly happened. Whichever the case, pilgrims still streamed to the sinking cathedral, many of them peasant penitents approaching it across rough paving stones on their bleeding knees to worship the virgin. Both she and the entire church that housed her were encrusted with gold and precious jewels. I couldn't help but wonder how many of these peasants could be fed and clothed with such wealth. (The shrine and surroundings are much changed today, with most of the historic elements absorbed into an anachronistically modern church across the plaza from the original shrine, still sinking lopsidedly.)

We toured the National Museum of Anthropology, considered to have the world's largest and best collection of pre-Columbian artifacts. In Chapultepec Park ("Chapultepec" is Aztec for "grasshopper") we saw young couples unabashedly necking on park benches, and I recall thinking, "How thoroughly civilized." At Teotihuacan, outside the city, we climbed the great Pyramid of the Sun. It was good to be back in time again, steeping ourselves in the past and the wonders of cultural diversity.

We had a contact in Puebla, a city east of Mexico City. He suggested we find a place to live in an Indian village, Cholula, about a half hour away by rickety bus. I later learned Cholula had been a thriving center of Indian culture and commerce, a sacred city to the Aztecs, but that in 1519, on his march to Tenochtitlan (today's Mexico City) to confront the Aztec emperor Moctezuma, conquistador Hernán Cortés sacked Cholula and massacred some 6,000 in five hours and destroyed the city. Think about it. That's 1,200 murders an hour. (The name, by the way, is not Montezuma, as most Americans believe, probably because of the U.S. Marine Corps battle hymn; it's more accurately spelled Moctezuma, or *Motēuczōma* in classical Nahuatl, the Aztrec language, but the anonymous 19th Century American who wrote the song had trouble with languages and spelling, I guess.)

I often walked the mile — and 456 years — to a 16th Century pyramid from that era. Archaeologists were digging around its base, unearthing the pre-Columbian city Cortés had sacked. I'd sit on the side of the pyramid watching them with envy as the dwellings of temple priests, servants and merchants emerged painstakingly from the soil. On more than one occasion Ann and I packed a lunch and picnicked there, watching the dig proceed.

Our apartment was in a complex attached to an RV park. Older folks, mostly American retirees touring Mexico by RV, would stop there for a few nights, their caravans parked in neat rows like cattle in stalls. Our neighbors in the apartment building were a young mathematics professor from Switzerland, who tried in vain to explain to me the abstractions of higher mathematical theory, and his wife, a physical therapist and thus far more utilitarian. The professor taught at the nearby *Universidad de las Americas*.

Other neighbors, Americans, had a son of about 13 who had the board game, *Risk*, and was a champion at it. We soon became addicted to his game.

From our apartment you could see Popocatépetl, a still active volcano more commonly known as *El Popo*. Its name means, unsurprisingly, "Smoking Mountain." Its story is shrouded in legendary Indian mythology, a variety of tales of rage at lost love. Mexico's second-highest mountain at 17,802 feet, *El Popo* has erupted more than 20 times since Cortés' scouts climbed it in 1519. A December 2000 eruption was said to have been the mountain's largest display of fireworks in thousands of years. Our Swiss friends suggested we climb *El Popo*.

We set out early one morning to make the five-mile trek to its base, toting backpacks. The climb was easy enough at first, along a winding dirt road. But I had the wrong shoes and soon my feet were growing blisters inside blisters. My back was aching, too. Here is where the mathematician's wife (I wish I could remember her name) came in handy. She lightly pressed the base of my spine with her fingertips. It was like lifting away 50 pounds of my own weight! The moment she released her touch, it was like having a sack of potatoes thrown into my arms. I have passed this little bit of physical therapy knowledge along to anyone with whom I've found myself climbing a hill, however modest.

But even her help wasn't enough. We stopped to rest and I took off my shoes. My feet were bleeding. A pickup truck came by and we flagged it down. I climbed in back and was taken to a lodge where we would spend the night, a short distance below *El Popo*'s icecap. The others continued on foot. The next morning, we climbed the rest of the way to the icecap, well above the tree line. The view was spectacular, but there was no way we could scale the ice without proper gear or climbing experience, and so no way to look down into Popo's cauldron.

Wolsey Semple and his girlfriend, Lynn, came to visit us at Christmas. They arrived Christmas Eve, and not long afterwards Lynn realized she had left her purse in their taxi, along with their entire stash of travelers' checks. They were pretty much resigned to never seeing it again when, Christmas morning, the cab driver, his wife, and his children all showed up at our door, dressed in their finest for Mass, and gave her back her purse. Not a thing was missing. They rewarded him handsomely, I recall. It taught us, as if we didn't already know, not to assume: you will find virtue in humankind everywhere, no matter the skin color or language or station in life.

It was on this visit also that Wolsey gave me the letter from Ralph telling me he was coming "out of the closet." I had to ask Wolsey what that meant and why Ralph was in a closet in the first place. Just because you have years, in this case 35, doesn't mean you have amassed knowledge.

Our Mexican visas were to expire in early spring and we were eager to get back to Europe and make our way, at long last, to Greece. We decided to see if we could hitch a ride on a shrimp boat to Key West or Miami, then fly to Europe. (The least expensive flights at the time were "no-frills" aboard Icelandic Airlines to Luxemburg.) We took a bus to the port city of Vera Cruz, only to learn that the shrimp fleet was at *Isla Mujeres* (Island of Women) near the tip of the Yucatan peninsula. That required more buses plus a ferry. Our bus passed by Chichen Itza, a magnificent Mayan archaeological site, but we could only see its pyramid from a distance. I vowed to come back one day. It's still on the to-do list at this writing.

At *Isla Mujeres*, as usual, we looked for the least expensive accommodations. We rented a tent in a campground on the beach. A dog prowled the grounds at night. She'd recently given birth to a litter and was protecting her brood fiercely, snarling and attacking anyone who stepped out of a tent at night in search of the rest room.

Worse than the dog was swine flu. Barely a day or two after our arrival, I had a full-blown case of it. We discovered that the people who had rented our tent before us had probably had it, too. Ann escaped, but I was feverish, throwing up, weaker than I could remember ever feeling before. We hobbled down to where the shrimp fleet was docked. The captain of one boat, a large round dark man who looked like he had just stepped out of central casting for the part, leaned out of his turret cabin and said the fleet would be in port for as much as another two weeks, there were major storms in the Gulf of Mexico.

We couldn't wait. We booked flights to Cozumel and Miami. The plane to Cozumel was a two-engine affair, and the captain asked some of us to switch sides to balance the weight. In Cozumel, they had no record of our reservation. We demanded our seats. Ann demanded to see the airport manager, then threatened to have me puke all over his desk if we didn't get seats on the next plane to Miami. She won.

My mother took us in and nursed me back to health. Unexpectedly, this presented me with yet another of those forks in the road. It was an election year and Jimmy Carter was running for President. I knew Carter reasonably well. As a reporter in Atlanta, I had covered his first run for governor of Georgia, the one he'd lost in 1968. *The Constitution* had endorsed one of his opponents, Ellis Arnold. I remember arguing with our editor-in-chief, Gene Patterson, that Carter was clearly the best we could get and the most electable. I didn't win the argument. Both Carter and Arnold lost, and Lester Maddox, the restaurateur who had notoriously handed out axe handles to his white patrons to keep Blacks out of his fried chicken emporium, became governor.

After that, I'd seen Carter at many events, state conferences of school board members or county commissioners, meetings of local governing bodies, nothing terribly important, but there he would be, sitting at the back of the room, taking notes. I asked him once what he was up to. "Just doing my homework," he said. He planned to run for governor again and needed to background himself on issues of local concern. He was nothing if not a brilliant student. Among other things, he had a doctorate in nuclear physics and had commanded a nuclear submarine. A few times we stepped out and shared a beer. I learned to appreciate his intelligence in ways the general public never saw. This, of course, was before he was "born again" and, I'm told, became a teetotaler.

Now here he was, in Miami, at the DuPont Plaza Hotel, a short walk from my mother's apartment. He and his entourage were campaigning before the Florida primary. I knew some of his people — Jerry Rafshoon, Jody Powell, Ham Jordan. One of his speech writers had been a reporter with me at *The Atlanta Constitution*. I flirted with the idea of walking those few blocks and seeing if I could meet Carter, possibly even join his campaign for a while. Who knew what might come of it? He probably wouldn't win, but if he did, might I land a job in the White House? Wouldn't that be a neat thing to add to my résumé?

The lure of the other unknowns, those so many intriguing parts of the world I'd set out for but had yet to see, stopped me from changing course. To this day, I've wondered how my life might have changed had I walked that walk. Instead, when I got over the swine flu, we took a flight back to Europe to resume our travels. This time, for sure, we would not miss Greece. We would start there.

Life, it turned out, was still pretty good.

Twenty-Four:
Steeped in History

We flew to Luxemburg, took a train through the Alps to Bari, Italy (where the original St. Nicolas, a bishop, had lived and distributed gifts to the poor), then a ferry across to Greece. Aboard the ferry, we met a young Greek fellow who invited us to his family's farm, not far from where we landed. They recommended that instead of going straight to Athens, our original plan, we rent an apartment in nearby Parga and return to join them for Greek Orthodox Easter, only a few weeks away. Of course we accepted.

Parga is a small, compact seaside town in northwest Greece. It was unexceptional in that it didn't comport with my idea of Greece, the ancient land I had come to see. That Easter on the farm was unforgettable, however. I helped chase a kid goat over the rocks and brush outside of town for our dinner, an incredible outdoor feast. I ate goat's brains like soup cooked in the goat's skull. During the Easter procession, the bearded patriarch blessed everyone and everything around, sprinkling us with holy water and incense smoke. We joined in the traditional game of egg-smashing, in which each person is given a raw egg to hold in his or her fist, then raps it end-first against someone else's. If your egg breaks you're out of the game, until only one egg is left whole. I learned there's an art to this egg-smashing thing, but darned if I can remember what it is. I don't remember what the winner won. The prize didn't seem to be the objective, anyway. Bragging rights seemed to be the whole point.

We hitched a ride from Parga to Olympus, the site of the very first Olympics, with a young German couple touring the country by van. Both joggers, Ann and I ran the race track at Olympus after touring the ruins. We also went to another archaeological site perilously perched at the top of a mountain, then continued on eastward toward Corinth. I don't recall what made us choose Loutraki, but choose it we did, a charming waterside village. At the local tavern we found someone with a room to rent on the edge of town, complete with yet another rooftop terrace.

Loutraki was famous for its spring, whose waters were believed uniquely healthy. People came from miles around to fill bottles and jugs with the water pouring out of the mountain, water we drank from the tap. You can buy bottled Loutraki water in stores all over Greece.

A short distance from town and a hundred feet or so up the mountain, I found a lovely spot under a shade tree. By moving a few loose rocks around I was able to construct a desk of sorts, one flat stone for a desktop, another for a bench, and some smaller stones arranged at my side to serve as a cool place to stash lunch and a beverage or two. Each day I walked up there and spent my mornings rewriting my novel.

My agent had been right; it desperately needed reworking. I did a new master outline. I infused the story with the rhythms and sensations of ancient Greece, its literature and its mythology (or tried to; I'm not sure many readers caught it). That ancient land was palpable all around me — in the deep blue of the sky, in the barren mountaintops where you could easily envision Pan merrily dancing around and playing his flute. Ancient gods seemed to lurk everywhere.

Below me spread the Gulf of Corinth, that narrow band of sea that nearly divides Greece in two, separating northern Greece from the Peloponnese, the peninsula of Sparta and Agamemnon, Helen and Heracles (the Romans changed his name to Hercules). Across the water was the modern city of Corinth, and up a mountain slope beside that, the ruins of the ancient city where Paul had preached to the Corinthians. I was at my stone desk under that mountainside tree one day when I saw our old friend the Canberra, unmistakable with its twin smokestacks, entering the Corinthian Canal.

It was Nero, the fiddler, who decided to help nature by digging the deep-water canal that today links the Gulf with the Aegean Sea to the east. Before that, seamen had to go either all the way around the peninsula or haul their ships those few miles overland. When Ann and I lived there, you could walk from Loutraki to Corinth just by following the seaside. When you reached the canal, you boarded a flatbed ferry that was pulled across the waterway by a windlass and chain. It could carry one or two cars, too. If a ship wanted to pass through, the chain was simply dropped to the floor of the canal. Today they have a more modern ferry system, a motorized bed that is actually an elevator: the entire bridge is dropped to the canal floor to let ships pass.

After I'd written my day's complement of the novel, I'd eat my lunch, then walk down to the water for a swim where we'd found a secluded cove. Sometimes Ann would join me there. It was a good life, but I overdid it, got too much sun, and came down with sun poisoning. My skin tingled with electricity if sunlight touched it. I became nauseous in any kind of daylight, even on a cloudy day, and had to remain in a darkened room for I don't remember how many days, until it passed.

I also spent a night alone in a cave near a monastery higher up that same mountain. I'd gone exploring, looking for what life might have been like those thousands of years ago when giants had walked this ancient land. I found a monastery up there and visited its chapel. The cave I stayed in was a short distance above that. The view was breathtaking, the serenity sublime. I don't think I've ever experienced quite the peace I did that night under the stars, gazing out from my cave, wondering about the long ago.

Ann and I visited many sites in Greece. Athens, of course, with its Acropolis and Parthenon, its agora and the museum with its golden treasures, including the supposed golden death mask of Agamemnon, the general who led the Grecian flotilla against Troy. We went to Delphi to consult the oracle, but the oracle wasn't home, I guess. I learned nothing of the future. But we did jog the race track there, too.

We went by bus to the ancient sites of Argolis, the thumb of the mitten-shaped Peloponnese. We went to Agamemnon's city, ancient Mycenae, and marveled at the hugeness of the Lion Gate, wondering how they could have ever lifted that 20-ton boulder to serve as the gate's lintel, let alone the even larger stone that rests on it, lions at either side of a column.

We visited Tiryns, said to have been built by Heracles himself. So huge were the rocks of its walls that it must have been built by such a giant as he. We stopped in Nafplion, then took another bus to Epidaurus. We fell asleep on the bus and missed our stop. When we awoke, we had gone several miles too far. We got off at the next town and had to take a taxi back to the site of the ancient outdoor theater, which claims to have the finest acoustics in the world. All the tourists were trying it: someone would stand on the stage and speak in a normal voice. Someone else would stand at the farthest row of stone benches that inclined up the hill and without fail could distinctly hear what was said on the stage.

The ruins of ancient Greece are everywhere. Walk into any town, stop at the first tavern, ask where the local ruins are, and they will direct you. We heard about an ongoing archaeological dig a few miles from the Corinthian Canal and walked there to watch the work.

At the Lion Gate, Mycenae, Greece (during a revisit in 1986)

I'd more than once thought of offering my services at such a dig, but I discovered this was not a paying job — it was one you paid, handsomely, for the privilege of doing. At another nearby site, this to the west of Loutraki, we camped overnight surrounded by stone walls thousands of years old, again communing with the stars and the ancients.

Before leaving Greece, we wanted to see Mykonos, one of the many islands in the Aegean. Its homes are all pure white, standing on the hillside like sugar cubes. We bussed to the other side of the island from its port, then walked with our backpacks a few miles along the shore to Paradise Beach. We'd heard about it and wanted to experience it for ourselves. To get there you cross several coves, each separated from the next by a rocky hill. At each cove the bathing suits became skimpier and fewer.

Paradise Beach is "clothing optional," as they say these days. Back then we were more honest: it's a nudist beach. Back from the beach is the campground. You can bring your own tent or rent one, or do what we did, rent a hutch, a thatch-roofed cement platform surrounded by waist-high plywood walls and screening. Showers were communal and open. There was a gift shop, a small pharmacy and a cafeteria. In those you had to wear clothing. On the beach, bathing suits weren't forbidden but they sure made you feel ridiculously out of place.

As soon as we parked our gear in our hutch I headed for the beach, stripped down and went for a swim. Ann was going to follow with lunch. The water was the cobalt blue of the Aegean, flecked with silver and gold from the sun, and cool on my body. There was a table of rock that spanned the cove about a hundred feet out from shore, with a gap across the middle. The rock was a foot or so below water. I climbed up on it, crossed to where it dropped another foot, as though nature had meant to provide a bench to rest on, then crossed to the deep water. When I heard Ann calling from the beach, I retraced my steps. That's when I stepped on a sea urchin, a ball of barbed black needles. The pain was instant. I lifted my foot and saw what was firmly planted in my sole, then hopped on the other foot to that underwater stone bench. I sat to dislodge the sea urchin from my foot and felt a sharp sting on my butt. I had sat on a jellyfish!

I did shake the urchin free but the barbed points of its thorns were still in the ball of my foot. I hobbled ashore and did my best to explain what had happened. Ann came to my rescue. Someone in the cafeteria gave her some olive oil, vinegar and a needle. I was going to become a Greek salad. She was told to pat the vinegar on the raw jellyfish welt on my backside. That brought instant relief to that quarter. Then she was told to put the oil on my foot to soften the skin and to carefully tease out the barbed needle points. She was warned to be sure to get them all because one could get into my blood stream and migrate to any other part of my body.

She must have worked on my butt and foot for an hour. I limped around for days thereafter. Years later, I felt a pimple on my chin, under my beard. Too old for acne, I inspected it in a mirror. It was black. I was able eventually to squeeze it out. It was one of that urchin's barbs.

We had one final stop in Greece: Delos, a tiny island a half-hour's boat ride from Mykonos. No one lives on Delos. It is the site of a grand temple to Apollo, one of the most beautifully preserved ancient sites of Greece. The small boat carrying our group of about 20 bounced over the waves. I sat on the floor at the prow and rode every bounce, feeling the sea spray over me. The captain enjoyed it as much as I did, I think, because he seemed to delight in cutting across waves to increase the effect and was grinning from ear to ear watching me get soaked.

It was time to leave. Our six-month visa was up. We booked passage on a Turkish ship bound from Athens to Barcelona, Spain. (My insurance agent back in Washington had told us he owned a time-share in a beachside cabin in Denia, about halfway down the east coast of Spain, and invited us to use it as he never did himself.) I bought a *Time* magazine and a small bottle of ouzo, then settled down in a deck chair to sip the milky, licorice-tasting liquor and watch the port of Pireaus slowly shrink into the horizon.

Thumbing through *Time*, my eye caught a small headline: "Mexican Peso Floats, Sinks." While in Mexico, I had learned that Mexican banks were offering 12 percent annual interest on Certificates of Deposit. The best I could do with my savings in the States was 7.10 percent on U.S. Treasury bonds. I'd contacted my banker in Washington and asked if it would be safe to move those funds into Mexico to reap the higher interest. He could offer no guarantees, of course, but he said the Mexican peso had been at par with the U.S. dollar for more than 20 years, and it was sound enough that the Japanese were investing heavily in the resort town of Cancun. Shortly before leaving Mexico, I'd sold the T-bills, converted the dollars to pesos, and plunked all my savings into Mexican CDs, now losing value fast.

Life was still good, but it was not at all clear that it would stay that way much longer.

Twenty-Five: Castle in Spain

By the time I was able to contact the Mexican bank and extract my savings, the $15,000 I had squirreled away was worth only about $2,000. We had a major decision to make: return to the States and resume a "normal" 9-to-5 life, or see what kind of housing $2,000 could buy in Spain. I usually tell this story by saying our decision was based on the flip of a coin, but the truth is there was no coin toss. Neither of us was yet willing to abandon the dream. We went house hunting.

Luckily, a neighbor of the beach house where we were staying was a real estate agent. He showed us some dilapidated farm houses, but we weren't much into farming. Then he took us to Benidoleig (pronounced Benny-doe-*layge*), a cute village on a mountainside overlooking a lush valley of orange, almond and olive groves. He took us to see the mayor, the local pharmacist, who said he knew of an abandoned house the owners might be interested in selling.

It was at the lower edge of the village. Vincente, the owner, was a quiet, silver-haired bachelor. He took us through. We didn't need a key to get in, it had no lock, just a makeshift wooden latch to keep the wind from opening the large double-doors, more suited to a barn than a home.

The house had been empty 20 years. After Vincente's father had died, he and his mother had moved to the father's more "modern" ancestral family home. The one we were looking at had been in his mother's family since it had been built, in 1379, almost 600 years before. It said so, carved in stone on an outside wall, a stone framed with thin red bricks. The whole house was made of stone. The interior walls themselves were a couple feet thick. It had no running water, no electricity. The wall extending from the front door to the corral in back had been rubbed black from waist down by generations of goats that had lived back there and, of course, had to be taken in and out through the house every day.

The place was thick with cobwebs and spiders. Mice and rats skittered about. It had but two small windows, one upstairs and one downstairs, both shuttered but without glass. Upstairs was unfinished. The roof was made of cane and sagged like an old gray mare. From the roofbeams hung homespun cords with coffee-can lids halfway down their length. Vincente explained that they used to hang tomatoes there for preserving during winter, and the coffee can lids prevented rats from getting to the tomatoes; whenever a

Our home's 'Birthstone' — 1379

rat tried to climb down the string to reach the tomatoes, it would get to the lid and fall off.

In the corral behind the house was an outhouse, now filled with extremely dry human waste. Above the corral, on the second floor, was a large open terrace overlooking the orchards and, beyond, the Mediterranean. That view, and the inviting fireplace in the main room downstairs, sold us. Vincente introduced us to his mother, Señora Presentación, a tiny, stooped lady in her 80s. She would sell us the house for our last $2,000 on one condition: we would live in it, not fix it up as an investment to sell off to someone else. She wanted to know her ancestors' home would be in good hands.

We promised her that is how it would be and shook hands. The next five years of our lives were now charted. With what little money we had left, we bought a broom, a shovel, some candles and a bucket. We cleared the cobwebs from an area at the front of the house and unrolled our sleeping bags. Water had to be hauled down from the town's fountain behind the church up the hill. The bucket also served as our latrine. It wasn't much, but we had a home.

I asked Vincente what a man could do to earn money around here. He told me the orange harvest was starting and every able-bodied person was heading for the orchards. On his advice, I went to one of the bars at the center of town and inquired about joining a *quadrilla*.

With Presentación & Vincente

Our 'Castle,' as purchased

The men didn't exactly laugh at me, but I think they found me a bit strange. An *Americano* who wanted to pick oranges? They suggested I go see "Juanito" and told me where he lived. Juanito gave me my start.

Over the next five years, I picked oranges from September to January. During the rest of the year I did odd jobs for retired foreigners who lived in chalets up the hill well outside of town — mostly house painting and clearing brush for gardens, the work I had so scornfully disparaged as a teenager.

The orange picking made me one with the villagers. *Quadrillas* of a dozen or so men would go out and pick for specific exporters. You left home at dawn, met at one of the three bars in town for a coffee and brandy, then worked until sundown. You used sharp little clippers to cut the oranges and *clementinas* from the trees, snipping cuts into your fingertips if you weren't careful. I eventually learned to be careful. You carried rubber tubs — *capazos* — of oranges or tangerines on your shoulder across the orchard to wherever the truck would pick them up, quite often a long slog over uneven terrain. You went home exhausted each night. If you weren't exhausted, you weren't pulling your share of the team's load. If your fingertips weren't bleeding, you probably weren't snipping oranges from the trees fast enough. You were paid based on how much the team had picked, so it was important that everyone pick at approximately the same rate.

Juanito's *quadrilla* was the slowest and weakest. While other teams picked the best orchards and consisted of the fastest pickers in the village, ours usually did the second pass of each orchard, picking the leftovers and, toward the end of the season, even the windfall fruit that would be processed into orange soda. That year our *quadrilla* had two women (ours was the only team that included women), a 72-year-old man and another who had only one arm — and myself, the neophyte *Americano*.

We picked six days a week, often 12 or more hours a day. When I reached home, I'd wash up in our bucket. Mostly this involved cleaning black *miel* from my face and arms; *miel* is Spanish for "honey," but this wasn't honey; it was the sticky spore of the white fly that coats the leaves of orange trees and comes off in your eyes, ears and, of course, all over your arms and clothes. Washed, I'd head uphill to the bars. It was important to be sociable. The whole *quadrilla* would be there, sharing *tapas*. If I went home for a quick dinner, it was back to one of the bars afterwards, usually Ishmael's and usually with Ann, to watch one of the few televisions in town — and have a few after-dinner libations, of course. Sometimes, we'd be there until well after midnight. The whole process would start over again the next dawn.

We made friends rapidly. Antonio "Parabales," our next door neighbor, became like a brother. Balding and gruff-voiced but tender-hearted, he was a bachelor and laborer in his 40s. He had painted a sickle and hammer on his *capazo*. I asked him if he was a communist. He said yes, matter-of-factly. As he explained it, the Communist Party was for laborers, he was a laborer, therefore he was a communist.

Antonio 'Parabales'

But he was also fiercely curious about America and democracy. Franco had died while we were in Mexico and King Juan Carlos had been restored to the throne. The young king had immediately reinstated democratically elected government. Antonio had a thousand questions. How did democracy work? What were you allowed to talk about? Should they change the way the village was governed? What was the best way to do that?

Invariably I had but one answer for him: democracy was not one thing, it was what you made of it. Spain needed to invent for itself the kind of democracy that would work best for Spain. The important thing was equality, that everyone, from the king to the lowest laborer, had an equal voice and an equal right to express an opinion about anything and everything.

I asked him about his nickname, *Parabales*. Literally, it means "stop the bullets" in the way that "parasol" is Spanish for "stop the sun." More accurately, you'd translate his nickname to "shield," I suppose. During the Spanish Civil War in the 1930s, it had been his father's trade: he'd made shields, so they'd given him that nickname. Antonio had inherited it from him.

As a teenager, Antonio had returned from the fields one day and found his mother dead, hanging from a roof beam. He had sealed that room up with bricks and never again entered it — until we made it necessary. He had lived alone in the house ever since.

That sealed room adjoined our bedroom, but our common wall was bulging dangerously inward on us and didn't look like it would survive much longer. With his permission I tore it down and rebuilt it. This, of course, made it necessary to go into the musty chamber of his mother's death, if only to remove rubble.

His home was identical to ours, ramshackle, dirt-floored and without plumbing or electricity. He had an oil drum on a windowsill upstairs behind his house where he collected rainwater. From that he drained the water down a hose into a tin can whose bottom he'd punctured with holes for a showerhead. If there wasn't enough rain, he'd refill the drum from the town's fountain, one bucket at a time.

Antonio passed away some years ago. He simply fell down and died while trimming a tree behind his property, we were told. That was his profession outside of orange-picking season: he was a trimmer of trees. He was also a wise and good man.

Near the end of the first orange harvest, ours was the last *quadrilla* still working, because we were cleaning up the leavings of the others. Some of the village's fastest pickers came to join us as the best remaining source of income, and our speed and earnings increased commensurately. My competitive spirit was ignited again and I tried to keep pace with them. We'd actually race each other to deposit our pickings at the scale, then run back to the next tree. After the season closed, I was approached by the foremen of both of the two *quadrillas* acknowledged to be the best in town. They asked me to commit to working with them the following season. I, of course, felt flattered. I had arrived as an orange picker. I chose the one on which I had the most friends.

In the spring of 1977, I prevailed on my mother to visit us. She'd never been to Europe. She loved her stay, pitched in as though she had been in a small village her entire life. She shopped the outdoor market, went into the woods with us to chop firewood. She didn't complain about the cold, just wrapped herself in a blanket and sat huddled in front of our fireplace. And of course she was a regular at the church and soon became a favorite of the parish priest.

At the end of her visit, we took Mom to France. Our first stop was Lourdes. Unfortunately, the buses were on strike. We arrived by train and Ann and I went off to find lodging. Mom stayed at the station to watch our luggage. While we were away they closed the station and made Mom wait outside. She was furious.

Lourdes was more carnival than religious experience. Street-corner barkers were selling little plastic statues of Our Lady of Lourdes filled with water presumably from the "holy" fountain where she is said to have appeared centuries ago to Bernadette. Religious trinkets and souvenirs were everywhere. The shrine itself was surrounded by souvenir stands.

From there we went to St. Malo, her ancestral home that had given her her family name, famed back then as the home of pirates and explorers. We walked its ancient walls, then stopped for a drink at a bar near the town gate. An old Frenchman "in his cups" started hitting on her, picked out her French accent as Canadian from the start. I think she was secretly flattered at having attracted his attentions, but of course she brushed him off.

The crowning experience of her trip, I believe, was Mothers' Day in Paris. The city was alive with flowers. We attended High Mass at Notre Dame Cathedral. She told me many times later that that trip to Spain and France had been the high point of her life.

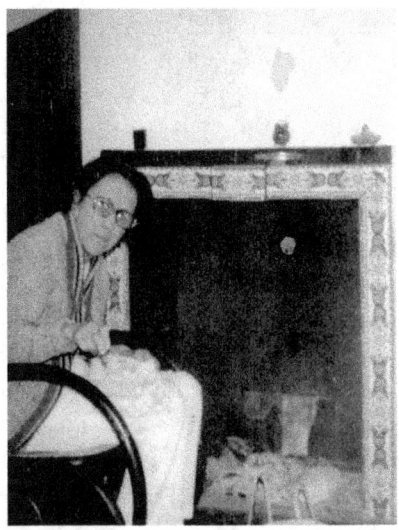

Mom sewing by the fire...

...At the market...

...Chopping firewood

The camaraderie among orange-pickers was special. As a *quadrilla*, we not only worked together, we had our morning coffee together, we broke for breakfast around 9 a.m. and ate under the trees together, then again for lunch. Afternoon siestas were for summertime only, so we didn't do that during the September-to-January orange harvest, but we worked until the sun went down and it was too dark to see, then reconvened at the bars for *tapas* and drinks. We had paellas together and end-of-season parties where it was not unmanly at all for men to be seen dancing with each other. I myself became fairly adept at the bullfight-mimicking *pasodoble*.

The custom was that the owner of the orchard you were harvesting would provide the day's wine, typically huge flagons of hardy homemade red wine to be passed around at breakfast (yes, *breakfast!*) and lunch. One day we were picking in a valley on the other side of the mountain and it fell to me to take my turn loading the truck. This meant that while the others continued picking until dark, I spent the final hour or so lifting cases of oranges up onto the truck bed where the driver would stack them.

I hoisted up a few cases, took a swig of the local red, hoisted a few more and took another swig. This went on for some time, swigs turning into chugs. What I didn't know was that this particular homemade wine had almost the potency of brandy. By the time the truck was loaded, so was I. Two of the other guys had to carry me home between them. When we entered the house, they just asked Ann, "Where do you want him?" That's all I remember about that night. Clearly, I was now part of the village family.

I also "arrived" as a housepainter. One day, as I was painting the outside of a chalet owned by the Hudsons, retired Canadians, I was approached by a painter from the village, a young man named Pepe, one of the two who had helped me home that day after getting loaded loading oranges. He and his painting partner, a gimpy old fellow named Geronimo, had been painting a house nearby. How much was I charging, Pepe wanted to know. I told him, and he said I needed to charge more, that I was under-selling the market. He told me the going rate and said if I didn't charge at least that much he'd have to report me to the Guardia Civil, the feared national police. I raised my rates. I was, after all, working illegally. I was there on a tourist visa, with no right to work. My customers were quite generous in understanding.

It wasn't much after this that Pepe came to me at the bar we both frequented and asked if I'd be interested in joining him and Geronimo. We'd make a heck of a team, he said. I could speak the languages of the *estranjeros* – English and French – and could solicit their business, while Pepe and Geronimo could bring in the village business and get our painting supplies at wholesale rates. I immediately agreed, but pointed out that the rules were a bit different when painting foreigners' homes. At village houses, the premium was on getting in and out quickly. The idea was to slap on whitewash and leave. The women of the house weren't interested in paying painters to clean up after themselves. If paint fell on the sidewalk or nearby bushes, so be it. They'd tend to it themselves after the painters left.

Not so the retired Canadians, British, French and Germans who lived in the chalets up the mountain. Indoors, we would have to spread drop cloths. Outdoors, we'd have to put drop cloths on sidewalks and even over garden plants. We'd have to use quality paints, not whitewash. And we would have to wipe up after ourselves. They had no problem with these rules. We would be paid by the hour, after all. A deal was struck, a very profitable deal for all of us.

One hitch was the Guardia Civil. They came calling with fair frequency. We weren't the only Americans in the village. One young couple drew attention, not because they worked (they didn't have to; he had won a bundle on the American TV quiz show, *$20,000 Pyramid*) – but because their Spanish was minimal and they did all their shopping in Denia, the nearby coastal city favored by English-speaking tourists. Another was a Canadian woman who was well liked and pretty much kept to herself. She, I believe, had legal residence.

We, however, were anomalies. The Guardia were curious. They'd inquire about us at the local bars and routinely be told not to bother us, that I was certainly not working, unless you called writing a book "work." I was at home, writing my books, they'd say, suggesting, I suppose, that I was the *"loco Americano."* If they heard a rumor that I was working as a painter at some chalet, they'd come to see.

Pepe had the hearing of a hunting dog. He could hear their car sputtering up the hill before anyone saw it.

"Ricardo! Rápido! La Guardia!"

I'd throw my paintbrush into a bucket of water, and go hide in the bushes until Pepe would whistle the "all clear." These interruptions were not uncommon. Perhaps the riskiest moment was when I was painting an exposed-beam ceiling, sloshing whitewash into a tight corner, and a big dollop of it splashed into my eye. For anyone who isn't acquainted with whitewash, it is a caustic mix of lime and chalk. When it hits mucous membrane, like that soft tissue that lines your eyes, it burns literally like hellfire and brimstone. I was rushed to a doctor who washed out the eye and applied some salve. For a while I thought I was going to lose the eye, that same eye I'd almost lost to handball many years ago in Gainesville, the one that had received more than its share of confetti at the Mexican Independence fireworks show, the one that was constantly invaded by white fly *miel* during orange harvest. What only occurred to me later was that this could have been just the sort of event to attract unwanted attention from the Guardia Civil, attention from which I couldn't hope to hide. Luckily, I saved both the eye and my career in Spain.

Another major event happened while house-painting that reminded me of all those boxes Cindy's mother had stashed in her home in Sevilla. We were painting a palatial home, this one belonging to wealthy Spaniards. I was up on a ladder painting away when Pepe called me down. As usual, he had a radio going while we worked. But the music had been abruptly interrupted. The Spanish army was attempting a *coup d'état*. Angered at the military's loss of control with the return of democracy, armed soldiers had broken into the parliament – the *Cortes* – and were holding the legislators hostage. They had also taken over the national radio and TV stations. Tanks were moving into positions in key cities, including Valencia barely 65 miles away. Revolution was suddenly no laughing matter.

Several days of tension ensued. King Juan Carlos refused to yield to the military's demands. He insisted their actions were illegitimate. A lesser man would have caved, I am sure. But sanity won the day, thanks to the King. He's had my admiration ever since.

Hours not devoted to picking oranges and painting other people's houses were filled with restoring our own humble abode. We discovered tiles under the dirt of a few rooms downstairs, so Ann set about mopping what was to be our kitchen, trying to get to the tiles below. Vincente happened to drop in for a visit just then and broke into laughter. She'd never reach paved flooring, he said. It was a dirt floor. So was the corridor from the front door to the corral that the goats had traversed every day for decades. It was all pure mountainside.

Self-taught, Ann and I tiled floors, scraped and painted walls, exposed ancient rough-hewn beams over doorways and brought them back to life with linseed oil, wired the house for electricity, and laid a water line under the floor from the street to the kitchen and on into the corral, where we built a real bathroom from scratch. Upstairs, we knocked out two walls and the floor of one front room to open it to the foyer below. We laid a new floor over the plaster of the ceiling below, propping up the downstairs ceiling beams with iron supports borrowed from a local mason. Ann mixed the cement in the foyer and I hauled it upstairs one bucket at a time to pour the new reinforced-concrete floor. Then we tiled it and put up railings to overlook the foyer downstairs.

We learned to be quite creative. We had the fireplace deepened and faced with new brick (we hired professionals to do this), broke open

Our Castle Restored

Upstairs…

Downstairs…

a closet wall between what had been a front bedroom and the living room and put in a few steps between them. The house, after all, was built on a hillside. I tried to move a boulder that was in the way and discovered it was attached to the mountain. Solution: build the steps around it. The same happened again when we built shelves into the recessed wall on one side of our new fireplace. Again, we cemented around the exposed mountain rocks to seal out any vermin, then varnished the boulders for easier dusting.

We scavenged pieces of furniture wherever we could find them. An abandoned old bentwood rocking chair was rehabilitated and straw-seated chairs were rewoven. We made a lounge chair of sorts out of plywood and cushions. I fashioned part of the upstairs into an office, complete with a custom-made desk for my portable typewriter. (I hired a professional carpenter to make the desk for me; I know when I'm out of my league.) We also hired professionals to put a new, solid roof on the house and refinish the facade, complete with a proper front door and glass windows.

Someone found a pair of old church gates rusting in a field outside of town. They were wrought-iron and stood almost two stories tall. We managed to get them back to the village and were given one of them. We sanded it, then painted it with rust-proofing, black paint and satin-finish varnish. The top of the gate was a peacock's tail of curlicues. We bolted that to the wall as our bed-head and turned other sections into window planters and wall hooks.

My body paid a heavy price for all this work. My lower back was killing me. When I returned from work, especially during orange harvest, I'd collapse into a chair. Standing again required help and then backing against a wall to force my back upright. I took to wearing a whalebone girdle to work. I've paid for it with back pain ever since. But our abandoned stone house was becoming a home, and that was worth it. We had something to be proud of. Life was good.

Twenty-Six: Beginning (Again)

I was up a tree. Literally. It was spring, but orange-picking time nevertheless for *clementinas*, small tangerines that grow in large trees. With most orange trees, you can pick the fruit standing on the ground or, at most, on an overturned orange crate. The trees are young and small. *Clementinas*, however, ripen in much larger trees, and to pick any but the lowest hanging fruit, you have to climb inside the tree. That's where I was when I heard Ann shouting my name as she came running through the grove. She was waving an envelope. I nearly fell out of the tree even before I knew what the excitement was about.

She had a telegram from my agent in New York, Chuck Neighbors. My novel, now eight years old and aging — written, burned and rewritten in Montreal, then rewritten yet again in Greece — had found a publisher! Someone actually thought it worth putting in bookstores. That someone was Larry Goldstein, owner of Dorset Publishing, a small publishing company in Toronto, Canada. Chuck wanted me to call him.

I don't think I picked my quota of *clementinas* the rest of that afternoon. And everyone in the village seemed to know about the good news by the time our work day ended. I went to my favorite bars and bought a round for everyone in the house, insisting everyone celebrate the great event. We were, after all, family.

We didn't have a telephone in our 600-year-old stone home so I had to arrange a phone call to Chuck through the town's central switchboard. Chuck said Dorset was offering a $1,500 advance against royalties, a paltry sum for eight years of work, but I wasn't going to quibble about money. It was getting the book between covers and into bookstores that I wanted. I'd need to go to Toronto to work with the editors, he said. Fine. No problem.

That spring, 1980, I flew to New York. Ann said goodbye in tears. She told me later she didn't know if I'd ever come back to her. The truth is, not long before this she had caught me in a dalliance I couldn't deny. Going through my wallet for some money to pay a bill while I was off painting a house, she'd found a few love notes from the young lady in question, the daughter of the Canadian couple with the retirement chalet up the hill. The daughter had been visiting, and I was smitten, I admit, but almost nothing had come of it. Still, the notes in my wallet were incriminating. No matter the truth or what I could say about it, Ann was not to be mollified.

Memory, as I said at the outset, can be a trickster, so I can't vouch that the sequence of events I'm about to recall about my trip back to the U.S. is precisely accurate. In general, however, this is what I remember of a very emotion-laden voyage.

In New York, I called Gail. I was back in country, I said. I wondered how my daughters were, and might I have a chance to see them? It was during that phone call that I first learned that Junior, the replacement husband who had adopted my daughters, had abandoned them barely a year after taking them from me. I wanted to kill him. For a moment, I think I even wanted to kill myself for letting him adopt them.

The girls were no longer living at home, Gail said. Teenagers now, they had been more than she could handle. She'd sent them to foster homes. Information about them came tumbling out of her like a cataract. It was more than I could readily digest.

I told Gail I wanted to come down to see them. She dropped the bombshell: Teri, now 16, was in a juvenile detention home in DeKalb County, on the outskirts of Atlanta. She'd been arrested for harboring a fugitive. Her boyfriend was wanted by the police and had been living in her apartment, or she in his — something like that.

That sealed it for me. I was coming to Atlanta. I don't remember how I got there. It was probably by Greyhound. I rented a motel room and a car and went to see Gail. She told me where to find Teri. She promised to contact Renée as well and ask if she would see me. I went to the DeKalb County juvenile home and they let me see my daughter. She was very quiet, very reticent to talk about herself, her life, how she had gotten into trouble. With Gail's permission, they let her leave the facility with me that evening. I took her to dinner and a movie. I confess I have no recollection what movie it was. It didn't matter. I was with my daughter again and that was the center of my focus. I do remember our dinner was at a restaurant downtown called the Land of the Midnight Sun, the finest I knew in Atlanta. We talked about her life, about mine in Spain.

Again with Gail's permission, I made arrangements for Teri to be released to my custody for the coming summer. She would spend that summer with us in Spain. Teri thought the idea wonderful, mostly I think because it would liberate her from the juvenile justice system. By the time she would return to Georgia she would be 17 and no longer a legal juvenile. I was taking the first tentative steps in what would be a long and rocky journey of re-assembling my family. I have to say, I felt good about it, and terribly frightened about whether I could pull it off. I knew, in my bones, that life was taking another abrupt turn. I concluded: let the rebuilding begin.

I also saw Renée. Gail had arranged for me to meet her at a local restaurant, a Dunkin' Donuts, I think. That didn't work out so well. We sat in a booth across from each other. Conversation was awkward and superficial, not at all like the exchange I'd had with Teri. Renée had tried her hand at writing, poetry mostly. I said I'd like to see some of her work. It was pretty good, I thought, and I told her so.

At one point she stared at me and said, "You're not my father. You don't know how to be a father." I had no answer for that.

I flew to Toronto and met Larry Goldstein. I was underwhelmed by Dorset Publishing. For one thing, it consisted of a few rooms in Larry's house. For another, Larry freely confessed he was having problems with his banker. He had a meeting at the bank one morning to go over some issues, such as unmade loan payments. He prepared for this meeting by – smoking dope. Now, I'm no prude about marijuana, but I don't think it's the wisest thing to do just before going to see your banker about money you owe him. Larry's attitude also seemed to require some adjustment. He bragged how he was going to lay down the law, to tell the banker *his* demands. Not a wise move for someone who owes several thousand dollars. But it wasn't my affair. I kept my mouth shut. Yet, novice that I was, I did start to have doubts about this publishing firm.

The staff was a small handful of young people, all working out of Larry's house. I slept in a spare bedroom for a week while we went through a major editing of the manuscript. Some years later, I told the story of my novel's perilous voyage toward publication in an article for a writers' magazine, *Byline*. I can't tell it any better today. Here's an excerpt:

> *We talked of paperback sales, translations, European rights, movie contracts, TV mini-series. Heady stuff. We zipped through the editing in a week, agreed we had a blockbuster on our hands, and I flew back to Spain with visions of $ugarplums.*

When we had finished the editing and were all happy with the end product, I collected my first $500 of the advance and we decided to celebrate by going to dinner and a movie. They suggested *Kramer vs. Kramer*, which had just won the Academy Award for best picture. Having no idea what I was about to see, I agreed.

Dennis Hoffman was the dad. Meryl Streep was the mom. They were divorced. And there was this little boy trying to figure out his place between them. I was in tears from beginning to end, and through the rounds of drinks that followed. I was supposed to be happy about the completion of my novel, its readiness for printing, and the check I'd received against royalties. Instead, I was crying a river and trying to explain how the movie had stuck a knife into my heart. They consoled, they were nice about it, but I don't think I got through to them. As I said, they were young.

When Teri arrived at the Madrid airport, I wasn't there. I'd taken a bus to meet her but it was late. She was wandering around the airport looking for me when we finally connected. Not a good omen, as openers go.

The summer was awkward, to say the least. Ann and I were drinking too much and fighting. Often the fighting was because I felt she was taking Teri's part in arguments about Teri's liberties. I was being your standard-issue protective father. Teri wanted freedoms. She wanted to go night-

With Teri, Vincente & Ismael (behind)

clubbing. There was this one guy in the village nicknamed *pistola*, because, even though married, he was known to have a roving eye. His eye roved in Teri's direction and he wound up taking her out a time or two, although she was still 16 and he was well into his 30s. I objected, as any dad would, but my objections seemed to fall on deaf ears.

There were good times as well. She went boating with Paulino, a nice guy who had spent some time working in the States. We went to the beach and danced in the streets during the town's annual fiesta. Tentatively, I was rebuilding my family, one baby step at a time. Teri was with me, and for that I was grateful. In September, when she turned 17, she returned home, no longer a "juvenile." I went back to picking oranges and painting houses.

That summer I also received the galley proofs of my novel and the second $500 check. The *Byline* story tells best what happened next:

> ...(I)n September 1980, a letter arrived "to inform you that Dorset is now insolvent...." Goldstein was driving a cab. Luckily, under terms of our contract, all rights to the novel reverted to me.
>
> As for my agent, I was informed the following February that he was now re-opening his own shop, which had also been closed since August. For six months I'd unknowingly been without an agent as well.

Chuck had closed up shop and gone to work for the Dick Morris agency, a large outfit that was agent to stars. The light at the end of my tunnel went out.

It was now early 1981. The house was done. It had a new roof, a new façade, proper windows and doors, electricity, hot and cold running water, tiled floors. The spiders and the rats and mice had been evicted. Everyone we knew had stopped by to marvel at how we had transformed it. Many who had predicted it would collapse over our heads were now applauding what we had achieved. When all had taken their turns saying how nice the place looked, they stopped coming. One evening, Ann and I sat across the living room from each other — and had nothing to say.

It was then that I realized we had spent the preceding nine years — from Montreal to France to Germany to Yugoslavia to Italy back to France to Spain to Morocco back to the United States to Mexico to Greece and finally back to Spain — filling our lives and conversations not with each other but with doing things, going places, experiencing experiences, including the experience of turning this 600-year-old stone house into a lovely dollhouse, lovely but a dollhouse nevertheless.

No publisher, no agent, the house completed, the relationship now seeming vacuous, it was time to go home. I could not face an endless string of years picking oranges and painting houses. I was approaching 41 and needed to regenerate myself. I had to make life live up to its promise. I had to make it good again.

Twenty-Seven: Back to D.C.

Ann and I kicked around a few ideas of where to go in the U.S. to reconstruct our lives: San Francisco, New Orleans, and a few others were on the list. Washington, D.C., won out as the most reasonable. We both had connections there that we could tap to find lodging and work. We made arrangements for our bank account in Benidoleig to pay ongoing utilities and taxes, had a going-away party at a local restaurant with our friends from the village, then closed up the house and headed "home."

In D.C., we stayed with Wolsey Semple in Mount Pleasant for a month while we searched for an affordable place to live, finally settling on a damp basement apartment just a hundred feet or so from the edge of the urban wilderness of Rock Creek Park, then shopped yard sales for furniture.

With a single notable exception, my old contacts proved useless in my job search. I'd been gone nine years and was completely out of the stream. Editors of magazines I'd written for no longer knew my name. I needed to start back at zero. The editor of *Washingtonian Magazine*, for whom I'd written many cover stories in the early 1970s, including the one that landed me on the *Larry King Show*, made it abundantly clear to me: I was yesterday's news.

He had a point, in a way. I probably couldn't name more than five or six sitting U.S. senators. I discovered you no longer stood in line to get your money out of your bank account from a person called a "teller," you went instead to a machine called an ATM. That was just the first of many new impersonal devices I had to learn how to use.

Another was the personal computer – PCs I was told they were called. My portable Royal typewriter was a relic. Faithful as it had been, writing numerous short stories, a novel twice, countless letters — it was an antique. Not only that, it was a broken antique. It had suddenly decided to stop capitalizing letters. The "shift" key stopped functioning. I went to the Yellow Pages looking for typewriter repair shops. They no longer existed. I found an office equipment supply shop that I thought might help. The guy laughed me out of the place. I located another promising repair service in the suburbs and schlepped my Royal out there, on Washington's no-longer-new Metro that I'd only seen in its early construction phase. Learning how to use its pre-pay farecard machine was a challenge in itself. The store I found turned out to be selling and servicing computers only. They laughed, too. They tried to sell me a computer. All I wanted was to have my Royal "shift" key fixed. As I headed out the door, one helpful guy said I could probably fix it with a paper clip, that the connecting link inside had probably broken.

At home, I looked inside the contraption and, sure enough, there dangled the broken little rod responsible for my problem. I replaced it with a straightened paper clip as suggested and, *voila!* My Royal worked just fine again, thank you. I even got the last laugh: I used that Royal to write a humorous column about my experience trying to repair the typewriter. I sent it to American Airlines' magazine, and damned if they didn't use it on their back page — a standard feature of nonsense.

The title I put on it tells it all: "On Getting the Royal Shift." My point, of course, was that if your personal computer broke down, you probably couldn't fix it with a paper clip. In the end, I bought a PC and taught myself how to use it, and forever after have wondered how I had managed to survive without one.

I may not have been up-to-date enough to find work, but Ann signed on with two temporary agencies and was immediately in great demand. Most places she was sent as a "temp" she was offered a permanent job. Within a month or so she accepted a position as a secretary in one of Washington's most prestigious law firms. I became a househusband — doing laundry at the local laundromat, shopping for groceries, cooking, house-cleaning. I was uncomfortable in the role, not because I found the tasks demeaning or difficult, but because I suddenly found it too uncomfortable to spend a dollar for a beer at the neighborhood bar while the laundry was churning next door, knowing the dollar was money Ann had earned. I had never learned how to spend other people's money.

We had some notable visitors in our basement apartment. Russell Mokiber lived in the house upstairs. An intense young man, he was one of Ralph Nader's lieutenants, living a Spartan life — nearly as Spartan as that of Nader himself on Nineteenth Street, barely a mile away. At the time Mokiber was national director of the student wing of the Nader-inspired Public Interest Research Group (PIRG). He's gone on to bigger and more nationally known roles as an heir apparent to Nader's watchdog-in-chief former status (before he became the perennial grouchy presidential spoiler and curmudgeon-in-chief).

Mokiber found a family of rats living in his kitchen and got rid of them. I think he caught one of them in his stove. The eradication of the rats unleashed a plague of fleas upon us all.

A colony of mice also lived with us, in the walls. While I was sitting on the john one day, a mouse scurried out a tiny gap below the baseboard, sat there looking at me for a few seconds, then scurried back inside his wall. One morning when I awoke and went to get the open-toed slippers I'd left near the living room sofa the night before, I stuck a foot in one of them and felt something squishy, and then something else skittered across my toes and under the sofa. That was the momma mouse. The blind little babies were the squishiness inside the slipper, where she'd given birth to them overnight. I counted a half dozen of them. They perished in a bucket of hot water. Cruel, I know, but when you live on the edge of the forest primeval — known in Washington as Rock Creek Park — it's survival of the fittest.

I went hunting the mother. When I pulled the couch from the wall she was still hiding there, but scampered behind my desk. I started extricating drawers as she jumped from one nook or cranny to another inside the desk. I had a broom at the ready when she finally made one last dash for freedom, charging straight at me as if to run me over. I backpedalled fiercely, swinging the broom in wild arcs trying to slam it down on her. Sad to report, I succeeded. Stunned by a few blows from the broom, she finally succumbed and joined her innocent babies in mouse heaven.

Then there was our opossum. We weren't sure what was upending our trash can outside the kitchen door each night until one evening I glanced out and saw him, standing on his hind feet, trying to nudge the lid off with his nose. He was huge! As I recall, we discovered that a ring of baking soda on the ground and a real heavy brick on the trash can lid would keep him away.

But surely the most curious visitor of all was Chuck Neighbors. My agent was back in business, he wrote, and wanted to come to Washington to discuss my publishing possibilities. Did we have someplace he could sleep? We offered him the sofa, now mouse-free. Here's how I recounted in *Byline* magazine the visit by my graying, 50-something agent and its sequelae:

(He) arrive(d) clad in denims, boots and Stetson. I soon learned that the object of his trip wasn't my literary career, as I'd supposed, but a new love, a 22-year-old Ringling Brothers elephant rider who was visiting family nearby. I was merely another unpublished author to console in exchange for a weekend's free lodging....

(My agent) and his petite circus performer danced the night away at Bronco Billy's, a popular urban cowboy watering hole, and I fed my fantasy with Scotch and tried not to notice that I was on my way down without ever having achieved more than an appetite-whetting glimpse of the top.

What should have been the fatal snip of the (Fates') shears came yet another half-year later, in April 1982: the agent wrote that he was moving to San Antonio and 'starting a new business that will be involved with motion picture productions.' I was again without an agent. By my own definition ... (A real novelist was published now and then. At the least he had an agent) ... I was no longer a real novelist....

I wrote myself depressing notes, blamed Reaganomics, considered a career as a housepainter. By June suicide didn't seem implausible....

In fact, I vividly recall one late afternoon, sipping beer at a sidewalk restaurant in Adams Morgan as I eavesdropped on the conversation of three guys at a nearby table. They were discussing the best methods of committing suicide. Guns were "too messy." Sleeping pills and sticking your head in a gas oven were "too slow" and offered too much opportunity to back out. They seemed to agree drowning might be best. I sat there silently contemplating each with them as though it was the most natural thing in the world to plan one's suicide. Walking home, I had to shake myself off that train of thought, literally frightened at what I'd been thinking and how calmly.

By then I was not only without agent, novel, or job, I was also without Ann. We'd separated after my year of house-husbanding. She was personally hurt by it, and I know it was all my doing, but I don't think we were ever going to build a happy, comfortable life together after the excitements of life as international vagabonds. I gave her what little savings we had and she moved in with Lynn, Wolsey's former girlfriend. In time, she went on to finer and greater things — her own graduate degree, a book of her own, a marriage and successful career in Toronto, Canada.

I moved into a group home on a one-way, one-block street on the seedy side of town, just off the Fourteenth Street corridor that had been devastated during the 1968 riots following the assassination of Martin Luther King, Jr., a neighborhood only now starting to be rebuilt. My street was notorious as a drug market. Taxis and cars crept down it each night waiting for the purveyors to come out of hiding and make a hasty sale through the car window, like the carhops at drive-ins when I was a teenager. The taxicabs typically were for the wealthy whites in the suburbs who wouldn't dare show their faces or have their fancy cars seen on our block.

The group home was peopled by students from nearby Antioch Law School, now defunct. They referred to it as a "grope" home. The owner, an architect, who had been living there a while, bought his own apartment in a nicer part of town and asked me to be resident manager of the "grope" home: my "pay" was to live there rent-free.

I was hanging out with Wolsey a good bit. We'd go to basketball games and tennis matches. I should note here that Wolsey is another of those figures in the background of my life who played pivotal roles. Indirectly, it is he who influenced me to stop smoking. During the early 1980s, his son Jeremy was a champion tennis amateur in the mid-Atlantic region, on his way to winning a tennis scholarship to Stanford University. Wolsey took me to many of his matches and I marveled at his powerful serve-and-volley game. He made it all look so smooth and easy.

I mentioned that to Wolsey and he said he could show me how to play. Wolsey is a tall, gangly, slow-moving, slow-talking man from Guyana in South America. He grew up in a prominent family there, then went to Massachusetts Institute of Technology and decided to remain in the U.S. He ended up forming his own computer services company in Washington and teaching computer sciences at Howard University, considered the "Black Harvard." Eventually, he became dean of the computer sciences department and an "insider" in local politics and government.

He was also a devoted tennis fan. He taught me the rudiments, but I was never very good. I'd huff and puff back and forth across the court chasing balls while he seemed a human backboard, easily slapping back anything I sent toward him, never breaking a sweat. After our "games," if you can call them that, I'd collapse and drag out my cigarettes. I told him I didn't understand how he could make it look so easy and I couldn't.

Two words: "You smoke."

I decided playing tennis well would be more fun than smoking. I was "dating" one of the "grope home" law students at the time, a strange young lady named Linda. On a Saturday in February 1982, we went downtown to a major intersection where I knew they usually had kids passing out free samples of cigarettes on every corner. Linda had a big purse, I had a coat with large pockets. We circled that intersection again and again, pocketing free samples at each pass, until her bag and my pockets were filled with sample packs, five cigarettes to the pack. Each pack also had a coupon worth perhaps a dollar or 50 cents off a full pack. I pooled the coupons and took them to my neighborhood liquor store, where I usually bought my cigarettes, and gave them to the owner. He tallied them up, then cashed them in for the cigarettes of my choice — at the time low-tar Carltons. I went home with I can't remember how many free cartons of cigarettes. Lots.

These I stacked on a bookshelf and pledged to chain-smoke them until finished, and then never smoke again. It took me a week or so. By the end I was smoking almost five packs a day — and hating it. I couldn't wait until I *didn't have to smoke!* I remember the last cigarette of my life was at about 12:35 a.m. on a weeknight in March. I had tapered off a little that day because I saw the end near and wanted the last one to be at the close of the day, just in case I'd be tempted to go out and buy another pack. David Letterman was on TV. Back then he had the "late late" show after Johnny Carson. He was doing his opening monologue when I smoked that last cigarette, stubbed it out, turned off the TV and went to sleep. The next day I threw away ashtrays and took window drapes and blankets and anything else that might retain the smell of cigarettes to the dry cleaner. I never smoked again. To this day, the thought of that episode gives me an urge to gag.

Wolsey also introduced me to the Trinidadian community of Washington, taking me to all-night parties during Mardi Gras one year, and the following year talking me into joining him for a trip to Trinidad to celebrate Carnival at its fullest. He had relatives and numerous friends there, most of them former students at Howard University. I met them all. I drank coconut water out of freshly cut coconuts and more than my fair share of Caribe beer, danced all night at parties, and joined in "J'ouvert," the opening bacchanal of carnival in which everyone gets covered in mud that is wheeled around in barrels in every parade. The mud is slung playfully at paraders and bystanders alike.

With Wolsey at Trinidad Carnival, 1991

One day, as I walked down the street with Wolsey and his friend (and now mine) Mike Holdip, people I didn't know kept waving as I passed, "Hi, Dick!" (Wolsey had met me before I reverted to "Richard" and so persisted in calling me that, so now everyone in Trinidad who knows me knows me as "Dick.")

"Mike, who are these people?" I asked. "They seem to know me. Do I know them?"

"Dick," he said, "they know you. You were the only white guy at the party." Mike loves repeating that story to this day.

I also made almost annual trips to Montreal and Québec in the 1980s and 1990s, sometimes with Gary, sometimes alone to visit Marthe. She had divorced and was down on herself. We spent a good bit of time on the phone. I'd tell her to run a warm bath, pour herself some champagne, light some candles — and then we'd talk late into the night. I urged her to love again, because a failed marriage did not mean the end of love. We became even closer than before, sharing music, laughing about the summer she had been in Miami Beach and I a teenage seminarian smitten by my cousin, the summer that ended with a bus ride back to the seminary, her makeup on my shirt.

Remember that notable exception to my lack of productive job-search contacts? That was Ralph Hoar, my friend from the Insurance Institute days who had "come out of the closet" in a letter transported to me in Mexico by Wolsey. He was still living with his wife, had two children, but was privately living a gay and dissolute life — public baths, back alleys, and drugs, both marijuana and cocaine. But he was also plugged into several federal agencies and regularly received assignments from them to edit or rewrite various reports and studies. He brought me on board for many of these as he considered my writing and editing skills superior to his own. He'd get the jobs and together over his kitchen table we'd work the nights away polishing up the awful grammar and syntax of governmental scribblings no one would ever read — annual traffic accident and fatality reports from the Department of Transportation, reports of the Legal Services Corporation that Reagan was hell-bent on dismantling, Census Bureau reports, obscure papers from the Office of Technology Assessment, and a massive report on the history of ETIP, the Experimental Technology and Invention Program, which had sought to leverage federal buying power to push corporate America into innovative solutions to problems and which Reagan was also terminating. Money started trickling in.

Ralph called one Friday to tell me someone he had met at a party the night before wanted me to call him. He was the editor of the magazine of the National Trust for Historic Preservation, and he had a rush job he needed done. Another writer had turned in what was supposed to be a cover story on historic American hotels, but it was a mess. The editor couldn't possibly publish it that way, but the magazine was set to go to the printer on Monday. Could I revise it over the weekend? I jumped at the opportunity, little understanding how much work would be involved.

I bicycled down to the Trust's offices (yes, I'd acquired another bicycle), met the editor, and received a large cardboard box crammed with brochures, advertisements, and assorted scraps of history on about a half-dozen hotels stretching from Memphis to San Francisco, plus the rejected original manuscript. I pored over the material all Friday night, Saturday and Saturday night, then wrote a fresh story on Sunday. I turned it in Monday morning, and the editor was demonstrably relieved. More than that, assignments for other articles started to flow in from him.

I was on my way back at last. And in more ways than one. Just before the Fourth of July, 1983, I received a call from Toronto. It was Larry Goldstein, the owner of the now bankrupt Dorset Publishing Company. He told me McClelland and Stewart, Canada's largest publishing house, was interested in my now 10-year-old novel! Back to that *Byline* article:

> *From the pits back to the pinnacles.*
>
> *Goldstein must have been toting the galley proofs around with him in his taxicab. He'd never stopped believing in the novel, he said, and had been hawking it among other Canadian publishers ever since his own company bit the dust.... (H)e'd offered it to M&S while temporarily engaged there as a reader. So far three editors had seen it. He told me to expect a call soon after an editorial board meeting scheduled for Monday, July 5....*

I spent that July Fourth weekend at Gary's, up in the Virginia mountains, full of anticipation. That Monday, the promised call came from M&S.

> *Valerie Thompson, the editorial director, said my novel had "the makings of a classic." I changed my address...to Cloud Nine.*
>
> *It was time to recruit another agent. After all, I had a sale practically in hand. Ten percent could be had just for passing Go with me.*
>
> *No such luck. In rapid succession two New York agents turned me down. They were already overloaded with clients, they said. One complained the advance would be so paltry his commission would be consumed by long distance telephone bills alone. I decided to fly solo. After all, John Updike had no agent.*
>
> *The best mail of all came later in July from Lily Poritz Miller, M&S's senior editor, introducing herself as my editor-to-be. "A truly remarkable book," she called the novel. "It makes me wonder who in fact (in the U.S.) had the chance to read your story.... A strong effort should be made to seek international publication."*
>
> *She even enclosed her in-house reader's report. More of that ecstasy that makes the agony of the writing life worthwhile even before the first royalty check arrives. "Master of the language...beautifully written...great command of dialog...an incredible work.... The author's knowledge of his surroundings...is impeccable, and the same skill exists in the creation of his numerous characters."*

From Cloud Nine to Seventh Heaven. This was the stuff boyhood dreams were made of.

Contracts were reviewed and signed, I received another $1,500 advance against royalties. Combined with the $1,000 from Goldstein's aborted venture, that made my take the princely sum of $2,500 for more than 10 years of on-and-off work and agonizing. I didn't care.

The new editing process made the one-week skim-over we'd done at Dorset look like child's play. This was a grueling six-month, total-immersion ordeal, often painful because it's never fun chopping up your own offspring, however ultimately rewarding.

We began talking of paperback sales, selling rights for co-publication in the U.S., translation into French, foreign sales. None of this came to pass. In fact, I received word that U.S. publication had been considered at the prestigious Boston house of Atlantic Little-Brown only to be rejected because, in the words of one editor on the board as passed along to me, "It's about French Canadians and everybody knows they don't read books."

About the time I was wrapping up the final revisions, fate stepped in again in the person of Ralph Hoar. He had a friend named Ted Johnson who was a management consultant to a little known national organization called HALT. They needed a communications director and Ralph had recommended me. Would I be interested?

A regular paycheck seemed enticing but I wasn't sure I wanted to hitch my wagon to an unknown horse. I met with the group's executive director, Matt Valencic. He explained the name and the agenda. HALT stood for "Help Abolish Legal Tyranny." The mission was to advocate reform of the legal system so people could do many routine things without lawyers and so that lawyers could be regulated by citizen boards, things of that nature. It sounded like a good enough cause. Its funding was all from direct mail appeals, however, and its funding base was admittedly right wing, the lawyer-bashing segment of the population who blamed lawyers for civil rights, women's rights, criminals' rights, and every other liberal cause in the country. The odd thing about it, Matt said, was that the entire staff was politically very liberal.

I agreed and we shook hands. Matt said he had to leave on a business trip the next day, but he wanted me to start right away. The staff turned out to be a bunch of nuts. They cheered my arrival as though I was coming to save their sinking ship. One woman couldn't handle pronouncing my name and had put up a big banner spelling it phonetically as "Herr—Bear." Another guy had a nervous tic in his eyelid whenever we spoke and never looked directly at me. They were not only strange, they were disorganized and seemed to like it that way.

Each had already carved out his or her turf to defend. One insisted that there were certain shops and restaurants they did business in and others they boycotted, suggesting I would be expected to follow suit. The finance director, a willowy blonde, invited me to lunch. Over our food she suggested we "get together" after work, that we were "so much alike," she could just feel it. I politely declined, not thinking that a wise first step in a new job.

I anguished that entire night, unable to sleep. I wasn't going to cut it with this bunch, I was sure. I returned to the office the next day and told the willowy blonde, Matt's second in command, that I had reconsidered and wouldn't be taking the position.

Matt's call came the very next day. He'd been summoned back to battle stations, apparently. Would I take on the job as a contract consultant, just to get them up and running so they could at least publish their quarterly newspaper that was due at the printer in another week or so? That, I thought, I could do, because it didn't signify a long-term commitment. A few weeks turned into a few months. In rapid order I learned how to use a computer and how to juggle staff personalities to produce respectable results.

Most of all, I managed to calm the willowy blonde's extracurricular expectations. My eye had caught on someone else, a part-time assistant to the legal department's director. Her name was Karen. We were dating within a month.

The Questing Beast was published during those first few months at HALT. I took a week or so off to go on a media tour in Canada. I know authors are supposed to say they hate these tours, hate having to sell their books on TV and radio talk shows like so much costume jewelry, hate the endless grind of the publicity business. I felt none of that. I loved it. We did late night TV shows in Toronto and Montreal, hopping from station to station, taking trains from city to city. It was exhilarating, a badge of having "arrived." Even after I returned to Washington, I did a show from the studios of the Canadian Broadcasting Corporation at the National Press Building, then went to New York to participate in a televised roundtable of authors discussing how their ethnic backgrounds had shaped their work.

I received clippings of the newspaper reviews. Here's a sampler of their headlines:

"Hébert's Story of Quest Among Best First Novels"

"Hébert Sets High Standard"

"*Questing Beast* Powerful Novel of Mythology"

"Vivid Scenes Lift a Québec First Novel"

Needless to say, for someone so recently in the dumps, I was riding pretty high.

Life was shifting gears again in other ways as well. Karen and I went to Benidoleig for a few weeks and stayed in the home Ann and I still owned. It was that visit, spent largely cleaning and making repairs to the house after it had been closed for three years, that convinced me I didn't want to own it any longer. Ann said she wanted to keep it. After a few more years we arrived at agreement and Ann bought my half interest. She still owns it and rents it out to vacationers.

In Karen I'd found another fellow traveler. In addition to Spain, we vacationed in Italy, Greece, Hawaii, Acapulco, Paris. When we weren't on one of those major voyages, every long weekend, from Memorial Day in May to the Oyster Festival on Columbus Day weekend in October, we spent on Chincoteague Island, Virginia.

What I didn't know is that while I was on my book-promoting tour in Canada, a power struggle had been raging back at HALT between its two co-founders, Matt and Paul Hasse. Hasse won. A few months after I began working there, Matt was gone and a new executive director was hired, Glenn Nishimura, a Hawaiian of Japanese descent who had been recruited from the Consumer Federation of America, where he had earned a reputation as a strong consumer advocate.

One of the smartest moves in office politics I ever made was with Glenn. Shortly after he came on board, I told him I wasn't staff, only a temporary contractor, so neither he nor the organization owed me anything. I wanted him to choose whether or not he wanted me to be his communications director. I would be his "hire," not someone he'd inherited. Glenn asked me to stay on. I stayed six more years.

We did some good work. We transformed the quarterly newspaper into a slick monthly magazine. We instituted annual awards to journalists who covered our issues well. We went to Florida and staged rallies to free an elderly woman who had been jailed for helping poor people file legal documents even though she wasn't a lawyer, even got her story told on *60 Minutes*. We held demonstrations against bar association practices in Annapolis, Maryland, in San Francisco, and in Chicago. I took Glenn up and down the state of California meeting with the editorial boards of all the major newspapers to promote our agenda. The activist in me had reawakened.

And not merely because of HALT. Wolsey also played an important role. Marion Barry was mayor of Washington. People were calling him "Mayor for Life," but everyone knew he was doing dope, groping women in elevators, getting "serviced" by the strippers at the back tables of downtown clubs. Ladies of the night in Washington talked freely about it. Barry himself declared he was a "night owl."

With Karen

Birthday Catamaran Cruise, Acapulco Bay, 1988

Chincoteague Oyster Festival, 1989

I discovered Wolsey was part of Barry's circle — not exactly a close friend, perhaps, but someone whose computer services company had benefited mightily from city business under Barry. He didn't so much defend Barry to me as tell me that if I didn't like the state of the city government, to get involved. "Do something or shut up" is what I think he said, if not in so many words.

I did something. I got involved, first in the failed race of a woman who ran against Barry in the mid-'80s, then in the failed race of a young lawyer who ran against our incumbent city councilmember, and ultimately, in another mayor's race when I volunteered to help the least well-known candidate among five seeking to succeed Barry as mayor. I didn't care. I was excited again. I could feel the rush of the challenge. Life was good again.

Twenty-Eight: Playing Politics

In the Spring of 1990, Glenn and his wife left to join the Peace Corps and I left to join National Public Radio. With Glenn's departure for Papua New Guinea, the handwriting on the wall at HALT seemed pretty clear. The new executive director and I had never hit it off. She'd been another department head. I thought her something of a bully, she probably held me in similarly low regard. We'd found ourselves on opposite sides of many internal battles over strategy. Besides, I'd been there a little over a half-dozen years and it was time to move on.

I knew I had to sanitize my résumé. HALT had some 150,000 members nationally at the time but was decidedly unpopular in Washington, which has one lawyer for every 15 people. Lawyers ran everything. You had to go through them for virtually any position or contract or favor. They openly described HALT as a "lawyer-bashing organization." Having HALT at the top of your résumé was not a good way to attract potential employers. NPR, however, was a revered brand, and NPR was looking for a media relations specialist to help launch and promote a new Specials Project. (NPR isn't particularly clever at naming things, I quickly learned.) I applied and was hired.

The project was to produce week-long special programming directed at a specific under-represented audience, in this case young people. NPR's audience consisted of aging, liberal Baby-Boom yuppies. The problem was they were not being replaced by younger listeners. We would go after the kids. The first week-long programming ran as segments on all NPR shows under the heading, *Prejudice Puzzle*. It asked if we were teaching a whole new generation of kids prejudice against people not like them (answer: yes). It interviewed Inuit kids in Alaska and native Hawaiian kids, American Indian kids and Black kids and Hispanic kids, and of course a battery of obligatory "experts" on related topics. We devised a smorgasbord of fun support materials to appeal to the young: rap competitions, poster and poetry competitions, and special educational tools and manuals for teachers to use in issue-focused classes.

My role was to produce the written promotional and support materials, edit the teacher's manual and work with the more than 400 local NPR stations throughout the country to promote the programming and its related activities in their local media. I worked with a great bunch of young people and we congratulated ourselves mightily at our success when the week of programming closed that following September with a two-hour long national call-in show on a Saturday afternoon, with calls from groups of kids in classrooms and libraries and community centers across the country.

We went to work immediately on our second "specials project," about the changing nature of what constitutes a "family." I came up with the winning title for it, *Family Stories*. (As I said, I learned quickly that they weren't into clever titles.)

Washington, D.C., was in the throes of the first mayoral election of the first post-Barry era. Marion Barry had been caught in the famous crack-smoking sting — he complained that "the bitch set me up" — and was in prison. Five people wanted his job. Three were veterans of the City Council and the fourth was the outgoing long-term (nonvoting) delegate to Congress, Walter Fauntroy, himself a civil rights hero of some repute. The fifth was a diminutive, light-skinned black woman, a Washingtonian by birth, named Sharon Pratt Dixon. She'd never held public office (although her ex-husband, Arrington Dixon, had). She had served admirably as treasurer of the National Democratic Party and as a vice president of the local electric utility, Pepco, and her father had been a highly regarded judge, but that was about it.

Her campaign beat on a single drum: she would "clean house," and she would do it "not with a broom, but a shovel." The shovel became her totem. She accused the City Council member candidates of being "three blind mice" who turned the other way rather than confront the sins of Marion Barry. Fauntroy I don't think she even bothered going after.

She was at barely two percent in the polls when I joined the campaign, but I liked what she said. Wolsey had said to "do something"? I did. I sent a $50 donation and a letter volunteering my services as a writer, editor and media specialist. I was asked to come in to her headquarters, met with some people, and was put to work. By the end of that campaign, I was heavily engaged in its every aspect in my ward, Ward I, the most compact and culturally diverse in the city. I was standing outside Metro stations at dawn handing out flyers to people going to work, putting up posters on lampposts and utility poles late into the night, canvassing door-to-door on weekends, staffing telephone banks at every free moment to call voters and cajole them into voting for Sharon. We took her through Adams Morgan, stopping in each restaurant to go table-to-table shaking hands and asking for votes. I recruited friends and neighbors to help, including Karen, who I don't think quite knew what hit her.

The biggest coup (and surprise) of all came the weekend before the election: *The Washington Post* endorsed her.

I also turned 50 that week. Karen surprised me with a magnificent party at a restaurant in Adams Morgan, renting an entire banquet room. It was our custom to treat each other to a fine restaurant meal on birthdays, and as she led me down 18th Street in Adams Morgan, she refused to tell me which restaurant she was taking me to. Then I spotted Wolsey in the distance. As soon as I saw him he ducked back inside. I found that strange, as he must have seen me, but it was not unusual for Wolsey to be on the streets of Adams Morgan, after all. He did live in the neighborhood. So the surprise element wasn't spoiled. When we walked in and they popped the surprise, I found it hard to believe Karen had rounded up some 30 or more people from very different sectors of my life — Ralph and others from the Insurance Institute of long ago, friends from HALT, neighbors from the cooperative where we lived, political types, and yes, Wolsey — and they all seemed to be getting along just fine. As they say, a great time was had by all.

It's a maxim in Washington that the primary is "tantamount to election," because whoever wins the Democratic primary always wins the general election over token Republican candidates, if any. On primary day, I was responsible for four voting precincts strung along the infamous, riot-torn Fourteenth Street corridor. I positioned myself at one precinct for an hour handing out brochures as voters went in to vote, then jumped into Karen's car and rushed to the next, then the third, then the fourth, then back again. This started at 7 a.m. and didn't end until 7 p.m. When I called in the final vote tallies and got into the car shortly after the polls closed, I flipped on the radio and learned we were winning! They had already tabulated the morning votes and Sharon was well ahead. Historically, the afternoon and evening voters had never reversed the tide of morning votes.

Jubilation ran high at the victory party downtown that night. Several people from other campaigns came up to ask how we had managed to recruit so many volunteers, that everywhere they'd gone during the day they'd seen Sharon's people working the voters. I told them it was the principle of the lone Indian hiding behind a hill, firing off a few arrows at a wagon train, whooping a war cry, then running to another hill to do the same thing again, over and over, proclaiming to the wagon train, "I've got you surrounded." On stage, Sharon Pratt brandished her sparkling new shovel and declared it was time to "clean house."

Then reality struck again, of course. Not long after Sharon took office, we were hard at work on *Family Stories*, trying to duplicate everything we had done for *Prejudice Puzzle*, when the first Persian Gulf War broke out, that international effort to drive Iraq's army out of Kuwait. Many people considered it "CNN's war," because that network, still young, had people positioned in Baghdad throughout, televising the war firsthand into people's living rooms as tracer bullets lit up the night sky and bombs exploded everywhere. Most Americans had never before seen war so up-close-and-personal.

NPR decided to try to compete with the major networks and sent about a dozen news correspondents to the Middle East. They broadcast wall-to-wall coverage of every aspect of the conflict for the two weeks or so that it lasted, and nearly went bankrupt in the process. After the war, forced to trim its sails, NPR went on a program-slashing binge. Some major programs were threatened with extinction or cut back severely. Our "Specials Project" was abandoned completely. I was on the street again.

I was unemployed about six months this time. I picked up a few scraps of work from Ralph, but it wasn't the same as it had been earlier. I used some of my unemployment compensation to buy a $400 acoustic guitar and re-taught myself how to play, mostly trying to mimic Eric Clapton's work from the songbook of his *Unplugged* album. Karen and I went to Paris at the end of August. On the way back we stopped in New York City a few days, staying in a cheap, seedy rooming house, and attending early rounds of the U.S. Open tennis tournament. Wolsey had secured tickets for us. Renée came up for a few days as well, to attend a poetry conference, and we rode the Staten Island Ferry together. Things were looking up a little in that department at least.

When we arrived back in Washington, my answering machine had a message for me from Paul Costello, a well-known name in Washington political circles. He had been press aide to Jimmy Carter's wife Rosalynn and Michael Dukakis' wife Kitty. He was now the new mayor's communications director. He had my résumé from the campaign in front of him when I returned his call and asked if I was employed. I conceded I was "between jobs." He asked me to come in to talk. I lost no time.

By the end of the week, I was the Public Information Officer for the District of Columbia Department of Public Works. I had very little idea what the job entailed. I knew only that it paid well and provided health care, annual leave, and even matching fund pension contributions; that I'd have a staff of two; that my boss would be DPW Director Betty Francis; that I'd have a DPW-issued SUV and cellular phone (a much bulkier thing back then than today's sleek little toys), and that I'd be working out of the Reeves Center, a new office building at Fourteenth and U Streets, part of the massive effort to rebuild the corridor. That put my office within a 15-minute walk of home. It would have been barely a five-minute walk from my "grope home" on the drug-peddling street, but I'd moved from there in 1987 to an Adams Morgan studio apartment in a cooperative. I'd bought the apartment when Karen had turned it down as too small for her furniture; then she'd bought Glenn's old apartment downstairs in the same building when he left for Papua New Guinea, so we became upstairs-downstairs neighbors.

My first day on the DPW job, the deputy director informed me I needed to be back at work at midnight for something he called a "snow drill." I told him he was kidding, right? This was some sort of initiation thing? He assured me he was serious. Then Betty Francis herself confirmed the seriousness of it. A year or so before, when Washington had been slammed by a massive snow storm, it failed to deal with the snow in any meaningful way and it later turned out that Mayor Barry had been at the Super Bowl in California and had stayed on a few extra days to party with friends — where he had been seen snorting snow of a different variety. Betty assured me this was never going to happen on her watch.

For two hours that first night, and twice again before snow season began, we went through the snow drill in our Command Center atop the Reeves Center, pretending we had a blizzard on our hands. Strategically placed thermometers sent data on local conditions on the streets and bridges to our Command Center computers. Snowplows and sand trucks patrolled the streets, dispatched here and there by Kirk Johnson, our emergency coordinator, as let's-pretend trouble spots erupted — an overturned bus here, an icy bridge there that had to be sanded, a derailed Metro train snarling traffic on the other side of town, a burst water main spewing a lake downtown that was rapidly icing over, make-believe fires raging out of control because fire trucks couldn't get through. I made let's pretend calls to make-believe media to issue updates, hammered out rapid-fire news releases that were never sent, held news conferences with no real reporters.

At one point, Betty and I drove around town to monitor how things were going at the igloo-like domes where sand and salt were stored, at the truck yards where plows were dispatched, and on the streets themselves. By the time we had finished practicing, we had the procedures down cold (pun intended). We were never caught unprepared by snow and soon were winning accolades from neighboring jurisdictions and even *The Washington Post* for our ability to handle major snowstorms.

Betty Francis was a regal, statuesque woman. She was the best boss I ever worked for. With a smooth, coffee-and-cream complexion and an unruffled manner (she told me she was a Buddhist), she was as beautiful as she was a tough manager, a very difficult combination to pull off when your empire consists largely of a rather rough breed of men — garbage collectors, water main maintenance guys, road pavers, sewage treaters, and parking enforcement officers. Her department was the most visible in the city. It ran the traffic lights and the parking meters, the Metro system and the roads, street paving and pothole patching, tree maintenance and street sweeping, water distribution and sewage treatment, trash collection and recycling (which we initiated), the issuance of drivers' licenses and adjudication of parking tickets. It was where city met citizen.

If anything went wrong in that empire, as it did often enough, it was my job to go before the people, usually on television, and explain how we had everything under control. Or would real soon because we were already working on it. I did this standing in blizzards and in floods from broken water mains, beside fallen trees and long lines at the driver-licensing bureau.

"Dr. Gridlock" wrote a weekly column in *The Washington Post* that griped about traffic problems great and small, usually with a bit of sarcasm toward the District of Columbia. (He lived in the Virginia suburbs.) His information usually was based on crank calls and letters he received from disgruntled readers. One column in particular irked me into action. He said driving through Washington was a "jaw-breaking" experience because of all the potholes. I responded with a letter pointing out our vast improvement over the previous administration's poor record by instituting a programmatic repaving program that was resurfacing streets throughout the city. I told him it was clear he hadn't driven in the District of Columbia recently or he'd have known better.

He printed my letter, then issued a challenge: who was right, he or I? He urged his readers to write in their experiences.

I went to work. I rustled up as many friends as I could cajole into writing letters praising our newly paved streets, naming streets in their own neighborhoods wherever possible. Some didn't want to be bothered but let me put their names on letters I drafted for them. I made sure I had people from all sectors of the city, none of them DPW employees. We flooded "Dr. Gridlock" with mail. The following week, an entire two—page spread of the newspaper was devoted to letters he had received, only one of which was negative. Many were those I had ginned up, but I was surprised to find quite a few supportive letters from people I didn't even know!

And we danced. The Public Works management style was very collegial. We went on retreats together, went out to eat together, had parties together. Inevitably, dancing would begin, typically a line dance, especially the Electric Slide. Now, I love dancing and feel I have good rhythm, but I never did quite develop the ability to dance in a line, making precisely the moves everyone else is making. I suppose I was hearing a different drummer. Again. This would amuse my almost completely African-American colleagues to no end. Until one afternoon at a local beer and sandwich place, Sade came over the speakers singing *Smooth Operator*. My feet started moving. Next thing I knew, I was "getting down" with Evelyn Shields, the smart and attractive young woman who was director of our recycling program. The others erupted in applause when we finished. They didn't make fun of my dancing again after that.

DPW Gang. Betty's on my right, Evelyn Shields behind her

I was feeling pretty good about myself when the Mayor's office called and asked me to come downtown to meet with her. This was about a year after I'd started at DPW. I was ushered into her private office not knowing what to expect. Was there something I needed to defend myself against?

She was on the phone when I entered. I waited nervously on the sofa trying not to hear her conversation. She apologized when she hung up. She said it had been an important call with Vernon Jordan, now regarded as a kingmaker in national Democratic politics. I told her how, back in the 1960s, Vernon Jordan's office had been across the street from *The Atlanta Constitution* and how we had met there several times to swap stories and news leads.

Then she came directly to the point: she was reorganizing the entire communications program; would I be willing to leave DPW and come downtown to work for her? I gulped. This I had neither expected nor aspired to. The idea was to sort the city government's entire communications operations into clusters of agencies, with one overall coordinator for each cluster. The biggest cluster would be called "Operations" and would include DPW, but also Parks and Recreation, Health, Corrections, Regulatory Affairs, the Taxicab Commission, and Administrative Services. She wanted me to be its coordinator. She'd been watching what I'd done at DPW and was impressed. I had taken the most maligned department in the city and made it the most respected. And yes, she had already discussed this with Betty Francis.

You don't tell the Mayor you are happy where you are and don't want to work for her, even if it's true, which it wasn't. I moved downtown. I continued to be the public spokesperson for DPW, even after they hired a young lady to take the official title of Public Information Officer. It was understood she would manage the information office at the Reeves Center, but in emergencies, she would defer to me as the public face of the department. Betty wanted it that way. Beyond that, I was also now charged with corralling the information officers of six other departments, each of whom had his or her own way of doing things that didn't necessarily conform to the overall script. Turf consciousness is one of the greatest diseases of governance, I discovered. Melding the seven information programs into a single coherent message machine wasn't going to be easy, and while I think I made some strides, when it was all over, I had to admit it still wasn't the well-oiled machine I had imagined or that the Mayor had wanted.

Meanwhile, Betty Francis had also laid another challenge on my desk. The Mayor had appointed a blue-ribbon committee to devise a master plan for making the District of Columbia more congenial to businesses, which had been leaving town for less troubled and less expensive suburban sites. "The Washington Committee," as it was named (again, not very original titling, I concede), consisted of bankers and lawyers, professors and business leaders – the city's *crème de la crème* – assigned to various working subcommittees. One group worked on taxation issues, another on business licensing and related affairs, another on public services. I was assigned to that last one, in other words Public Works. That subcommittee dealt with such things as parking availability, shuttle bus access, traffic patterns, other services that might make doing business in the city a bit easier. Betty wanted me on that subcommittee as her eyes and ears. I said OK, of course. I was flattered.

Then she told me she thought a prominent public relations guy on the committee was something of a loose cannon. He'd need to be curbed. She didn't want me starting any fights with him, just to keep him under control and keep her informed about any issues that might need to be headed off. I asked his name. Art Schulz, she said.

I don't remember if I told her then or later — maybe never — but I knew Art from my Atlanta years. He had been a reporter for WSB Radio during the 1960s when I was with the *Constitution*. Now a tall, balding, somewhat brash fellow, he and I quickly renewed friendship. He introduced me to Famous Grouse Scotch whiskey, for one thing, but was best known for having driven the red light district out of downtown Washington a year or so earlier, a success story I told him I didn't exactly applaud.

In the end, it was Art Schultz and I who wrote the final Public Works subcommittee report during many late nights in his offices, and then editing and refining the overall Washington Committee Report. We won high praise for the work, and Art proved easier to "control" than anyone had imagined. We worked well together, based on a long history of mutual trust. All I needed to say if I saw trouble ahead was something to the effect that "I don't think we want to go down that road" and he'd back away from a pet idea he'd advanced. But even that happened very few times, I recall. I suspect he had picked up that I was somehow Betty Francis' man and, by inference, the Mayor's as well.

I think we put out a pretty good report. It certainly received high praise from the Mayor and the chair of the Washington Committee, and when I visit Washington these days, I can't help but notice some of our proposals actually in operation — municipal parking garages in areas where parking was always the biggest problem, or the shuttle service to and through highly congested Adams Morgan. Whether they have resulted in attracting more business, I'll probably never know.

In the Mayor's office I also joined the statehood movement, a new group called Citizens for New Columbia (CNC). Every Thursday we marched to the U.S. Capitol, then stood side by side across Independence Avenue and poured out a coffee urn of iced tea – our own version of a Tea Party to protest taxation without representation. Each Thursday we were arrested, held for a few hours in a holding room, then released after posting a $50 fine. While in the large holding room we would sing freedom songs and do snake dances, to the great amusement of our jailers. One day we snake-danced to the door and almost made it out of the building before the jailers realized what we were doing and herded us back inside, with considerable banter and laughter.

We had wanted to confront the federal government in court, but it turned out that blocking the street was a city offense and we would be prosecuted by the very city we were trying to free. The city prosecutor, John Payton, today the head of the NAACP Legal Defense Fund, agreed to drop all charges if we promised never to block the street again. He also told us the way to get into federal court was to block a federal office building entrance instead of a street. That's what we did for another dozen Thursdays. Sometimes we were as few as 12 or 15 protesters, but sometimes 25 or 30. The Rev. Jesse Jackson marched with us once. So did the Mayor.

For those offenses we were prosecuted by the U.S. Attorney General, by the office then headed by Eric Holder, who would go on to be Attorney General himself under Barack Obama. They tried 23 of us together, one jury trial for all charges. When I took the stand in my defense, the prosecutor kept trying to get me to say I sat down in the doorway of the House of Representatives office building to prevent congressmen and staff from going inside to do their work. I kept saying no, I sat down there to make my voice heard in the Congress, my right under the Constitution, because otherwise I had no vote and no voice. The judge kept telling me to stop making political speeches and to answer the question. Then the prosecutor would ask the same question again and I'd give the same answer. I don't remember how many times we went back and forth this way, but ultimately the judge threatened to find me in contempt of court if I didn't answer the question. This time I did answer it. I simply said, "No."

The jury found us all not guilty. Then they took us out to lunch. Several asked if they could join our organization. A few years later, I became the third chairman of the group, succeeding Bernard Demczuk, then the mayor's legislative liaison, and Mark Thompson, an activist who had earlier led student demonstrations for African studies at the University of the District of Columbia and went on to be a prominent radio commentator. I left the chairmanship of CNC when I moved away from Washington in January 1999.

Life was not an unbroken string of success and activism during those years, however. On March 23, 1992, Gary suffered a massive heart attack. I was on my way home from work when I received the call on my DPW cell phone. Gary had gone to retrieve his mail and when he reached his hilltop A-frame again, felt that telltale pressure on his chest. At the hospital they ran tests and decided to keep him overnight. His then girlfriend, Monika, was on the phone at his bedside giving the news to his mother in San Francisco so she wouldn't worry if she called and found him not at home, when his eyes rolled back in their sockets. A trained nurse, Monika hung up, ran out of the room and intercepted his doctor, who just happened to be coming down the hallway. By the time I received word, Gary was being transferred from the little hospital in Front Royal, Virginia, to the much bigger medical center in Winchester. I headed for Winchester, near the West Virginia line.

Gary is only a year or so older than I. We've been like brothers most of our lives, with all that suggests, both the quarrelsomeness and the shirt-off-your-back devotion. We are very unlike each other in so many ways: he's of the mountains, I'm of the sea; he's military and bellicose, I'm a peacenik; he seems to prefer being alone, I need social companionship. But we are of the same blood, the same family. We share cousins, aunts and uncles, and a grandfather and grandmother we never knew — his mother's and my father's parents.

His family gathered at the Winchester hospital. Gary was in a coma. His heart was functioning at only 14 percent capacity. It was unclear whether he would live. Doctors said they had done all they could. Then someone — Gary's brother-in-law Ron, I think — said, "Hell, no" and called a lawyer friend of Gary's. The lawyer said that as an Army veteran, Gary had sufficient insurance coverage to demand and get the best. Within hours Gary was being flown by helicopter to Fairfax Hospital, on the outskirts of Washington, D.C., where one of the nation's leading heart surgeons was in residence.

We caravanned to Fairfax Hospital. There we waited endlessly. Tensions rose. I was not immediate family and wouldn't be allowed in to see him. Yes I would, said others. I was admitted, eventually. Gary was on his back, cold as a dead fish. Wires ran from electrodes on his body to monitors, where green lines wavered, almost flat. Late at night, his sister Carol and I engaged in racing wheelchairs up and down the corridors while we waited, to the clucking disapproval of elders like Aunt Florence.

This went on for a week or more. I'd go to work, then return to the hospital every evening I could to sit with the family. Slowly, Gary came awake. He would live, but he needed a new heart. They put him on the list for a transplant just as soon as a compatible heart could be found.

For four months he lived in the hospital hooked up to an IV bottle. Monika took up residence in a facility the hospital provided for family members. Again, I visited every evening I could after work, sometimes alone, sometimes with Karen. We'd take Monika out for dinner to give her a break from the depressing life of the hospital. Gary regained some of his old bravado, then lost it, then regained it. He told Monika that if he ever got out of the hospital he would marry her. If there ever was a Florence Nightingale reincarnate, Monika surely was it.

Lying in his hospital bed, Gary also asked me one favor: if he got out alive, would I bring the family back together, gather all the far-flung cousins in one place to celebrate family and life, just as my father had done year after year with those backyard clambakes in New England? I gave him my word.

The heart arrived by helicopter in an Igloo cooler on July 12. We watched them take it out of the chopper and hurry it into the hospital. We were told it had belonged to a 23-year-old male who apparently had been killed in a car crash in Southeast Washington, D.C. It was coming from a hospital in that sector of the city, at any rate, and that area was almost 100 percent Black in population. The next time we saw Gary, he was alive and well with a healthy heart. He called his new heart "Jerome." He went home nine days later, on July 21, 1992.

He'd told Monika he would marry her, but there wasn't room for her in either his home or his life. She left not long afterward to return to her life in Chicago and, later, San Francisco. He told me he would write the story of his experience of near-death and rebirth. He never did. What can I say? He's my surrogate brother. Our lives have gone separate ways. We disagree about pretty much everything now and never speak to each other. I know, at least, that I was there when it mattered.

That year, 1992, was remarkable for yet one other reason. In November, my fourth and last grandchild was born. Renée wanted to name her Victoria. I suggested that if she did, she give her the middle name "Lareine," which in French means "the queen," thereby naming her after England's longest reigning queen. Teri, whose middle name is spelled "Laraine," wanted to know why she hadn't been so honored. I had to admit it hadn't occurred to me at the time. But I also have to say that, considering my daughters and grandchildren were once again "with" me, I was feeling that life was, indeed, good. And promising to get better.

Twenty-Nine:
Reunions and the Grim Reaper

Teri and Nic came to visit me in Washington in 1991. He was a ball of energy and fun, until he ran out of both and was cranky. In other words, a normal kid. We took him to the Air and Space Museum to see the planes and rocket ships. We took him to the zoo down the hill from where I lived, where seals and monkeys seem to run free. He chased Karen all over the park across the street from my apartment. We took a cruise down the Potomac to Mt. Vernon, George Washington's home. I thought he seemed especially fascinated, but then I may have been reading my wishes into him. From the photos that survive, we all seemed to be having fun.

December 1994: unemployed again. Sharon Pratt Kelly (she had married Jim Kelly soon after becoming mayor) lost her race for re-election to the released-from-prison and self-proclaimed "redeemed" Marion Barry. After serving his term for crack cocaine, the "Mayor for Life" had come home triumphant, like some Roman general returning from the conquest of new lands, and claimed a seat on the City Council, from which perch he had caused no end of problems for our upstart mayor and, in the end, snatched his throne back from her. (I should note that in this newest — and his last — term as mayor, he would bankrupt the city and send it into federal receivership.)

Before leaving office, Sharon called her inner circle into her conference room and said the usual wonderful things you say to a staff that is about to disband. She served snacks and we all wished each other well in our future pursuits. Most had already made preparations for new careers. As we broke up, Mayor Kelly asked to speak with me in private.

Cruising the Potomac to Mt. Vernon with Nic, 1991

She asked if I knew what I'd be doing next. I had to admit I hadn't a clue. She said I had been hired as a political appointee, so I had none of the civil service protections that some of the others had that would assure a job in city government no matter who was mayor, but she could "squirrel" me away somewhere. Barry might not find me for years, she said.

I reminded her that I was a "public" information officer, with everything that the word "public" suggested. I wasn't going to drive a truck or go into seclusion somewhere to push paper around. It was in my nature and talents that Barry would find me quite soon, I was sure. For one thing, I never had acquired the skill of concealing my opinions.

She nodded softly. I remember her look just then. She seemed so sad for me. I was touched. But you don't get up and hug the mayor. You do what I did. You bite your lip and say you are prepared to take your chances out in the world, because you know you've done it before. I thanked her for her thoughtfulness.

She invited me to lunch a few times after she left office, usually at one of her two favorite restaurants in Adams Morgan, one French and one Italian. Over lunch we discussed ventures she was planning, the most notable of which was to build a multi-service network for young businesses interested in investing in Africa. Could I help her build a web site? Could I help draft the necessary documents? I wanted very much to help her, but honestly, international finance and negotiating with international agencies for the rights to distribute widgets in Angola just wasn't my strong suit. In any event, I think she was trying to help me more than asking me to help her. We parted as friends. I have nothing but the highest admiration and respect for her to this day.

Gary had asked for a reunion. It was time to keep my promise. With his agreement, I planned a small gathering at his house for June 1994, inviting the cousins I could locate. Nicole and Jean-Pierre and Marthe came down from Canada. Gary's sister Carol and her husband Ron Bloom came from their country home in Boiling Springs, Pennsylvania. And of course I was there, but arrived with a surprise. Without telling anyone, I'd asked Elaine to fly up from Miami and be with us. We enjoyed a wonderfully relaxed weekend celebrating Gary's new lease on life and vowed this was so much fun, we'd do it again. We didn't think we could pull it off annually, but why not every two years?

In 1996 we convened again in Québec, at Nicole's home with an even larger group. Karen and her sister were with me, having driven up earlier to tour Québec City. I rode up with Gary. We picked up Elaine at the Montreal airport. The entire Canadian wing of the family was there.

The surprise this time was from California. Adelard, my father's older brother, had raised his family in Miami. One of his childen, Rose de Lima, named after our grandmother, had migrated to California with her husband, Jim Snodgrass. Everyone knew her as Titi. I have no idea why.

Jim had researched his own family tree and was working on Titi's. He had contacted one of the Canadian cousins, Chantal in Thetford Mines, and she had suggested he contact me because I'd already documented the genealogy back to the first French colonist in Canada, Louis

Hébert. Jim had emailed me and I had sent him my chronology of the family's history as I had been able to reconstruct it. In the process, I'd told him about our "cousins" reunions, as we'd come to refer to them. So Titi and Jim, and several of their kin, came to Québec City as well.

I think we were around 20 or 22 people at that reunion. We rode the *bateau mouche* on the St. Lawrence River, had our family photo taken standing beneath the "new" Louis Hébert monument that now graces the city just below its landmark hotel, Château Frontenac, and had a "family" banquet at the Louis Hébert restaurant just outside the historic center of the city. It was a memorable reunion. Jim and Titi were so pleased, they promised to host the 1998 reunion at their home in Costa Mesa, California.

Obviously, much more was going on during those years than family reunions. To start with, I was unemployed again, foraging for income wherever I could find it. It was déjà vu time. I circulated my résumé. Again.

I heard that Coventry House was looking for a communications director to promote its program. The organization collects abandoned and runaway children and teenagers off the streets and seeks to give them an anchorage in life, values and caring. The D.C. Executive Director was Vince Gray, the former head of social services under Mayor Kelly and himself a future mayor. I'd enjoyed cordial working relations with him, including a joint appearance on the local government-access TV channel during a nasty snowstorm. He was nice to me at our interview but honestly explained he was looking for someone younger.

Marion Wright Edelman of the Children's Defense Fund gave me pretty much the same answer. They needed a younger person for the job.

The National Organization for Women seemed impressed by my credentials. At the interview, I was asked to write a sample press release based on some canned information they gave me. I did it in a few minutes. I can't remember exactly why they didn't pursue further, but the impression I had was that it had little to do with my gender, lots to do with the silver in my hair.

I remembered my first venture into looking for work in Washington, in 1969, when I was either too liberal or too Democratic or too white for whatever position was open. I determined this time to fight back, not from anger, but with a strategy. I invested in a product called Just for Men. I'm not a vain person, never have indulged in hair styling or tinting. I am who I am. But the message I was getting was that I had to indulge in a little duplicity if I wanted to get a job. My hair was clearly getting too gray. I combed that stuff into my hair, mustache and beard until they became unnaturally black. I looked strange to myself in the mirror, but at the very next interview I was hired.

Sort of. The Center for Science in the Public Interest (CSPI), a Ralph Nader-inspired think-tank and advocacy organization, asked me to be its communications director, but under a contract. No insurance, no sick leave, no vacation, but the pay was good. They wanted me to hold down the position for a campaign they were waging against olestra, the non-fat substitute Proctor & Gamble was putting into potato chips and test-marketing in three cities. The problem was that the stuff ran through your body without being absorbed, as fat is, and gave you diarrhea. On its way out of your body it also washed out other vital nutrients. Nasty stuff. We held press conferences that received national news attention, and ran media campaigns against the stuff in the three test markets, Eau Claire, Wisconsin; Cedar Rapids, Iowa, and Colorado Springs, Colorado.

I also became involved in a host of other campaigns against fatty foods, CSPI's specialty as the self-proclaimed "food police." It was CSPI who warned people about McDonald's Big Mac fat, theater popcorn's fatty butter, the fat in Cinnabons, even Fettucini Alfredo, which it dubbed a "heart attack on a plate."

After about six months of this, I received a call from across the street. The Center for the Advancement of Health also needed a communications director, but a full-time staff person. It had never had a communications program and needed someone to start one from scratch. The Center's deputy director, Rena Convissor, was friends with one of the CSPI vice presidents, but that wasn't how she'd found me. Mike Pertschuk, a former chairman of the Federal Trade Commission and director of the Campaign for Tobacco-Free Kids, had come across my résumé and passed it to her. I had known him from my years at HALT. That's called networking, the most valuable asset a job-seeker has. I had a job again — with benefits.

The Center's mission was to promote the science behind behavioral health — how stress can kill you, how most of our modern illnesses could be controlled and even reversed by changing our behaviors from risky to healthy. Many small research societies were engaged in this science but couldn't compete with the publicity machine of the biological medical community, the pills-and-surgery crowd of the American Medical Association.

My job was in part to correct that imbalance by working with the small behavioral research societies and promoting their work. In the spring of 1997, we decided to bring the editors of their journals together for a day-long media training session to show them why it was important, even necessary, to talk with the media about what they were doing. The overall objective was to fashion a strategy of pooling their resources and ours. Rena and the Executive Director, Jessie Gruman, were nervous. They wanted to see a script; I gave them an outline. They insisted I practice what I would say in front of them. They drove me crazy with over-preparation. I could understand their nervousness — they'd never seen me in operation before an audience, and they feared I was going into a den of "alpha males," scientific prima donnas who would eat me alive. They told me so in just so many words.

When the day finally came, in mid-May, the program went off without a hitch. My "class" of a dozen or so scientific editors seemed to enjoy themselves and take away the intended message. My bosses breathed a sigh of relief. So did I, although much more deeply. A few days later, as I took my first sip of coffee at the office, I suddenly felt a pain in my chest, like a blow from a sledgehammer. I broke into a cold sweat. I knew instantly that I was having "the big one," as Gary had called his heart attack. I started believing that numbness was creeping down my left arm. I "felt" all the symptoms I'd ever heard of. I was 56 years old, almost 57. I was certain it was my time.

I called my doctor. He told me to go immediately to George Washington University Hospital, he'd meet me in the Emergency Clinic. I had a car now, a Saturn bought the previous November, but it was at home because I usually walked to work. I asked Rena if someone could drive me to the hospital.

"Take a taxi," she said.

So much for behavioral health. I flagged down a cab. They were waiting for me at the emergency clinic and rushed me into a private room. I changed into a hospital gown, and as I bent over to take off my shoes, out came a massive burp. When I straightened up again, my chest felt fine. It was just heartburn. They kept me there all day for tests anyway. I called Karen's office at the courthouse, where she now ran the Small Claims Court mediation program, and left her a message, telling her staff not to interrupt a meeting she was running, it was nothing serious. I just didn't want her worrying if she happened to call my office and found out I'd gone to the hospital. Maybe I didn't sound convincing enough, because the next thing I knew she was running into my hospital room.

You can do a lot of thinking in a hospital between stress tests and all the pokings and measurings of your vitals. I can't say the weeks of stressful preparations for the media training program had anything to do with the heartburn, but it sure felt like it. I took the heartburn as a warning. I was simply involved in too many things, from my job to campaigning for various city candidates to organizing demonstrations for statehood to serving as president, then treasurer, then vice president, then president again of the cooperative where I lived.

I needed to slow down and change course. Again.

The following week, Karen and I made our customary trek to Chincoteague, Virginia, for the long Memorial Day weekend. We stayed at The Year of the Horse Inn, a bed-and-breakfast we had stayed in every trip the past few years. I was pacing the lobby floor one morning with a cup of coffee, telling Carlton Bond, the lanky, white-haired B&B owner, how much I envied his lifestyle. There he sat on the sofa, feet up on a coffee table, relaxing without an apparent care in the world.

"You want to buy the place?"

I hemmed, then I hawed, then I said, "Let me think about it."

When I returned to the office, I told everyone I was considering buying a bed-and-breakfast in Chincoteague. They thought me nuts. Karen said I'd never be able to stand living there year-round.

The "cousins reunion" of 1998 in Costa Mesa, California, was even bigger and better than the one in Québec. Many more of the California contingent came, of course. I brought Teri to this one. All the Canadian cousins were there, including Chantal and Marthe, who now had great trouble breathing because of her progressive emphysema. Elaine couldn't make it. Mom had had a severe heart attack the previous November and we'd had to put her in an assisted living facility. It was a beautiful home. She had her own apartment, a chapel for daily Mass, pleasant grounds, regular outings for shopping. But now she was weakening and Elaine didn't want to leave her alone.

The reunion was over the Fourth of July weekend. The Costa Mesa fireworks display was spectacular, but it left Marthe gasping in the cordite-filled air. We drove to San Diego and took the Tijuana Trolley to Mexico, then walked across the border. Dust was thick in the air, again rendering it almost impossible for Marthe to breathe. We bought tee-shirts, found a quiet sidewalk café and had Margaritas, but on the walk back across the border, so many cars were idling in line waiting to cross, the dust-laden air was now thick with exhaust fumes. I put my arm around Marthe to help her, carrying her weight and coaxing her every few steps, assuring her she could do it. I know the other cousins were watching. I didn't care what they thought. Marthe was in trouble.

By then I had thought myself into the decision to buy the Year of the Horse Inn. A few weeks before the reunion, Carlton and I had agreed on a price, contingent on my being able to secure financing. In Costa Mesa I announced that the 2000 reunion would be at the B&B, dates to be determined.

The summer of 1998 turned abruptly into a summer of loss. The day after I returned home from Costa Mesa, I received word from Elaine that Mom was dying. She had had another heart attack and was in the hospital. If she survived, we'd have to put her into a nursing home.

I flew to Miami. Elaine and I went to see a few nursing homes, hating the thought of what we'd have to do. Early the next morning, the hospital called: my mother's kidneys were shutting down, her vital signs were weakening. We hurried to the hospital. Mom was in and out of consciousness all day. At one point she asked me if I was still in the seminary. Later she asked if I was married.

Early in the evening, Elaine and Lise went to the cafeteria. I stayed by my mother's bed, holding her hand, gently rubbing her forehead as though trying to reawaken the brain I knew was still alive. It seemed clear to me she was fighting death with all her might. Whenever I asked her to squeeze my hand if she could hear me, she would squeeze it ever so slightly.

I told her, "Mom, it's okay. We'll be okay. You can let go. You don't have to fight anymore."

She let out one deep sigh, and then she was gone.

I had Elaine paged. She ran into the room shrieking, refusing to believe. She fell on the bed hugging my mother. I finally had to almost carry her out to the hallway so the nurses could do their work. Lise and I cleared the room of my mother's things.

The family gathered: Renée and Teri, Ronald and David, Lise and her daughter Cortney. Karen came down from Washington. I broke down trying to give a eulogy in the church. I just couldn't get the words out. Tears kept getting in the way. The one thing I remember saying was that Mom had always believed in saving "for a rainy day." I glanced out a window. "Mom," I said, "it's raining now." At the cemetery we each laid a flower upon her casket. It was hard to say goodbye.

Renée had a mid-afternoon flight back from Ft. Lauderdale Airport. Teri was flying later from Miami International. After dropping Renée at the airport, Teri, Karen and I went to Ft. Lauderdale's beach to relax for a few hours and get some lunch. On our way off the beach I showered away the sand near the perimeter wall, then attempted to climb over the wall to the grass. My wet feet slipped on the smooth painted cement surface and I cartwheeled off the wall, landing on my left wrist and forearm on the sidewalk beyond. I asked a lifeguard to look at it and he said it was broken, that I should put some ice on it.

We went to the sidewalk café across the street, The Sloop John B. (It has changed ownership and name since then.) The bartender brought ice and a towel to wrap around my wrist, and we sat there for an hour or two eating raw oysters and drinking beer. Karen changed her return flight reservation and took over the driving. When we reached Elaine's in Miami and told her what had happened, she drove me to Mt. Sinai hospital on Miami Beach while Karen drove Teri to the airport for her flight home. They put my arm in a temporary cast.

When I finally arrived home, I learned that Jim Snodgrass, the host of our California reunion just a week before, had died in his sleep.

Debbie, Gary's oldest daughter, came to visit him. She was 33 and dying of bone cancer. I hadn't known her until we'd met at the hospital while waiting for Gary's heart transplant. I'd taken an instant liking to her. She was a rebel of sorts, and now she was dying too soon. She had always been slim, with lively eyes. Now she was frail, walking as cautiously as someone in her 80s or 90s. When I tried to hug her, she warned me not to hold her tightly. Her bones were fragile. She died that December.

Labor Day weekend 1998, Carlton and I formally shook hands on the purchase of his B&B. I'd bargained him down from his $395,000 asking price to $330,000, and negotiated a sweetheart mortgage with a local bank and an even nicer second mortgage with Carlton himself. Carlton had run the place for 20 years and wanted out. For his own tax purposes, he asked that we close the deal only after New Year's Day. We did it in a lawyer's office a few days into the New Year and I returned to Washington to wrap up my affairs.

About a week before I was to move to Chincoteague, a long letter arrived from Marthe. She wrote: "I had learned on November 26…that I had cancer cells in my lungs." She had kept it secret until after the holidays because she didn't want to spoil the season for others. "I still have so much love to give, so many things to do…. I like to think that what we shared was beautiful love." She thanked me for loving her, for being "the only man who really made me feel beautiful, lovable, good and even sexy.

"You have given me so much love and tenderness. Every time we met, I could feel there was something special between us…. I cherish the memory of all the tender care you have shown me…. My heart is so full of beautiful memories."

The feeling was very mutual.

Before leaving Washington, I invited some 50 friends to join me at a local restaurant for a going-away party. They came from the smorgasbord of my D.C. life — previous jobs, like Ralph and Dolores, and some from HALT; neighbors at the cooperative; Wolsey Semple, of course; friends from Millie & Al's bar; friends from political campaigns and the campaign for statehood and my work in the mayor's office. Bernard Demczuk from the mayor's office wrote a series of six haikus for the occasion.

I left hanging desperately on to the belief — against all the evidence of death and dying around me, and the sense deep in my heart that I was leaving the exciting pressure cooker of Washington for what was beginning to look like my own final resting place — that life was still good.

Going-Away Party: Mark Thompson (center) & Bernard Demczuk, my predecessors as chair of the statehood movement

Thirty: Innkeeping

Thus it happened that this journalist/author/writer/media specialist became an innkeeper, as though beckoned by ancestors. After all, my father's father had owned and operated a succession of hotels in Québec, as had others of our clan, apparently. In Québec years ago, I'd run across more than one other hotel that carried our family name.

It wasn't long before I realized that running an inn was not going to be the laid back experience I'd anticipated. Within a month I discovered the heating and air conditioning system was woefully inadequate. Electric bills were shooting through the roof of my bank account. I brought in an engineer. He took one look at the air handler in the attic and pronounced it all but dead: it was rusted, leaking condensation into the ceiling space below, right over lighting fixtures; it was on the verge of setting my inn on fire. And the air ducts in the attic were a patchwork of duct-taped tubes leaking like a massive sieve.

The solution: a complete overhaul. A new air handler, an additional air conditioning unit outside, new air ducts, and conversion of heating from electricity to propane gas, a separate heater in each room so that during the cold-weather months when paying guests were fewer I wouldn't have to heat the entire building all the time, just the rooms that were occupied.

And there was the pier, a rickety affair I'd known needed replacing. Well before I bought the place it was posted, "No trespassing." It was already sagging into Chincoteague Bay. By the time they finished ripping it out and replacing it with my new deck over the water, the entire yard had to be re-landscaped.

I enlarged the little pond in the side yard and stocked it with goldfish. Unfortunately, all the fish died: I'd refilled it from the hose with chlorinated water. Goldfish, apparently, do not like chlorine. In effect, I'd bleached them to death. From then on, I kept buckets of water in the garage to let the chlorine evaporate for a few days before topping off the pond.

I bought a cell phone. I had resisted that technology as long as I could, but now I had no choice: I was losing business because I couldn't be at home to take calls all day, every day. When I'd come home from shopping, I'd return calls only to learn the callers had booked elsewhere. With a cell phone, I could forward my calls to it regardless where I was.

I didn't make many friends on the island, but those I made were good and true and remain friends to this day.

Chuck and Carol Kalmykov, who owned the Island Manor House, sold their inn the same month I sold mine and now live in Sarasota. Chuck's grandfather had been a Russian ambassador under the czars, before the Bolshevik Revolution, and had escaped with his family, including an infant son who became Chuck's father. Chuck enjoys many of the same things I do, word-play and bad puns, old movies and singing along at the top of our lungs to music from what we like to think of as the Golden Age of our youth.

Barbara and David Wiedenheft had had two inns, Miss Molly's and the Channel Bass. After I moved away, they sold the first and now have only the second, but they come to visit me almost every year. Barbara is British but had been married to a Dutchman before coming to the U.S. and marrying David, so she had lived in Holland (and Tunisia). We shared travel, curiosity about other cultures and lands, and a decided liberal bent. She had also an emotional, even volatile personality, not unlike my own. David, on the other hand, was even-keeled and conservative. Together they seemed to me to be Exhibit A for the maxim that "opposites attract."

Many on the island thought Barbara and I were carrying on, but that was all it was, gossip. We were friends, even soul-mates. Barbara would come by my inn in the evening after chores were done to sit and sip wine and watch the sunset, and we'd share innkeeper stories or observations about the state of the world. When we could in the mornings, we went for power walks together. I wouldn't call that an "affair." We simply enjoyed each other's company. And for good reason: I was craving intellectual stimulation, and Barbara was good at that. Karen had predicted this about Chincoteague, that I would "dry up" there for lack of the excitement and even turmoil I'd grown used to in Washington.

One telling example: Early on, I became a weekly habitué at AJ's restaurant and lounge, where Ron Cole played his guitar and sang old favorites every Friday night. One evening, the woman sitting next to me at the bar struck up a conversation. She'd heard I had bought the Year of the Horse Inn. Carol was a bartender at a nearby restaurant. Naturally enough, she asked my background. When I told her I was a writer and former newspaper reporter, she said, "Oh, then you're part of the island intelligentsia. There are three of us who meet here every evening to watch *Jeopardy*!" She introduced me to the other two "intelligentsia" — the elderly librarian at the NASA base on nearby Wallop's Island and an English teacher at the local high school, who was cute as hell but seemed incapable of stringing together an intelligent sentence. She seemed to have mastered the clichés, but not much more.

The B&B was good to me, once I put it on a sound footing. Everyone agreed I had the ideal location, right on the water, with magnificent sunsets over the marshes. I was also on the route of the annual wild pony roundup, swim and parade up Main Street to the fairgrounds. Many couples sought my place out for their wedding ceremonies — always to be held out on the dock, at sunset. My upstairs guestroom balconies offered the best view of the annual July 4 fireworks, so much so that each July 4 I held a "Margaritaville Party" up there for all my guests and invited friends, serving up munchies and huge batches of Margaritas, one year even giving out filled salt shakers labeled, "Your lost shaker of salt, found at the Year of the Horse Inn."

We seized on any excuse for a party, not only the Fourth of July fireworks, but Memorial Day and Labor Day weekends, birthdays, Oyster Festival weekends. Whenever I could, I hired Ron Cole and his two fellow-musicians (they called themselves "The Suds Brothers" back then) to play for us. The drummer was Glenn Wolffe, my doctor, and the lead guitarist was Keith Mann, the fellow who set up my web site.

The best party of all at the Year of the Horse had to be the Hébert Cousins Reunion in 2000. We had around 35 people. I shut down the inn the entire weekend after Labor Day and turned it over to the family. They filled the place with fun. We went on Captain Barry's "back bay" boat tour in shifts; had a feast in a room to ourselves at Wright's waterfront restaurant, my favorite seafood restaurant; volunteered for "coastal cleanup weekend," walking the beach and picking up trash (yes, that can be fun, too), and capped it all off with a Saturday night crab feast in my yard, under tents. I had baskets of steamed crabs, raw oysters for shucking, steamed corn, and of course all the beverages you could handle. The Suds Brothers were there, and Ron Cole let me play his guitar during an intermission to do my (rather amateur) version of Eric Clapton's *Tears in Heaven*, in memory of those we had lost since the reunion in California – my mother, our California host Jim Snodgrass, Gary's daughter Debbie, and Marthe.

Marthe had come down my first summer as an innkeeper, 1999, with Nicole and Jean-Pierre. Gary joined us. It was to be our last goodbye. By then, Marthe was walking around linked to an oxygen tank by 25 feet of plastic tubing. Her spirits were still high, but you could see her energy was gone. It was simply too difficult to breathe. We made the most of our short time together.

As it turned out, that wasn't our last goodbye. In October, Gary called. "Let's go see Marthe," he said. "We won't have her much longer." By mid-October, the tourist traffic usually slowed to almost nothing. I agreed without hesitation, closed the inn and drove up to Québec with Gary. We had a wonderful weekend at Nicole's house, where Marthe had moved, did some touring and visited our favorite Belgian restaurant for a feast of mussels.

Our last day, I sat with Marthe in her room for more than an hour, talking quietly about the good times; mostly we just held hands and looked into each other's eyes. I was inhaling as much of her as I could. We really didn't need to speak. We both seemed to understand that. It had all been said.

Then it was time to leave. Goodbyes were said. I looked into Marthe's eyes again, and we hugged. That hug lasted and lasted and lasted.

Last meal with Marthe (l). On my right: Eric, Gary, Nicole --Québec, 1999

Someone behind me quietly wondered would they ever get us apart, or something to that effect. I had to let her go. As soon as I did I rushed out to the car without saying another word. Gary said his goodbyes and came out a few minutes later. I don't know how many miles we went without speaking a word. I cried silently to myself watching the countryside roll by.

She died that December. Nicole told me she had a smile on her face. At the funeral, December 27, Marthe's picture was beside the funeral urn. As they played an "Ave Maria," a ray of sun from a window reflected off the picture and "just hit my eyes," Nicole told me. "I felt it connecting me directly with Marthe to give me a last goodbye." I had had mine.

The best part of inn-keeping, I found, is the people you meet — the beautiful and the strange and the otherwise memorable. Ziggy, the blues-guitarist/singer/pharmacist from Boston who jammed with Ron Cole both at AJ's and at my inn, and his wife Chris, the yoga massage specialist who worked all the kinks out of my body one afternoon, carrying me around the living room stretched across her back. The former Soviet tank commander, he of the shaggy gray hair and gap-toothed grin, who regaled us at breakfast with stories of rusting Russian tanks abandoned in Siberia and, when I asked if he wanted "caf or de-caf" for breakfast, boomed, "Decaffeinated coffee is like dehydrated water!"

Bernard Demczuk was a frequent visitor. He usually came with a friend, Larry Rubin, a city councilman in Takoma Park on the outskirts of Washington. From 1961 to 1964 Larry had been an activist registering Blacks to vote in South Georgia and Mississippi. Mississippi newspapers ran his picture on the front page, branding him a communist. Like so many other civil rights volunteers, he did not escape Mississippi without being attacked violently. But at my inn, what made him stand out most was that he was a fan of Tom Lehrer, the iconoclastic balladeer of the early 1960s who had made famous such satirical songs as *Poisoning Pigeons in the Park* and *We'll All Go Together When We Go*. I have a complete collection of Lehrer's work and would break it out for breakfast whenever Bernard and Larry were there. Larry knew every word of every song and would sing along heartily.

Ralph Hoar and Dolores Smith came down often, too — at first. They surprised me my first Easter weekend by booking all my rooms without my knowing it, using the name of Dolores's friend, whom I knew only as Gigi, not as Elizabeth Lytle. Two years later, Ralph called and told me his prostate cancer had metastasized. He'd had himself castrated years before to prevent just this. He said it was the "gold standard" of prevention. Yet here he was, telling me he was dying. He and his friend Francisco visited one last time that summer. They were planning to come again in September to cement their vows with a ceremony at my inn, but he fell ill. I received the news of his death the Friday after that horrible day, September 11, 2001. I went to Washington for a memorial service for him a week or so later and read a eulogy. Ralph was the definition of a good, lifelong friend.

Nine-eleven, of course, is indelible in all our minds. My inn was full. Guests were seated about the lobby eating breakfast. There was a TV in the lobby but it was almost never turned on. We generally preferred conversation. Shortly before 9 a.m., Barbara called: "Turn on your TV. A plane just crashed into the World Trade Center."

We all watched in shock as the second plane struck, then the Pentagon. Rumors flew. The White House was evacuated, and the Capitol. Another plane crashed in Pennsylvania. An eternity later, it seemed, the Twin Towers slowly collapsed, as though choreographed.

On January 14, 2002, I received the gift of a lifetime: I got a daughter back. Teri had retained a lawyer and we went before a judge in Gwinnett County, Georgia, where I officially re-adopted her. Soon after that, we went to Canada together.

Teri had expressed an interest in getting to know the place from which our family had sprung. I told her the best way to see it was during Winter Carnival. It might be "Mardi Gras" in New Orleans, and

"Carnaval" in Rio, but in Québec, it is "Winter Carnival." Teri climbed piles of snow as high as houses. From a ferryboat in a lashing, icy wind we watched international teams take practice runs with their canoes across a St. Lawrence River clogged with ice floes, in preparation for the actual race during the carnival itself. She repeatedly had to re-warm the camera under her coat, against her breasts, to keep it from freezing.

Trust me, that's Teri and I at the Hébert Monument

Teri also wanted to sleep overnight in a teepee, but Dad wasn't so sure that was a wise idea and, of course, prevailed. We did go tobogganing, and visited an Indian village reconstruction. We toured the ramparts and rode the horse-drawn sleigh and saw all the ice sculptures and ambled about the *Hotel de Glace*, an actual hotel constructed entirely of ice, down to the chandeliers, the wedding chapel's alter and pews, and even the blocks of ice in which drinks are served in the bar. The hotel beds are bearskins on huge blocks of ice.

And we paid the obligatory visit to the Louis Hébert monument, now a lofty structure near the Chateau Frontenac.

What the Year of the Horse Inn was not very good at was nurturing my love life. That started falling apart my first summer and went downhill from there. The Sunday morning before July 4, when Nicole, Jean-Pierre, Marthe and Gary were sitting around the lobby chatting, getting ready to leave, one of them poked a head into the laundry room where I was working and said I had a guest at the front desk.

I went into the lobby and did a double take. Make that a triple take. I was bewitched by a vision from the past.

Some historical perspective is needed. When I had been in Italy in the 1970s, there was a flurry of controversy about "Jesus Jeans." This company decided to promote its jeans by putting its cut-offs — the skimpiest, tightest little cut-off jeans I'd ever seen — on billboards all over the country. The billboards were simple: a close-up of a nicely rounded feminine butt in teeny-tiny cut-off jeans and the words, "Jesus jeans...come, follow me." The Pope had a fit over that. Within a week those billboards disappeared.

She had her back to me. And she was definitely wearing come-follow-me apparel. The cutest butt in the world was packed tightly into the world's tiniest denim cut-offs. Then she turned around and flashed this great big smile. Her eyes were blue sparkles. Her name was Brenda, she said, and she'd like a room for a night. She had driven all the way from Cocoa Beach, Florida, and just needed to de-stress. I looked out the front window and saw her car — a new white Corvette.

I know I made eye contact with her far too often and let my fingers touch hers a moment too long when I handed her the registration form to sign. And I'm reasonably sure the cousins still sitting around the lobby were taking it all in with assumptions dancing in their heads.

The next morning, when I cleaned Brenda's room and made her bed (I didn't have a housekeeper at all that first summer, determined to do it all myself to learn the ropes), I left a note offering her the room for half price if she'd stay until Thursday and let me take her to dinner that following night. Beginning Thursday, the room was booked for the July 4 holiday.

The next morning at breakfast she said yes. That night, walking back to my car from Steamers restaurant, I told her upfront that, if it wasn't yet obvious to her, I was hitting on her. Did she mind? She said she knew. And no, she didn't mind. Let's just say things escalated from there.

When Karen came to visit in August, I had to tell her someone new had walked into my life. She took it hard. She was angry, with good reason. But our relationship had already grown stale, at least for me, and she had her career and life in Washington, a three-hour drive away. I needed more than that. I didn't tell her this new woman lived even farther away, in Florida.

Brenda was divorced, a regional service manager for Sears Roebuck, and a reformed smoker — until she became stressed about something and needed another cigarette. She came back two or three more times. When I was in Miami to visit Elaine and family at Christmas, Brenda drove down to meet us at a dance club in Ft. Lauderdale. Everyone thought she sure was cute. I was riding high.

Back at the Inn for New Year's, Brenda called. She wanted out. She wasn't ready for a relationship. It was over. Just like that. Ever since, I've referred to her as "Brenda Briefly." I have neither seen her nor heard from her since. But yeah, she sure was cute.

After that, the women seemed all to "come and go, talking of Michelangelo," like the women in T.S. Eliot's mournful *Lovesong of J. Alfred Prufrock*. I was beginning to revert to those crazy years in Atlanta following my divorce.

Chris, an old friend of Barbara's, was visiting from England. She was lonely. Barbara brought her to my inn one evening and she begged to stay the night. She became quite tearful. Maybe she'd had a little too much to drink. She didn't stay, not that night, but soon enough. In February, I went to visit her at her country farmhouse in what's known as England's High Peak District (not that I saw any peaks there worthy of the label). It was a centuries-old stone house with a magnificent hillside of open land.

She owned a convertible Alfa Romeo Spider, a nifty little sport car, and in it we toured an England I'd never seen before. She took me to York, where after viewing the historic cathedral ringed by statues of England's famous kings (Ann, who had been there, had told me that the statue of Richard the Lionheart bore a striking resemblance to me; I didn't see the resemblance myself), we stopped at a pub for a few beers. I'd read about the place; when they'd dug under it to make a wine cellar, they'd found the ruins of Roman baths. The owner let us go down to see them.

Chris also took me to Warwick Castle, and to Stratford on Avon, Shakespeare's home; to Glastonbury where it's said King Arthur's tomb was found at an abbey (historians doubt there was ever a king by that name and believe the good monks had made up the story of the grave to attract Medieval tourist traffic); to Tintagel at the far edge of Cornwall, a fortress built on a cliff overlooking the Atlantic, said to be where Arthur was born and raised; to the Roman palace at Chichester and the historic cathedral at Salisbury; to Stonehenge, where all I could do was pop out of the car and snap a few pictures from a distance because Mad Cow Disease was running rampant through the land and guards were everywhere shooing tourists away from pastures like those that surround the ancient Druid monument.

Chris also loved to invite people to dinner parties, but then almost always drank too much and passed out. I'd show the guests out, clean up the dishes and put away the leftovers. Often this would take until 2 in the morning or later. That ended that.

We're still friends, of course. She has since sold her place and moved to Spain, where she now owns and runs a bed-and-breakfast of her own.

Lois and Ingrid and "Bitsy" all came via the Internet. Yeah, I signed up with one of those match-making services, I was so desperate for some form of companionship.

Ingrid lived in Georgia near Teri and on one trip I helped her move to a new apartment. It lasted one weekend. We weren't a good fit at all.

Lois, a secretary at Virginia Commonwealth University in Richmond, lasted only slightly longer. She started off the relationship by lying about her age. I could see that the moment I met her. After a few weekends together — at her place and at mine — she drove down to Georgia to spend New Year's with me. She made something of a scene at the New Year's party at Teri's house, in effect telling me my own daughter wasn't behaving properly and I should say or do something about it. I did: our relationship ended then and there.

"Bitsy" was the weirdest. Her real name was Carol. What I didn't know at first was that she had a husband named Dallas back home in Stafford, Virginia. And she liked to taunt truck drivers sexually over her CB radio. She sent me a photo of herself that had to have been at least 20 years old. Next thing I knew, she was on my doorstep. She had packed all her belongings, including her plants, and driven the length of Virginia, uninvited.

Dallas called and begged me to send her home. I put her on the phone. I certainly didn't want to get in the middle of that! Next, yet another "boyfriend" showed up at my front door looking for her. I sent her out to talk to him. She said she told him to get lost, but I think she privately promised to contact him later. I had to go to Washington for some business (having to do with evicting the guy I'd been renting my D.C. apartment to; he rewarded me by trashing the place) and was staying with friends. She found the number and called, but when my friend's wife answered, Carol leaped to the wrong conclusion, exploded and left a message that she was leaving. She wound up with the "other" guy, I guess, or perhaps some third or fourth "other," on a ranch in Canada, last I heard. At least she left behind the plants she'd brought from Stafford.

Holly had visited from Washington. She worked for the National Institute for Mental Health and had vacationed at my inn. We struck up a friendship that continued off and on for a while, then evaporated. She has ADHD and talked endlessly about it. Another bad fit.

And so I lurched from one semi-relationship to the next. Slowly the idea of getting out of the inn business eased its way into my brain. I'd bought the B&B with a seven-year horizon in mind. But now, only three or four years down that road, I knew I'd made many improvements to the place and had turned what had been a summers-only business into an almost-year-round enterprise. Occupancy was up, income was good. I put it up for sale.

On one of my holiday-season trips to Miami, I visited an old friend in a retirement community in central Florida called The Villages and thought it a neat idea. It had a vibrant social center where seniors truly seemed to enjoy a life of free movies in the village square (memories of Bark Street School!), even a lounge with a large dance floor. Everywhere older people seemed to be having fun. It didn't look or feel at all like an "old folks home." (I was told later that The Villages has one of the highest rates of VD, including AIDS, in Florida, but that turned out to be bogus.) I started looking for places like it closer to the ocean.

On my drive back north from Miami, signs along I-95 in the St. Augustine area caught my eye. I'd always liked St. Augustine, ever since my first childhood visit and my days at the University of Florida when a bunch of the guys would pile into a car with a case or keg of beer and head to its beaches. I found a real estate agent online and she started sending me materials on homes for sale. In all, I think I made three visits to St. Augustine to look at properties. Teri was with me for one of them. I looked at a lot of single-family homes and cottages, but they all conjured up weekends spent mowing lawns or repairing the roof. More house-and-garden keeping was the last thing I wanted.

I settled on an apartment in the Conquistador Condominium, in St. Augustine Shores south of the city itself. Now all I had to do was sell the inn.

I've intentionally left out one guest I met at my inn. She came Memorial Day weekend, 2001, with her two daughters. They were quiet, well-behaved, even shy. We had our usual party with music by the Suds Brothers. And then the weekend ended and they were gone.

If meeting interesting new people is the biggest reward of running a bed-and-breakfast, watching them leave is the biggest drawback. "My guests always leave me just when I'm getting to know them," I told so many people in Chincoteague they must have grown weary of hearing it. But this particular family came back. Sort of.

She called. "My name is Eliane Wauthier. My daughters and I stayed with you over Memorial Day. We're thinking of coming back for the Pony Swim." I remembered her only because of the French accent. Unfortunately, I was already booked solid for that last week of July. That was okay with her, she said, they had a place to stay in Virginia Beach. Could they just drive up for the day of the swim and park in my yard?

I'd already planned to open my yard to public parking for $5 a car, all day, so I said sure.

They did the same thing in 2002 and 2003, simply parking in my yard for the day while they enjoyed the festival. Each year, when the saltwater cowboys drove the wild ponies up Main Street right past my inn, we'd have a crowd on and around my front porch and I'd pass out free iced tea and maybe some snacks. Eliane and her daughters joined in each time.

After the hoopla had died down in 2003, I told her she would have to find somewhere else to park next year because I had sold the inn, and the new owners had no intention of keeping it as a bed-and-breakfast. They wanted it to be a private vacation home where they could have friends over for parties.

The kids begged me to say it wasn't so. I remember Olivia, in particular, hugging me and pleading.

"What are you going to do?" Eliane asked.

"I've bought a condo in Florida. I just want to go down there and find some comfortable old lady to relax with like an old easy chair and enjoy the rest of my life. I've had enough excitement, I think."

"When are you leaving?"

"The closing is right before the Oyster Festival. I'll leave right after that, probably October 13."

"My birthday is the 14th. Some friends and I are going hiking up in the mountains. Why don't you come by Chapel Hill on your way to Florida and go hiking with us?"

I confess I had no idea where this was going. All I could picture was the turmoil of uprooting my life yet again, loading up a rental truck with whatever I could take from the inn, hitching my car behind it, driving to Florida, unloading and setting up housekeeping in my new home. "Going hiking" didn't seem to be able to squeeze into that schedule. I told her so.

"You could park the truck in our driveway," she persisted.

"I don't think so. I just want to get down there and be done with it all."

"Well, we're planning to go camping in Key West next Spring Break. Maybe we can stop by St. Augustine and see you on our way down?"

We left it at that. I told Barbara about the conversation later. "Richard, she doesn't want you to go hiking with her. That's not what she's after. She's after your bones."

We had one final grand party that last night at the inn. Dolores and Gigi came down from Washington, Ron Cole played his music, our innkeeper triad was together one last time — Barbara and David, Chuck and Carol, and myself.

I didn't detour through Chapel Hill, I didn't go hiking. I moved directly to St. Augustine. After unloading the rental truck, I drove to Miami to meet with another former inn guest, Maria Anderson, a member of the Coral Gables Town Council. She put me in touch with the head of the John Kerry presidential primary campaign in Florida, and before I knew it, I was deeply involved in the Kerry campaign.

I was not so deeply involved, however, that I didn't follow through on one thing. I had brought a bunch of email addresses with me, those of friends I had made as an innkeeper and before. Among them was Eliane's. As soon as I had a telephone number and an email address, I sent an email to all of them letting them know. An answer came back from Eliane within a half hour.

From there, emails flowed daily between us, then blossomed into telephone calls, which grew longer as the weeks went by. Finally, sometime in mid-November, I told her I didn't want to wait until Spring Break and her planned trip to Key West to see what this was going to become. I wanted to know now. Could I come up to visit her, perhaps after Thanksgiving?

The Florida Democratic Convention was held the weekend of December 4, and I'd been asked not only to be a Kerry delegate, but to be his driver during that weekend. But after that, I was free.

I drove up to Chapel Hill December 12. We met outside a Borders bookstore. She was standing outside her car when I drove into the lot. She wore a long black coat with a large fluffy black fur collar that seemed to circle behind her head halo-like, reminiscent of Tudor English ladies of the court. I got out of my car. She was smiling. My heart stopped. I was speechless. Life was suddenly very, very good.

Thirty-One: Retirement

I'd like to end it about here. The rest is still so close in time it is hard to see with the clarity and perspective that time and distance can give. Let it merely be said that I was wrong that day out on the lawn of the bed-and-breakfast when I told Eliane, "I've had enough excitement."

I haven't, and I hope I never have. New sparks have come from unexpected quarters. Never in my wildest imaginings did I think years ago that I would live to see my grandchildren grow up. Now, for the most part, they have, and they've each found ways to make me proud, if sometimes perplexed. Beyond that, I have even seen the arrival of a great-grandchild. "Little Zach" is the new generation in the making. I now hope I will live to see him through his formative years, through school, and perhaps, some day, into college. It is important to dream big dreams.

Since retiring, I've been through hip replacement surgery and other surgery to correct recurring Dupuytren's contractures in my hands. I ache a bit more than I used to and in new places, but I'm at the YMCA working out three times a week, trying to get a brisk

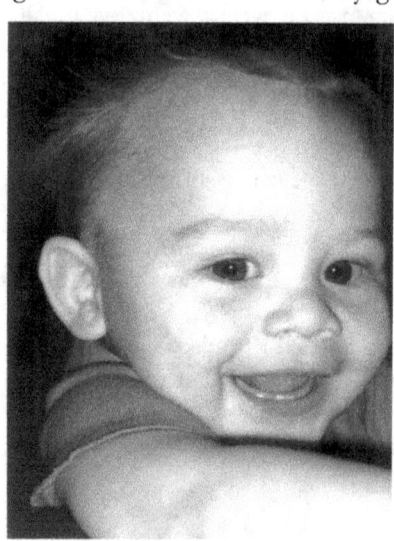

Zachary Chase Pope, 8 mos.

walk or swim in on other days. And I continue to be politically active, in the mid-term elections of 2006 and even more so in the historic presidential election of 2008, when I put it all on the line for Barack Obama. I believe he is the answer to the prayers I have been praying since the 1960s when, in rapid succession, I saw the lights — and the promises — of John Kennedy, Martin Luther King, Jr., and Bobby Kennedy extinguished.

With Eliane at Machu Picchu, Peru — July, 2007

We did take that Spring Break camping trip to Key West. I went with Eliane, her daughters, and friends. We were caught in squalls that finally drove us to take motel rooms and do some canoeing in the Everglades instead. We've white-water rafted the New French Broad River's rapids in western North Carolina, kayaked around Tybee Island near Savannah, snorkeled over the coral reefs at Key Largo. We went to Winter Carnival in Québec where we rode a toboggan down an icy rampart and toured the ice hotel just as I'd done with Teri. We parasailed over the ocean near St. Augustine and swam with manatees on the gulf coast. In 2008, I attempted to repeat the Key West, Key Largo and Everglades experiences with Teri, during the height of hurricane season. Let's just say the weather didn't cooperate very much, but we had quality time together, and that was what mattered most.

I've continued to try to satisfy my lust for exotic travel. We lived on a catamaran for a week hopping among the islands off the coast of Belize in Central America, including snorkeling the great barrier reef, then spent several more days exploring Maya ruins on the mainland (Appendix C). We went to Paris for Eliane's 50th birthday and dined on a night cruise of the Seine under the illuminated city. We went to Florence, Italy, for her 52nd and immersed ourselves in the great art and sculpture of the Renaissance.

We had a fantastic trip to Peru in 2007 (Appendix D) — 10 days in the Amazon rainforest living in thatch-roofed lodges, visiting native villages, walking canopy walkways among the treetops, fishing for piranha and swimming in the Amazon not far from where dolphins played. We went to the Andes for an additional five days and satisfied a lifelong dream, a visit to the mystical Inca city of Machu Picchu. I followed that with another visit to the jungles of South America, this time in Venezuela with Jo, a guy I know in St. Augustine, and Wolsey, my old friend from Washington. Wolsey and I extended that trip by revisiting Trinidad for Carnival, where I again danced in the streets until I couldn't dance any longer.

The lust for life goes on. It is always good, and always getting better.

Postscript — 2011

Just after the first printing of this memoir was delivered, my social life abruptly reverted to Square One, again. Eliane ended our relationship, jolting me back to harsh reality. When she explained her reasons, I understood. She had no choice.

Her younger daughter, Olivia, had morphed from a sweet child into a troubled teen. At 16 she had a succession of maladies real and imagined, from bulimia (imagined) to fainting spells (some of both, I suspected). She was arrested for shoplifting from three stores in a single mall. She did house-sitting for vacationing neighbors, including the local congressman, into whose home she allowed friends from high school, who proceeded to trash the place to a reported $5,000 in damages.

Eliane said she needed to devote all her time, attention and energies to setting Olivia back on a path toward responsible adulthood. I had to agree. The net effect for me, however, was that I became a septuagenarian searching again for my soul-mate. Have I found her? I believe so. Hope springs eternal.

Epilogue: What's It All Mean?

We live our lives on so many levels. We are family members — children, spouses, siblings, cousins. We are working members of society, whether plumbers or printers or professors. We are social beings, working and interacting with our communities, neighbors, even people we don't know, or don't know well. We are emotional beings. And, we are supposed to be *thinking* beings, *homo sapiens*.

I've tried to weave all of these layers together into a single fabric to give an idea of just what it was like to be me, to *become* me. For, as Alfred Lord Tennyson put it in the voice of his poetic Ulysses, "I am a part of all that I have met." It is that which makes each of us unique, because each of us has met different people, different experiences, different sorrows, different joys. They all combined to shape us into whom we eventually become. And so it was with me.

I know some will probably find a few words here and there that they consider too long, hundred-dollar words when a good old fashioned dime word would perhaps do. I will say in my defense, I don't use big or lesser-known words just to show off my vocabulary (although I find nothing wrong with having a large and ever-growing vocabulary and being proud of it). Rather, I use those words when they state precisely what I mean to say better than any collection of single-syllable words could. So if you stumbled over a word here and there, I suggest you do what my father told me to do all those many years ago: go get a dictionary and look it up. You might surprise yourself and become *enthused*.

On to more serious matters.

Some may say, with justification, "Richard, you never settled down. You never put down roots. Don't you miss the stability and purpose that gives to life?" To which I can only answer that I am skeptical of stability, at least for myself. Perhaps I'm a throwback, a genetic hiccup from the distant past. Humankind began as nomads, wanderers, adventurers. Humans always wanted to see what was beyond the next ridge. They wanted to fly. They wanted to people the heavens.

We are a *yearning* species. It was only when humans began to till the soil that they had to stay in one place, at least long enough to reap what they sowed. I guess I never saw any good reason to spend all of my life in one place, doing the same thing over and over again, tending crops. Besides, I've long felt that stability is not a place but a state of mind, a basic knowledge of one's place in the universe, and of one's connection with others — especially family. Although quite tenuous at times, I feel I have maintained that connectedness with all those who would accept it and reciprocate it.

How did I wind up on this path through life? I can't say I chose it. I think it became mine by default. I was forced to grow up fast, long before my body or brain was ready. The loss of my father at age 18 (a very young 18 by today's standards) cast me out into an adult world I didn't understand and was determined to conquer, even if I didn't know how. I had no weapons, no models to follow, no comprehension of what it would take. I just stubbornly determined I would go out and do it. That's too strong: I determined that I had *no choice* but to go out and do it. There was no other map for me through the storm that had overtaken my life. Early on, I thought I was doing a pretty decent job of it, in fact: checking off the prescribed boxes. Job and career: check. Marriage: check. Kids: check. Nice house in the suburbs: check.

I know now I wasn't up to the task. Growing up isn't a matter of checking boxes, of simply moving up the rungs of a ladder. I eventually began to understand better — if slowly — during my wandering and searching, and came away with what I believe are some pretty good guiding principles.

Moral compass: All that early mortification, I've wondered whence it came. Dad? The best thing was to hear him tell you he was proud of you. Even better, to overhear him say it to someone else. The worst thing to hear from him: "I'm disappointed in you." I heard it often enough, with conviction, whether in those exact words or not. It got so you could see it in his eyes, he didn't have to say the words anymore. When I told him I was too busy to help him drive to Canada that last trip of his life, he didn't have to tell me. I *knew*.

Faith vs. reason: Reason won, despite the best efforts of nuns, Christian brothers, and a summer camp baseball coach to make me memorize things, to make me let that first pitch pass as instructed.

Why did reason win? First, the seminary — and that brilliant little book, *Adventures of Ideas*, that I found and read while there — taught me to think and to ask, and that led me into journalism. Journalism taught me to question authority. The civil rights and anti-war movements taught me I was right to do so. Travel broadened the kinds of questions I asked, gradually eliminating the glib assumptions I'd been taught. I think my sister suspects a priest may have molested me when young, and that that is what turned me against religion. Never. Not even close. I guess our parents were right: I, like that atheist relative I'd heard them talking about, simply "read too much."

Opinions: Like assholes, everybody has one. I have many, I know. That's no great revelation. Unfortunately, too many opinions in our democracy are based on ignorance, rumor, or worse, demagoguery. I've tried, before forming an opinion, to go out and learn the facts. I've read, listened, studied. I believe my opinions are based on evidence and reason. There are others similarly well-informed. But too many people are woefully uninformed or misinformed. I believe it is our responsibility to inform ourselves and then to act on that information. In this age of information technology, there is no excuse not to. Which takes me to...

Intolerance: Most of all, the 1960s in Atlanta taught me about hate and how it poisons. I saw it in cross-burnings and Ku Klux Klan marches, in mob violence and unsanctioned war. I saw man's inhumanity to man up close. And I did not like it. I lost all innocence. Which is not to say I lost my idealism. If anything it grew stronger. The only thing I will not tolerate is intolerance.

Changing the world: In the grand scheme of things, I don't think my life has been important to the world in any major way, but I do believe I've tried to leave things in slightly better condition than I found them. Pretty early in life, I set out to change the world. I suspect that lay at the heart of my intention to become a priest (after all, priests were the most powerful role models I had back then) and, later, to go into journalism, which seemed a more direct route, and after that into direct action and political activism.

Have I changed the world? Not much, I think. Others will have to judge. All I know is that I tried. I'm not naïve. Humanity seems to have an unlimited capacity for ignorance, hate, and violence, the three-legged stool of intolerance. I had a small hand in electing as President a person I believed could transform the world only to witness in reaction a well-documented surge in the number of hate groups — neo-Nazis, neo-Confederates, anti-immigrant nativists, white supremacists; in crimes of racial violence; in stockpiling assault weapons and ammunition.

In my quest for a better tomorrow I made my share of mistakes, but at least I know I tried. I have the knowledge that I kept working at it, and that is all one can do. I have lived life fully, I've enjoyed the trip, and I plan to keep drinking from life's ever-refilling cup and savor it to the very end.

Now a few tips for a good life, for what they're worth. After all, books like this are *supposed* to wind up with some of these, aren't they?

Treating others

In dealing with others, start with tolerance. Other things (charity, trust) will come. Don't tolerate intolerance. Reject racism, arrogance, self-righteousness wherever you find them, in yourself or in others. And do not accept bread-and-circuses as the rule of life, consumption for the mere sake of consuming. It's only stuff, after all.

Do not fear those you don't know, those not like you. Seek them out, learn who they are, what they have to give. Whether race, language, culture, religion or skin color, differentness is beautiful. If Pat Buchanan and Glenn Beck and the other xenophobes of the anti-immigrant movement had had their way back then, my father would have never been allowed to walk across the border from Canada in the 1920s, would have never met my mother, would have never conceived me. We would none of us be here. We are living proof that America should be open to everyone.

Treat women well. I think the male version of maternal instinct is to be protective of women. Maternal instinct is genetically wired into women, to preserve the genetic line; for men, their genetic history tells them to protect family and home, but especially the female, as the embodiment of family and home. Defend, console, protect, and shelter her, not because she isn't capable of defending herself — she is — but because she deserves it. Nothing enrages me more than hearing of or seeing some guy abuse a woman. It demeans all men. And it painfully reminds me of how hard-hearted I was to Gail, who deserved much better from me.

Treating yourself

Excel. There are many ways to say it. When I was a kid, the word "Excelsior" was enshrined on a wall in every classroom. The U.S. Army tells you to "be all you can be." But my favorite are the lines from Robert Browning's poem, *Andrea del Sarto*: "Ah, but a man's reach should exceed his grasp, or what's a heaven for?"

I would add a corollary: don't compare yourself to others. Compare yourself to what you believe you *can* be. The others will only drag you down. It's a cop-out. Life is not graded on a curve. It's an arrow, and it should be pointed upward if it's to go any distance at all.

Above all, be true to yourself. And that means being brutally honest with yourself as well as others. (I've tried to do that in this volume. I'll leave it to others to decide whether I accomplished that or not.) You won't get many chances to prove you are a person of your word. Break your word two or three times, you may find you are never able to convince people you are worth dealing with again.

Treating your country

The dictionary tells us all we need to know.

Monarchy (from Greek: *monos* "alone" and *arkhein* "to rule") — undivided rule or absolute sovereignty by a single person, typically a king or queen.

Plutocracy (from Greek: *ploutos* "wealth" and *kratia* "rule") — government by the wealthy.

Aristocracy (from Greek: *aristos* "best" or "most fitting" and *kratia* "rule") — government in which power is vested in those thought to be the best, often by reason of wealth or station.

Oligarchy (from Greek: *oligoi* "few, small, little" and *arkhein* "to rule") — government by a small group, especially for selfish purposes; a debased form of aristocracy.

Democracy (from Greek, *demos* "common people" and *kratia* "rule") — government in which supreme power is vested in the people and exercised by them directly or indirectly through a system of representation (a republic), usually involving periodically held free elections.

When the convention that wrote the U.S. Constitution had completed its work, it is said that Benjamin Franklin was stopped by a woman as he left the hall in Philadelphia.

"Dr. Franklin," she asked him, "what have you given us, a democracy or a republic?"

"A republic, Madam," he answered, "if you can keep it."

What he meant was that a republic — representative democracy — can stand only as long as the people protect, defend, and participate in it. Since that day, our Republic has repeatedly been in danger of slipping into one of the other forms of government, from the time that supporters tried to make George Washington a king (he declined), through the successive waves of "robber barons" who wrested power for their own selfish ends. We see it happening yet again. Only the people have the power to prevent it — not by bullets but by ballots, their most potent weapon.

We love to sing the praises of our "rights" and "freedoms." We shout them from rooftops, brag about how our brave troops defend them, salute the flag for them, pledge our allegiance to them. Most of all, we *demand* them. Democracy requires more of us than that, more of us than righteous speeches, flags and symbolism. It demands civic responsibility. Ours is a government of, for, and by the people, as Abraham Lincoln said. In a democracy, the people get the government they deserve.

I learned these lessons from journalism. Journalism gave me something of great value, an understanding of the journalist's role in a democracy: to speak truth to power and to inform the public so that the people can make intelligent decisions about how they are governed and by whom. It gave me a deep appreciation of the *wisdom* of democracy and made me a far better citizen than I might otherwise have been. And for all that I guess I have my Aunt Lorraine to thank for suggesting it as a career path all those many years ago. I have been privileged to have been a journalist, to be a lifelong student with a front-row seat on the world and humankind. Whatever else I called myself at any given time in life — freelance writer, author, media relations specialist, innkeeper — at bottom I was always and always will be a journalist. Done right, I can think of few professions that are nobler.

Treating the planet

We don't own it, we occupy it. Treat it as you would want a visitor to treat your home.

Go out and discover it. I highly recommend travel. Lots of it. I do not mean to denigrate the value of a formal education. For a good start at a good life, you can't beat it. But I'd urge everyone, if at all possible, to go out and see the real world as well. Ingest all its wonderful diversity — of places and climates, of cultures and peoples, of languages and customs.

With due respect to Ann Eyerman's parents, No, you cannot find everything you need in your own back yard. When you return home, I can guarantee you will never look at your home country the same way again. You will understand and appreciate more deeply than ever your country's strengths and, importantly, its flaws. Unless we see the flaws in ourselves and our ways, how on Earth can we ever hope to correct them?

Final thought

Eleanor Roosevelt once said that inside every great man there lives a little boy. She mentioned Winston Churchill and her husband, Franklin Delano Roosevelt, among those who had that little boy inside them. Lord knows, I achieved neither fame nor greatness. I never got that Nobel Prize for literature that I coveted as a child, not even the Pulitzer I coveted as a young newspaper reporter. And I certainly don't consider myself anywhere close to the league of FDR and Churchill. Walk down any street in any city I've lived in and ask 100 people if they had ever heard of me. Chances are you won't find one who'll say "yes."

When I was a child, oh yes, I believed. I *knew in my bones*. I *knew* many things, among them that God existed, that only Catholics would go to heaven, and that I was destined for greatness. Well, years have a way of both adding to your storehouse of knowledge and stripping it clean of mirage. I'm no longer sure about the first thing I absolutely knew to be true, pretty sure the second is a gross misrepresentation of what any hereafter might look like, and convinced that the third was a youth's flight into hubris. But then, that is what youth is meant to be — a shout into the future that we *can* do better, that we can and must defy the odds and achieve greatness.

I didn't. And it doesn't matter. The goal in life, I now know, is not to achieve greatness, but to strive toward it. And I do know that I tried to keep alive inside me that little boy who dropped his sister's hand to run across that busy highway in defiance of every law of kinetic energy. I tried. It is up to others to decide to what degree I succeeded or failed.

Wherever I look in my apartment I see the memorabilia of my life, family photos past and present, artifacts collected in my travels. They remind me every day how fortunate I've been, what a good life I've lived, how much I have to be grateful for.

Only a single gaping hole remains to be filled in my life. I would love to see my family reunited before I leave it. It has been fractured, and I deserve some — not all, but some, perhaps much — of the blame for that. I try to make amends. Important strides have been made.

The bond between Teri and me, I believe, is stronger than ever, built over the years after Nic was born, and alongside it grew my bond with her husband, who became a son more than a son-in-law. I feel a peculiar warmth inside each time Tony calls me "Dad."

The bonds between Renee and her family and me are still very much a work in progress at this writing. Travis made the first overture, but I still don't know from one day to the next where his loyalties lie, what his life is like or what he wants it to be. I tell myself to be patient.

Zach reached out when his own son was born. Then Tori, who may well be the sharpest of them all. We are slowly building trust in each other. We have started closing the gaps with our hearts open wide and all the vulnerability that implies. I pray the building continues.

We Are Family! Four generations — Christmas, 2008

One big thing I've learned is that you can't turn a group of related people into a family by fiat. A family consists of individuals, each with a unique history, each with stresses and loves, tugged and pushed by both bonds and rivalries that date from the dim past. Each is free to participate in the family or not, and if so, to participate how and how often we wish. None of us can force the others. To be received we must wait, open-armed, open-hearted and patient.

Above all, we must maintain hope, the driving force of family for me. Hope keeps family alive and meaningful. It is reciprocal: my family gives me hope, and I have hopes for my family. My family is my bedrock. It may be cracked, but it still stands under me like a reliable foundation. Hoping for nothing but the very best for my family seems the least I can do. I have seen important signs of progress. Yes, there are setbacks. We aren't there yet, but I believe we one day will be.

Because life is truly good, every blessed minute of it.

Appendices

Appendix A:
Canada's First Colonist

(The following is a translation from French of material supplied by the late Jim Snodgrass in 1997. Snodgrass, husband to my cousin Titi, died in his sleep shortly after hosting the "Cousins Reunion" of 1998.)

Hébert, Louis: first colonist in Acadia, born in Paris, 1575, died in Québec, Jan. 25, 1627. Son of Nicolas Hébert, apothecary to Queens Catherine and Marie de Medici, and Jacqueline Pajot. His shop was located on the back side of what is now the Louvre Museum, but which was then the royal palace. Louis spent his youth in Paris where, from 1600, he was known as a merchant apothecary, a grocer and a townsman. One of his cousins, who had married Jean de Biencourt de Poutrincourt in 1590, often evoked in front of him the charms of New France (later Canada), where Jacques Cartier had founded the first French establishment on the Isle of Ste. Croix.

In 1604, Louis decided to associate with his cousin and with Pierre Du Gua, Lord de Monts, to start a new establishment in Acadia. All three went to the Isle of Ste. Croix, then to the Bay of Port Royal in 1605 (now Annapolis, in southern Nova Scotia). The explorer Samuel de Champlain was with them. Marc Lescarbot, a French author and lawyer who met Louis at Port Royal in 1606, spoke about Louis Hébert's talents as a healer and the pleasure he took from cultivating the land. They stayed in Acadia until 1607, but then were forced to go back to France due to lack of support from their French backers; the concessions assigned to Lord de Monts had been annulled.

In 1611, Hébert came back to Port Royal with Poutrincourt. Lescarbot, who accompanied them, wrote that he himself "planted wheat and planted grape vines with the help of Louis Hébert who understood a lot about farming." But the English from Virginia, commanded by Samuel Argall, attacked and destroyed the village. They had to return to France in 1613.

In 1608 Champlain himself had returned to Canada and founded Québec, having given up on Acadia: he knew what disappointments

Hébert had encountered, but he also had a lively appreciation of his qualities. In 1617, Champlain persuaded Louis to emigrate to the shores of the St. Lawrence, with his wife, Marie Rollet, and their three children, Guillaume (3 years old), Guillemette (9) and Anne (14), and lived out the rest of his life in Québec City.

Hébert contracted to work for two years for the "Company of Canada" with his family, that is to say his wife Marie Rollet, three children and brother-in-law; under the contract, he had to take care of the sick for free. The company, however, did not honor its part of the bargain and Hébert, in addition to serving as apothecary, devoted much of his efforts to farming, which the "Company" vehemently opposed because land-clearing interfered with its fur-trading.

He cleared a century-old forest, not without hard labor, but screamed often at the bad will of the Company. It forced him to work with the fewest manual tools; he didn't even have a plow.

As Champlain recounted, "He worked without cease for others and not for himself." The autumn after they arrived, his daughter Anne married Etienne Jonquet, who also came from Normandy; they both died in 1619 without children. On August 26, 1621, Guillemette Hébert married Guillaume Couillard and gave him numerous descendants.

Hébert had been named the king's representative, which permitted him to ask Louis XIII to stop the abuses by members of the Company. In the document that Hébert sent to Louis XIII asking for the land that surrounded his lodging, it is stated "that Louis Hébert is the first head of a French family who has inhabited this country since the start of the century." The Duke of Montmorency gave him, in the king's name, the fiefdom of Sault-au-Matelot on February 4, 1623. Three years later, the Duke of Ventadour gave him the one on the St. Charles River.

Louis Hébert maintained good relations with the Indians; in effect he saw in them not fur traders but brothers to enlighten; his home was always open. His agricultural activities were also very useful, as Champlain bore witness in 1620: "I visited the places, the worked land that I found sowed, loaded with beautiful wheat, the gardens loaded with all kinds of beautiful vegetables."

Hébert did not get to enjoy the fruits of his work. At the end of 1626, he fell on icy ground and, after suffering cruelly, died in Québec in 1627. After having sheltered many orphaned Indians, his widow died on May 27, 1649.

In the gardens of the city hall in Québec is a monument representing the first Canadian colonist offering to God his first sheaf of wheat, and on the house where he was born in Paris (129 rue St.

Honoré) is a plaque recalling that he was the first colonist of Acadia and Québec.

The statue is part of a triptych that also includes his wife and children on one side of him and his son-in-law, Guillaume Couillard, with his plow on the other. During the 1980s, the ensemble was moved to *Parc Montmorency* overlooking the St. Lawrence River, just a little downhill from the Chateau Frontenac in Québec City.

Appendix B:
My Father's Diary

These are my father's diary notes, reproduced as written, mistakes and all, on payroll index cards. They tell the story of his life year by year, his birth and the years from age 12 to 25, with a clarity and succinctness I could never hope to achieve. The 16 cards (1922 covered two cards) were found by my mother among Dad's belongings after he died, June 17, 1959. They were in an envelope completely sealed in cellophane tape. That envelope and those cards were the only things I asked her to leave me. She honored that request.

Notes:

1. My father's 15 brothers' and sisters' names are in bold-face.
2. Marianne is his oldest sister, not to be confused with "Marraine.".
3. "Marraine" means "godmother." She is Rose Annette, his second oldest sister, who became a nun, Sister (Soeur) St. Jean du Sacré Coeur.
4. "Thérèse" is a sister for whom my daughter Teri was named. She tried to become a nun but was taken from the novitiate by Rose Annette.
5. Marthe was yet another sister, who also became a nun (distinct from my cousin Marthe, daughter of another of my father's sisters, Gerardine.)
6. My father had *two* brothers named Rosaire, one born 11 years before him and died when he was only three months old, the other his youngest brother, retarded and the only male who lived much past age 50. He died in his early 60s, not long after I met and talked with him in 1972.
7. Dan (Daniel) was the brother closest to my father in age and temperament; they were close all through life. Dan ran a nursery and introduced my father to gardening and landscaping, which he loved more

than anything. He died at age 50, just like Dad, a few years after we moved to Florida.

My comments and clarifications are enclosed in brackets = [ ]. On the envelope, Dad wrote: "To be opened February 1953." We believe he expected to die when he went to Miami in early 1953 seeking relief from what they had erroneously believed was arthritis. He didn't die then. Instead, he regained health and vitality, decided the Florida climate — and gardening advantages — had "cured" him, and moved the family to Miami Beach. The envelope wasn't found and opened until after his death, in 1959. Here's what he wrote.

1909

Born, June 3rd. What a night! 2 o'clock in the morning. My Sister **Marianne** hated me so.

1921

We sell The Central Hotel. Pa buy the corner of Notre Dame and St. Alphonse Sts. He builds the Manoir.
Mother's very sick. We have to take our shoes off when we get in the house.
Last Christmas with both Pa and Ma, they knew it.

1922

January: Innauguration [sic] of the Manoir Hébert. All relatives (over 100)
February: Mother's very sick, she's going down.
March: Around the 10th we change Ma from her bedroom to another one in the Hotel dept. The 24 it's her birthday. She wants us to play the piano and sing. **Marraine** does sing for Mother. The 25th Mother leaves us for heaven. She dies Sunday morning like a saint.
Avril [April]. I'm very sick with "Inflamation des poumons" [pneumonia], go very close to the grave. Big fire and I want to get on the roof of the hotel to see it. The maid takes me from my bed, get scolded good for it.
September: I'm sent to a boarding school at St. Ferdinand, takes piano and violin, loves it.
Christmas: Everyone is sick. **Maurice** very much, big fire during night. I'm sick, then Pa is sick. Sad Christmas.

1923

March: The 5th. Pa dies in St. Joseph's hospital 2 o'clock in the afternoon, answering the Rosary (we were saying it out loud). He must have seen somebody from the other world before he died. He had gone to the hospital from church, just after the last night of his mission.

June: The 19th. Big fire lasting about 5 days. The asbestos mines at St. Maurice, Thetford. We see it from St. Ferdinand.
*Sept.***:** Sent back to boarding school.

1924
January: Romeo Turcotte (lost his father and mother like me at the same time) we are great friend. He tells me he's going to be a brother.
March: I go to be a brother, to join my friend Romeo. (Best time of my life, at the "Petit Novitiat."
Flor [**Florence**] and **Marthe** are in Lambton Boarding School. **Marthe** as [sic] taken painting and is a little artist.
Thérèse goes to be a nun, stays 5 or 6 months and then **Marraine** has her sent out. **Thérèse** gives trouble to **Marraine**.

1925
July: I am transferred to Montreal "Grand Novitiat." Gerry [his sister **Gerardine**?] comes to see me. **Dan** and Ralph [a friend] too. I show them my grave. [The novitiate assigned a gravesite to each novice.]
*August 15*th: Receives the brotherhood garments.
*Sept. 10*th: **Maurice** who was at Villa St. Martin drowns in an artificial pool. He had his violin. He was to become a priest. I can't go to the funerals [sic].

1926
Marthe goes to join **Marraine** in the Sisters of Charity. Nobody is surprised. **Marraine** would like me to go back to be a brother
August 15: Gives my 1st vows for a year, then I'm sent to Québec. Chemin St. Foye. Brother Magloire. Nobody likes him.
Rosaire is in Québec. Poor little brother hasn't a chance. At Scholartisat I like the teaching, but outside of that it doesn't appeal to me. I'm now 17.

1927
July: Renew my vows, and I'm sent to Nicolet, I'll never forget.
Brother Adolphe who used to teach **Dan**, is my co-worker. He's good to me. I love the kids but hates the life. I am not so pious.

1928

February: Meet Ivonne Florent. I kiss in church. She wants to be a mother to me.

June: I leave the brotherhood. Go to GrandMere. Meets **Florence** at the train. Good time at the "chalet." **Adelard** comes from Waterbury [Connecticut]. I go to Thetford. Refused money. Goes to Three Rivers to work. I have a wild time for a few months until I get hold of myself one day.

*Sept.***:** Work in 3 Rivers. **Adelard** sends me $100.00. I leave for U.S. Stops at Montreal and arrive 4 days late in Waterbury with $2.00 on me. Bad start. Very sad Christmas.

1929

All summer works with **Adelard**. Have an accident. Blood poison, 2 months. [His right hand was sliced open by an electric saw. After surgery, he was sent to a dairy farm to milk cows to regain strength in the hand.] Work at the Boys Club. I like it. Then work on a farm and another one and one more, in Washington, Conn. Have trouble there, get only part of my money. Go to Bridgeport, best job of all, Airplane factory. $300.00 stolen. Trouble at the end of November and all December. Christmas very sad.

1930

*Jan. 10*th: Start for NY and get there in about 2 days and half. Get no job so I walk back to Bridgeport, 45 miles. Take a train few days after and go back to NY. Mr. Keppel takes care of me. Hope I can see him some day.

March: Leave NY for Pawtucket [Rhode Island]. Work with Dan. Live at the Mansion. Stuck on blonde Dorothy.

June: Dan gets married. Hm-mm.

Dec.: I leave for Block Island. Saddest Christmas of all.

1931

July: Leave Block Island, go to New London, New Haven, Hartford, Bridgeport, Poughkepsie [sic], Albany, Cohoes, NY

Oct.: Works a while for a Wrecking Co.

Nov.: Get a job at Ten Yeck Hotel.

Dec.: Buy present for Gisele, Marianne, Charley. We have a good Christmas time.

I dance to [sic] much at a party and make believe I am dying, close to reality.

1932
Works at Ten Yeck unto [sic] March, then go with my brother-in-law. The woman and the kid in trouble, almost put myself in trouble.
Summer work for Undertaker Boivin.
I meet Felicia Widgowsky. Correspondence.
Christmas is poor but happy. Steel [sic] Christmas trees and don't get 'em, instead got a bad cold, in bed for 10 days about.

1933
March: I leave Cohoes [New York; **Marianne** and her husband Charley and daughter Gisele lived there] and come to Pawtucket [Rhode Island], works with **Dan**.
I try for a couple months to get Dorothy back, but then turn my nose up when she first looks at me. I agree to go out with girls just to fool them and do I do it. I meet Bill Gervais. Good times together.
We wreck a Cadillac on the road to Woonsocket.
Labor Day. We go to Johnson Pond and for 3 rainy days oh my oh my. Break up with Sweet Violet. *Tough*. Christmas up to **Dan** & Gervais.

1934
February. Transferred from Curtain Factory to Guyan Mills.
March: Move to Mansion.
June: 2 wild weeks. Almost drown myself at Lincoln Woods.
July: Have a big date for the 4th. Go to Revere Beach all night [with Lillian, my mother, who was then working at Guyan Mills, too].
Sept.: Lill is quite sick. Lill goes to the hospital. She doesn't die.
October. Lill goes to see Dr. Condi. He's wonderful.
Christmas: Best one I ever had. I get a wristwatch from Lillian.
I don't think I'll go back   to   be   a   Brother.

[He spaced out the final words just that way.]

Appendix C:
Belize, December 2005

Ship's Crew

Joe	*Skipper*
Smaranda	*Navigator*
Bill	*Dinghy Captain*
Natasha	*Apprentice Skipper*
Eliane	*Ship's Cook*
Richard	*Scribe*
Mihnea	*Sleeper*
Olivia	*Ship's Entertainer*
Alexandra	*Ship's Entertainer*

Saturday, December 17

The December Belizean sun smacks us like a blast furnace as we step out of the airliner and descend to the tarmac. Eliane had repeatedly cautioned some of us to pack sweat shirts and windbreakers against chilly nights on the water. The likelihood such gear would be needed suddenly seems as remote as the North Carolina pre-dawn wintry chill we left behind a few hours ago.

After a disorderly blur of scrambling for luggage, a flotsam of human specks swirling toward the funnel of Customs, helpful hands snatching our bags unasked, rapid-fire negotiations with a taxi driver (can we squeeze four adults, a teenager and two pre-teens into a single taxi?), more helpful hands tossing our luggage about, tips leaping from our pockets into theirs, all seven of us cramming into the taxi for a 20-minute herky-jerky ride to the water taxi terminal, yet more hands slinging our bags to the sidewalk, into the terminal, onto the deck of the water taxi, all unasked and, of course, to the accompaniment of yet more tipping, at long last we are water-borne, on our way across the sun-flashing sea to paradise.

Olivia and Natasha find my multi-colored baseball cap particularly un-cool. (For the most part, the adults graciously keep their opinions to themselves.) Having already discarded into a Miami airport trash can my straw hat (which everyone thought resembled that of a plantation boss) because it was shedding a steady drizzle of strawdust after languishing in my closet so many years, I'm not about to abandon my one remaining protection from the tropical sun. This is also about the time I remember leaving my sunglasses in my car back in Chapel Hill.

Before long, most members of our travel-weary band are lulled asleep by the roaring drone of the boat's engine, the dreamy aroma of gasoline fumes, and the rock-a-bye-baby bouncing of the waves.

A few vow, "Never again! When this is over, we're flying back to the mainland."

We are all awake for the brief stop at Caye Caulker, where we are introduced to the gospel according to Belize. While a few passengers disembark, a gaunt Belizean leaps onto the rear deck and peeks into the cabin. "Welcome to Caye Caulker," he calls out with a broad toothless grin. "No shirt, no shoes, no shit – no problem!" We are soon to see this on signs and tee shirts everywhere in the islands, except for the "no shit" line, which was all "Papa's" (we learned his nickname later), an element from which he takes special merriment by asking if anyone has any (without elaborating, of course), and then musing that having none just might pose a problem after all. We are no longer in Kansas.

San Pedro at last. Our first destination, Ambergris Caye, is the most developed of Belize's more than 175 islands (Cayes). But the fun part will have to wait a while longer. First, we have to trek more than 100 yards up the soft-sand beach dragging our bags, a feat that occasions more than a little grumbling but all of which silences as soon as we spot our 52-foot catamaran — the *Silver Lining* — gleaming white in the sun beside the TMM Charters pier.

Unfortunately, someone else has left shirt, sandals and bag on board. We surmise it's a previous renter. It certainly couldn't belong to Joe Kelly, Bill's friend from Annapolis who is flying in from Baltimore, because his flight was to arrive after ours. Besides, there's also a pack of cigarettes with the bag, and Bill assures us that Joe, a chum from his school days, doesn't smoke.

It turns out they are Joe's belongings, after all, because in due time all six-foot-six of him comes striding up the beach. He's beaten us to San Pedro. And yes, he does indulge in an occasional smoke, although not once during the trip will any of us report seeing him do so. We are, if nothing else, a health-conscious group.

We sort ourselves into shoppers and beach-goers. Our first provisioning at a local market runs up a bill of $566 Belize ($2 Belize equals $1 U.S.). Surely we will have food enough for our week of island hopping. Besides, there will be other stops along the way for restocking if we run out of anything, won't there? The market agrees to deliver our provisions to our boat in the morning.

Meanwhile, Olivia and Alexandra, both 12, are exploring the beach, repeatedly returning to the *Silver Lining* with treasures of bleached coral.

The eyeglass gremlin begins playing tricks. Joe has also forgotten to bring sunglasses. Bill says he's lost his reading glasses and goes looking to buy replacements.

After a briefing about the boat by "Andy" of TMM Charters, we head out in search of dinner — our first in Belize — and settle on a beachside restaurant, Caliente (Spanish for "hot"). During dinner, Olivia and Alexandra "assign" each adult a role based on what they think we resemble. Bill, they decide, is a sailor, Smaranda a "candy store" lady (the striped shirt she wears somewhat suggestive of candy canes?), Joe an architect, I a "wise book person" librarian (the scruffy beard?)...

We are a contented crew as we settle in for our first night of sleep aboard the *Silver Lining*.

Sunday, December 18

Joe and I go shopping for sunglasses and return with identical pairs of black plastic wraparounds. Eliane and I stop for breakfast at another beachside restaurant, Estele's, where we have our first taste of a Belizean staple, fried jack, a kind of puff-pastry dumpling. Eliane's, stuffed with mango, is scrumptious. It isn't long after this that I discover I've now also lost my reading glasses, but Bill finds me a replacement pair similar to those he'd bought himself, slim glasses that come stuffed into a tube in which you'd expect to find nothing bigger than a thermometer.

Back at the *Silver Lining*, the groceries have arrived. One bag isn't ours so it is sent back, but it later appears that some items we did buy aren't in our delivery. We never did find out what happened to them, and in any event we are too focused on our upcoming adventure to care.

Yesterday we made an issue with Andy, in jest of course, about not having a blender on board. Bill had found mention of one in the ship's log. How are we supposed to make Piña Coladas or Margaritas without a blender? A week of sailing seems rather pointless without an adequate supply and variety of alcoholic beverages. Today, Andy arrives with a blender under his arm — a defective one, he says, but a blender nevertheless. We now have all we need for setting sail.

After another briefing, this one on navigating the Belizean channels — "Watch for the sticks!" but don't worry about the ominously named Porto Stuck — Andy takes us out for a trial run to demonstrate proper seamanship. Our true sailors — Joe, Smaranda, Bill, Natasha — pay close attention. The rest of us luxuriate in ignorance.

Andy is picked up by his mates in a skiff and we are at last on our own, headed into the blue yonder for our first layover, Caye Caulker. We'll remain anchored there until Tuesday, when Mihnea will arrive (Smaranda's teenage son had stayed in Chapel Hill to compete in a Battle of the Bands), then island-hop our way south and be back to San Pedro by Christmas Eve.

Our first exploratory trip ashore at Caye Caulker settles one thing: snorkeling the coral reefs, one of our primary objectives, won't be as simple as we thought. Much of the reefs around the inhabited cayes are marine preserves, accessible only with special permits or tour groups. To be sure we don't miss out on some snorkeling, we book a Monday tour with Easy Boy Tours, which operates out of a hut on the beach.

It's happy hour aboard the *Silver Lining*. Libations are poured and we break out the island music that Eliane and Richard brought — Belafonte (Day-O!), Jimmy Buffet and, of course, Bob Marly. But it's a tune called *Blue Summer* that energizes us. If you don't listen too attentively, it sounds very much like, "Oh-oh-Osama!" Eliane and Richard sing along and dance to its Reggae rhythm on the aft deck while Bill videotapes it all from the dinghy.

Caye Caulker's main street runs beside the beach the length of the island and is lined with bars, eateries, inns, guided tours, beach snorkeling and kayak equipment rentals, and, more than anything else, gift shops and tables covered with home-crafted jewelry and carvings — a feast for ladies of all ages. No stroll down the beach goes uninterrupted by frequent stops to examine jewelry.

Dinner is at the Sand Box, yet another beach-front establishment, accompanied by annoying sand fleas that peck at our legs under the picnic table. We are getting accustomed to tables set on sand, and to that ubiquitous sign: "No shirt, no shoes, no problem!"

Monday, December 19

Joe awoke with a headache early this morning and took a Tylenol with a swig of what he, like many of us, thought was a bottle of Gatorade or grape soda left in the head by one of the kids. It is "Fabuloso," a tile and toilet disinfectant in a plastic bottle that resembles nothing so much as Gatorade. Needless to say, this did not rest easily on his stomach and, by his account, lurched out of him immediately. Thus is born the longest standing joke of the adventure. From now on,

Fabuloso will be the all-purpose remedy suggested for whatever needs healing, correcting, cleansing, or any other treatment. Joe, it should be noted, has a degree in medicine and is a de-frocked doctor.

Communication is becoming a problem. Smaranda is trying to telephone Mihnea to tell him to fly to Caye Caulker after he arrives in Belize, but cell phone connection is iffy at best here, we are learning. She manages to leave a message for him, but when Mihnea tries to return her call, he reaches a different boat. Apparently we don't even have the right number for our cell phone.

We gather at the Easy Boy hutch at 10:30 a.m. to collect fins, masks and snorkels, then climb aboard for what we are sure will be our first of many coral reef visits. First stop, Shark and Ray Alley. As we swim about, faces submerged with only our breathing tubes poking out of the water, a school of sting rays gathers, lured by the promise of chum. Some are fully six feet across. It's shallow enough for us to stand and the rays brush our legs, seeming to ask to be petted. It's clear they are quite accustomed to human company. Olivia has a love-dread affair with sharks; she is usually afraid to get into any unknown waters for fear sharks may lurk within. But when someone spots a nurse shark about 100 feet away, intrepid Olivia is the one to chase after it, albeit unsuccessfully.

Our second snorkeling stop is at the South Channel, where Ian takes us on a guided tour through a wonderland of coral canyons and underwater mountain ranges, bottomless chasms walled by eerie arms and spikes, polyps and antlers of coral, huge lacy globes of brain coral, all a-swarm with tropical fish, brilliant blue tangs, yellow-striped butterfly fish, others with camouflage ability to change colors to blend in with their shifting backgrounds almost instantly. Ian stops here and there to point out rare fish hiding amid the twists and curls of coral. We are gliding through a fantasyland.

At the third stop, called the Swash, we are free to explore the reef on our own. It is less dramatic, but each of us finds his or her own area to explore. Eliane stays on the boat — snorkeling makes her seasick. She can take the undulating swells of the sea when she is in the boat, but not when she is bobbing among the waves. Exhausted and our curiosity sated, we at last climb back on board and head ashore.

We've decided to have dinner with "Bouncer," or so it says on his soiled tee shirt. He's a huge mound of a man who works a grill on the beach and feeds his guests at picnic tables under the palm trees. Tonight's offerings: fresh snapper and barracuda steak. The aromas emitted by his grill are all the convincing we need: we reserve the second seating.

While the women indulge in more shopping, Bill, Joe, Natasha and I retire to a pub across the street from Bouncer to sample the local

Margaritas. When the drinks arrive, they are sky blue — the precise color of Tidy Bowl toilet cleanser. (I once tended bar at the Atlanta Press Club where anyone ordering a drink with Curaçao in it was deemed to be ordering a "Tidy Bowl.") Joe, fully recovered from his encounter with Fabuloso and now fueled by a Margarita, demonstrates the art of skipping rope to some youngsters on the beach as we await our dinners. The meal is all we'd hoped for. Life is good.

Tuesday, December 20

Eliane prepares a breakfast of French toast. Everyone agrees she is the ship's best cook, a role she gladly accepts. After breakfast, Bill begins a dinghy taxi service to and from the Caye Caulker pier. Eliane, Olivia, Alexandra and I walk the length of the beach — with mandatory stops at tables of jewelry — to the Lazy Lizard at the northern tip. It's a tiki-hut beach bar reminiscent of Key West before Jimmy Buffet upscaled it all. "My kind of place," I declare. Ordering "a beer" here automatically brings a Belikin. There are others brands, but they must be ordered by name. It turns out the owner of Belikin brewery also owns the Coca Cola franchise for Belize and, we are told, sells shrimp to the Red Lobster chain of restaurants. While we enjoy our Belikins, the kids enjoy the lagoon waters. I reminisce about a limerick my father taught me: "A wonderful bird is the pelican, his beak can hold more than his belly can."

The others, meanwhile, make a quick run to Caye Chapel to top off our reservoir of fresh water, which seems to be draining all too rapidly. We are cautioned to take only quick showers. Bill and Joe shave in the sea. I simply don't bother shaving.

After lunch at the Sand Box, Smaranda and Bill head for the landing strip to meet Mihnea and by mid-afternoon, we are a full crew at last and heading south under full sail.

We fall easily into our roles. There are clearly two classes of humanity on board: seafarers and landlubbers. Joe, Smaranda, Bill and Natasha are the seafarers. They actually enjoy hoisting anchors and sails, tinkering with persnickety engines, and untangling ropes — excuse me, lines. Eliane and I, although we proclaim everlasting love of the sea, are fundamentally landlubbers. So is Mihnea, apparently. (It has yet to be determined what Olivia and Alexandra will become, although they do seem to take naturally to water, if not to boating chores.) The seafarers patiently explain to the landlubbers that all those ropes are not ropes, they are lines. That starboard is to the right and port is to the left. Or is it the other way around?

Joe is a natural at the helm. Smaranda takes her post beside him, navigating our route with charts and binoculars. Mihnea sleeps on deck. He's had a long trip, but we soon enough discover he will do a lot of sleeping. It's a teenage thing. Bill and Natasha take their posts on the catamaran's twin prows to watch for the sticks — mere branches stripped from local trees, it seems — that mark our channel. Bill is particularly dramatic in pointing out sticks to starboard and port. (How do those fragile sticks manage to stay in place through all the tides and vicissitudes of sea weather?) Olivia and Alexandra are practicing a new song and dance routine. Eliane and I practice luxuriating in absolutely nothing to do. All is right with the world.

We make it through Porto Stuck without getting stuck, as promised. It, after all, has a real channel marker. Not long afterward, a dolphin swims alongside and accompanies us for some distance, then swims off to our left (port?). Soon afterwards, our delightful afternoon of sailing turns to panic. We've run aground. Suddenly all hands are busy. Joe dives in to look for deeper water. Bill jumps into the dinghy and tries to nudge the Silver Lining from the side, the way a rubber ducky might try to move you to one side of the bathtub. Next, we toss out tow lines and Bill tries pulling us out of the shallows. Not a chance. On the fore-deck Olivia and Alexandra rehearse a new dance routine, a "crisis dance." Bill is still doing his David vs. Goliath from the dinghy when a fishing boat putters up, three lobster fishermen aboard. They offer to help. Tow lines are attached to both the dinghy and the fishing boat, but repeated efforts still fail to budge us. At one point the mere inertia of the catamaran spins the fishing boat back against us; its outboard motor slams against our hull.

We try another tactic: backing off the sandbar. This time, the fishing boat succeeds in tugging us free. Why didn't we think of that first? Pure human stubbornness? Before departing, the fishermen ask if we'd like to buy some lobsters. Confident that we have enough to eat on board and will be re-provisioning soon in any event, we decline, tip them generously and ask them to guide us back to the channel and a safe anchorage off Caye St. George. The dolphin apparently knew the channel better than we or our charts, which made it clear we were in deep enough water when in fact we weren't. So much for relying on maps and sticks when you are in Belizean waters.

"I could see we were getting into pretty shallow water just before we hit bottom," confides Bill. He was on lookout at the bow just before we ran aground. Note to Bill: When a lookout sees an approaching risk, such as shallow water, the lookout should say something about it — *before* we hit it.

We drop anchor off Caye St. George and an expeditionary force goes ashore in the dark — Bill, Smaranda, Natasha and I. We are hit by a surprise shower on the way but, damp yet undaunted, refuse to turn back. After we dock, two young men, Chris and Kris, are waiting for us on the beach. They give us a flashlight-guided "tour" of the island, a walk along a pitch-dark path that snakes beside expensive looking vacation homes, all of them shuttered and in darkness. Our guides explain: St. George has two functions. It is home to a British military barracks used by soldiers on rest and recreation leave (reminding us Belize used to be a British colony, British Honduras, until a bloodless revolution achieved its independence), and it is a vacation resort for the aristocracy of Belize. There is the vacation home of the owner of Belikin Beer. There the governor's. It is Christmas week; none of the aristocracy is here tonight.

We are led to one of the island's two hotels, where about a half-dozen patrons are drinking without merriment. We order drinks and sit on the balcony looking out to sea. The drinks are poor, expensive and meager. We leave our young guides, already well on their way to inebriation, and make our way back to our dinghy and the *Silver Lining*. It is clear no provisions are to be had on this island.

Eliane does a masterful job of assembling dinner from leftovers and canned tuna, and we toast the night with Margaritas made with the last of our tequila. Smaranda mentions that the spots on Bill's face are pre-cancerous so he has to be careful in the sun. "He should use my 45," Eliane advises. We all point index fingers at our temples, leaping to the assumption that she means a .45 caliber pistol, not her 45 SPF sun block. "Eliane's 45" becomes our second most popular punch-line. Whatever ails you from now on, if "Joe's Fabuloso" doesn't take care of it, "Eliane's 45" will.

A storm comes up and the *Silver Lining* pitches and rolls throughout the night. The dinghy keeps slamming its motor into the hull just outside Eliane's and my berth. In the morning we can see its scars. From now on, we'll hoist the dinghy out of the water overnight.

Wednesday, December 21

We start out early under a forbidding sky. Eliane makes a breakfast of "Mexican" style egg-McMuffins. A skiff of the Belize Port Authority stops by and gives us tips on finding the channel south. On the horizon we watch three large cruise ships, floating hotels, move slowly as ghosts through the haze.

Under full sail again, we make it to Bluefield Range, which our guidebook says is a "resort" island, but all we can see on the island's shoreline is a row of large blue boxes, like cargo containers. Three other yachts are anchored in the harbor, including one from Montreal.

The sky is still ominous. Worse, we are almost out of food. We are down to a half dozen eggs, some Ritz crackers, Cheerios, and a dill pickle or two. Joe goes ashore in the dinghy to search for food. Using mostly sign language, he buys seven lobster tails from fishing boats tied up there. We steam and devour them.

Another expeditionary force goes in search of food. Smaranda and Eliane stop at one of the other boats and explain our plight. Our neighbors are generous, handing over a box of spaghetti and a huge conch they've caught, even explaining how to extract the meat. Smaranda saves the conch shell as a trophy.

With the food they bring back dire news: this storm is part of a large front that has closed in from Cuba and is expected to stay around for three days. We need to have the *Silver Lining* back in San Pedro by Saturday noon. We will not be able to go further south, and in any event there is nowhere to buy more food short of Tobacco Caye, some 100 miles to our south. All the islands between here and there are deserted, we're told. It is time to start thinking about heading back.

Eliane works her magic again and converts the gleanings into a delicious spaghetti sauce. We may not be good planners, but we are resourceful — some of us, anyway.

As dusk descends we enjoy the very last of our alcohol on deck and examine our options. We'd hoped to do considerably more island hopping, but logic dictates a return to Caye Caulker. Empty rum and scotch bottles join the empty tequila bottle in the recycling hold below deck. Smaranda weaves both Alexandra's and Olivia's hair into French braids and they don identical tie-dyed shirts. Some wile away the evening playing poker, using the last of the Cheerios as chips. Joe husbands his final few Cheerios to the bitter end, waiting for the perfect hand that never comes.

We spend another night rolling on the swells of a turbulent sea.

Thursday, December 22

The sun is back, but it's windy. Bill, always the first to rise, races off in the dinghy. He spotted a fishing boat leaving the harbor and is chasing it down to ask if they have any fish to sell. They don't, but tell him that another boat, across the harbor and heading off in the opposite direction, has some. Intrepid, Bill chases it down as well, and when he returns he has 10 pounds of snapper filets. Persistence has paid off.

We finish the last of the eggs for breakfast with the last of the lobster tails — yet another Eliane recipe conjured on the fly — confident that now, at least, we have food for yet another day. No vegetables, no bread, no booze — but plenty of fish and more gallons of spring water than we can ever drink. At least we will not perish of starvation or thirst.

Our portside battery is dead. That engine won't turn over. We have been unable to communicate with the TMM office, either via the ship's radio (we're out of range) or cell phone.

The seafarers among us set to work attempting to solve the accumulating problems. The others sit and watch, fretfully. There are efforts to switch batteries from port to starboard, to wire them together, to do other things that people who understand engines do in situations like this. At last we do achieve communication with TMM and are advised to "clean the solenoids." Joe and Bill seem to understand what this means and, to a standing ovation, get both batteries — and engines — working again.

It now also appears the bilge pumps are not working. Pushing a button in the head is supposed to suck our shower water out to sea. Instead, the accumulated dirty water just sits there, slowly seeping into the hulls. As the boat pitches and yaws at night, those of us in the rearward berths can hear the slapping of water suspiciously close by, but it takes a few nights of this for us to understand that the sound is coming not from outside the boat, but inside: our used shower water is sloshing around in the hull under our bunks, just under the false floor where our bags are stored. Extra blankets and much of our "clean" clothes are smelly and damp from it. This is one problem the seafarers are unable to solve.

It's decision time. Do we head straight back or make one last stop at the nearest island, Rendezvous Caye? The Caye is surrounded by shallow water and coral reefs. The chart makes that pretty clear. Smaranda and Bill want to try it. Joe says it is "a stupid idea." Eliane says this is the only time we will ever have this opportunity, don't we want to make the effort at least? Joe is outvoted and we slowly, cautiously nudge our way toward a speck of island, a mere sandbar with no more than a dozen palm trees out in the middle of the sea. Bill and Natasha watch for coral heads ahead of us. Joe, coaxing the *Silver Lining* forward among the outcroppings, keeps mumbling, "This is a stupid idea."

At last we drop anchor. Joe stays stubbornly on board while the rest of us pile into the dinghy and head for a floating pier just off the island, then wade ashore. On the way, the wind rips from my head my cap-of-many-colors and sends it out to sea. I'd left with two hats. Now both are gone. As are the reading glasses bought in San Pedro, but Bill has found his original pair so I can continue reading. As for my new plastic wraparound sunglasses, they broke in half. The glasses gremlin is still hard at work.

The shallows and beach of Rendezvous Caye are littered with conch shells. We collect shells, each larger and more magnificent than the last.

Smaranda calls Joe on the walkie-talkie and tells him he is missing out on the fun. He concedes he is jealous and joins us, then swims off to explore the nearby reef. Joe is very much a march-to-my-own-drummer kind of guy. The water is murky near the reef, he reports back, and it's hard to see anything.

By 10:15 a.m. we are setting sail for Caye Caulker again, now laden with conch shells and happy to be heading toward civilization. As we leave, a large tour boat pulls up to Rendezvous Caye and disgorges crowds of tourists. Our timing was excellent.

Smaranda, content with her "trophy" conch whose meat we'd eaten, didn't bother collecting a shell from Rendezvous Caye. Unfortunately, a remnant of meat is still attached inside her shell and is starting to emit a rancid odor. In an effort to scour the last of the meat from the shell we are towing it behind the *Silver Lining*. At high speed it is skipping over the waves.

The trip to Caye Caulker is a sunny, pleasant run powered by motor, without sails, and with a single hiccup. As we approach Porto Stuck, Joe radios an oncoming catamaran to ask if it will pass us to port or starboard. Natasha answers by radio from inside our own cabin. Joe repeats his question, she repeats that she doesn't understand. Somewhere in the mix-up, she finally confesses her prank. "We have a deranged crew member," Joe informs the oncoming boat. "Understood," says the other skipper. When nine people are spending a week together in the confines of a boat, a sense of humor is mandatory.

At Caye Caulker, we re-provision with eggs, a case of beer, and other essentials. I head for my preferred slice of civilization, the Lazy Lizard, and assay a "Panty Ripper," a fruity rum concoction. Mihnea joins me while others indulge their insatiable appetite for jewelry shopping or, in Bill's case, some more locally available if questionable "fast" food. Later, we dine at Romie & Jim's, on the usual floor of sand. The music is loud, the food is good, and a sudden downpour is unable to dampen our restored spirits.

Friday, December 23

We wake to brilliant sunshine. Joe solves yet another, ill-defined engine problem. I try my hand at breakfast — 19 eggs scrambled with grilled onion, garlic, and mushrooms. The others are generous with their praise, but this meal clearly does not rise to the high standards set by Eliane.

We separate into two groups. Eliane and I go ashore to rent kayaks and explore the shoreline of the northern half of Caye Caulker. The island was split in half by a long ago hurricane, and the northern section is largely deserted. It is densely wooded, laced with lagoons and narrow waterways, with here and there a hurricane-damaged and abandoned shack. Nature has reclaimed it for the wildlife.

The others set sail in search of a reef for snorkeling. Mihnea, after all, has yet to experience the reefs. They encounter choppy waters but eventually find a place to snorkel for a few hours. On the way back they stop at Church Caye to replenish our fresh-water tanks yet again.

Eliane and I discover that the walkie-talkie fails to communicate with the *Silver Lining* — it appears to have collected internal moisture during our kayak trip — so we stand on the pier waving beach towels to summon the dinghy. The others come ashore for a late lunch. Joe heads off somewhere with Bill and when they return, Joe has a bag full of lobster tails bought on shore for $5 a pound, less than half what we had paid at sea when they were our only recourse. Dinner is a seafood feast of red snapper and lobster, rice and vegetables. Civilization, we agree, is better than deserted islands.

Joe whips up a batch of Piña Coladas in the blender, and over drinks we discuss the next day's return-to-base strategy: do we tell all, or stay silent and hope they don't notice Olivia's lost snorkel and mask, the floatation cushion that blew away in the night after Smaranda left it on the fore-deck trampoline, or the cracked hatch over the starboard head? Perhaps we should point out the water damage caused by the bilge pump failure. And our communication problems. Being honest liberals, we will confess all, of course.

Joe, Bill, Smaranda, Mihnea and Natasha go into town for a final visit. After their return, Joe goes back to the island yet again to sample its night life. Our sea adventure is drawing to a close.

Saturday, December 24 – Christmas Eve

We are again without water for showers. We haven't a clue why, unless that humming sound we hear nonstop is a pump draining the tank. After a quick trip ashore for breakfast food, we set sail for San Pedro. When we arrive, Olivia and Alexandra head back to the beach and we meet with Randy. Bill confesses all, but Randy makes light of the damages, until a quick inspection informs him of a much more serious problem: a cracked keel, no doubt caused when we ran aground, perhaps when that lobster fishing boat slammed against us while trying to drag us off the sandbar. They tote up the damages and agree to settle all claims by keeping our $400 deposit. We revisit this conversation *ad nauseum* all afternoon.

Olivia, meanwhile, slices open the sole of her foot on the beach, apparently by stepping on razor-sharp coral. When her mother arrives, she is bravely trimming away a flap of skin from her own heel. She is fearless!

We taxi to our motel, the Blue Tang Inn, a deluxe place on the beach. While Olivia and Alexandra have their hair braided and beaded at poolside, Natasha and I head up the beach in search of a sports bar. It is a critical weekend for NFL games, the second to final game of the season and both my Washington Redskins and Natasha's Carolina Panthers are in the hunt for playoff berths. We find Cholos on the Beach and are in luck: the Panthers game against Dallas is being broadcast. We stay through the game, tracking the scores of the other games. The Panthers lose to Dallas, but the Redskins beat their nemesis, the New York Giants. (Both teams will make it to the playoffs, where both will eventually lose to the Seattle Seahawks.)

I tell Natasha it's time to rejoin the others but she wants to stay to see the scores of other games. This brings on a moment of angst. Mistake number one: I leave Natasha there alone. Eliane is furious. When I return up the beach to look for Natasha a short while later, she is gone. Only after yet another return trek to the bar do we see Natasha and Bill coming down the beach; he had come by and taken her with him in quest of yet another cheeseburger. Blame is distributed, rules established, apologies rendered, and forgiveness granted.

As soon as we settle down in Smaranda and Bill's room in the Blue Tang Inn for a relaxing evening of cocktails, Alexandra and Olivia arrive to invite us to their room for "Margaritas." There they serve us coffee, juice and Cokes — all in Margarita glasses. Smaranda distributes gifts she has bought for each of us, all with appropriate speeches. Good Christmas spirits reign as we head out in search of dinner.

We agree on the Bait and Tackle Bar & Grille, a deck restaurant perched over the water. A reggae band strikes up as we finish our meal so we hang around for a bit of music and photography. On the way back Alexandra prevails on Joe to carry her piggyback down the beach, and Eliane carries Olivia, still limping from her injured foot.

It is nice to linger in a real shower and sleep in a bed that does not roll with the sea. But it is easier to leave the sea than to have the sea leave us. We all still have our "sea legs." We can feel the sea's swelling and receding deep inside our muscles' memories.

Sunday, December 25 – Christmas Day

Eliane's party (call us RENO: Richard, Eliane, Natasha and Olivia) rises early to catch a cab to the water taxi terminal. The others will fly to Belize Airport from here rather than repeat the unpleasant water taxi ride we had upon arrival. Except this time, the water taxi is an open power boat, faster, more comfortable, and fume-free. We careen over the waves and reach Belize City at 9:10 a.m., arrive at the airport by 9:30, then have to wait for the Budget car rental office to open. A friendly fellow from an adjoining office uses his cell phone to reach the Budget representative for us while (can there be any doubt?) the girls go shopping in the airport terminal. They return with ice cream and fruit.

Our car is a Mitsubishi SUV. We're ready when the others arrive. Joe is flying back immediately to the U.S., eschewing the joys of jungle life. Smaranda is distraught: her conch trophy, arguably the most cared for and cherished sea shell in modern memory, protectively wrapped for the long trip home, was left in the refrigerator in her room at the Blue Tang Inn.

We now number eight. Squeezing ourselves into the SUV as cheek-by-jowl as sardines in a can, the little ones curled on adult laps, bags crammed into every available corner and crevice, we head north to Orange Walk. As advertised, it is a town of no tourist amenities. Smaranda had booked rooms at St. Christopher's Hotel and I had booked a boat tour to the Maya ruins at Lamanai with Reyes & Sons.

Unfortunately, we are forced to rely on my unreliable memory, as the copious notes I brought do not include the names or telephone numbers for the tour. Our hotel hosts come to the rescue. Yes, they know Orlando Reyes, but he isn't home. Instead, they call in Fernando and Vicente de la Fuente, operators of New River Cruises based just across the river from Reyes. We follow them to their base camp, establish that, yes, no one is home at the Reyes base, and happily agree to terms for a tour and a meal, the same deal we had thought we had arranged with Reyes & Sons.

Food is a high priority as no one has had a meal today, Christmas Day of all days. Smaranda is particularly adamant: she is going nowhere until she has first had a meal. Vincente's family epitomizes Belizean hospitality: without ado, Señora prepares us a "typical" Christmas meal of Maya tamales (essentially cornmeal in corn tortillas) and we dine alfresco under a picnic pavilion by the river.

We are on the river by 1 p.m., headed for Lamanai — Mayan for "sunken crocodile." As we ride the meandering river, hemmed in mostly by dense jungle, Vincente points out young crocodiles sunning on riverside logs, a rare night owl, and a meticulously manicured farm that appears as if by magic out of the jungle. It is owned by a colony of Mennonites, and all the young Mennonite men, identically dressed in candy-striped shirts, ties, straw boaters, and slacks, are standing on their riverfront dock as if posing for photographs.

Lamanai is impressive. Vicente leads us on a tour of its Pyramid of the Mask, its ball court, its other pyramids and courtyards. We scamper up pyramids like ants. We listen for the "howler monkeys" we are told live in the forests surrounding us. They are said to be heard for miles around, but they aren't heard today. This place has been a center of civilization since 1500 BC, long before Greeks and Romans "invented" civilization. These pyramids are contemporaries of their more famous Egyptian counterparts. Lamanai remained a cultural center until the Spanish arrived in the 1500s AD, and for a few hundred years after that.

The boat ride back to Orange Walk is another delight. We take narrower channels and a maze of tributaries. Anyone who had not grown up on the river, as Vicente did, would be lost within minutes. The boat banks around tight curves, under canopies of trees. Vincente brakes the boat and points out an iguana high in a treetop. He's not easy to spot, but in this setting all is believable.

When we dock, Señora de la Fuente offers us yet another "typical" Mayan meal, called "black soup." It is truly black, fashioned with a kind of black bean paste, but with chunks of chicken and dressing. It is quite spicy. And filling.

Back at the hotel, Bill and I go out in search of orange juice (for the gin) and some rum (for Smaranda). But it is Christmas. As forewarned by Vincente, the only businesses that are open are the few restaurants and convenience stores operated by the local Chinese.

Monday, December 26 – Boxing Day

Eliane and Natasha both awake with diarrhea, probably brought on by the previous day's spicy diet. Fernando and Vicente de la Fuente are again at the hotel. They have come to invite us to breakfast. It is Boxing Day, they explain. No restaurants will be open. We are reminded again that this was not so long ago a British colony. Who but the British still celebrate Boxing Day?

Breakfast in the open air beside the New River is a "traditional" meal of eggs, ham, fried jack, and tortillas. Our solicitous hosts tell us of their plans to expand their touring business into a restaurant and, eventually, perhaps a motel or cottages for rent. We wish them well with their garden spot by the river.

Next stop, Altun Ha, a Maya site just off our route back to the airport. It is a "new" town by Maya standards, dating back only to about 600 AD, the dawn of the Mayan Classic Period. I miss the turnoff to Altun Ha and only at a police checkpoint several miles away do we get pointed back in the right direction. Altun Ha is yet another impressive archeological site. More pyramids, but now in a beautifully manicured setting. We follow one trail looking for more structures, only to dead-end at an ominous swamp and pond.

Bill has to fly back to North Carolina today: work summons. But we plan one more stop before leaving him at the airport: the Baboon Sanctuary, a preserve for "howler monkeys." Our guide escorts us under the jungle canopy. At his call, the monkeys come down from the trees and hang there, eating out of his hand. The guide roars in what we assume to be howler language and the alpha male soon appears. So does a new mother, her baby on her back. The monkeys seem to pose for us as our cameras zoom and click.

After waving Bill off at the airport, and potty breaks for all, we pile back into the SUV, now with a little more leg room, and head west to San Ignacio, a few kilometers from the Guatemala border. Martha's Guesthouse is a beautiful, three-story, hacienda-style hotel with numerous balconies and artful woodwork. We arrive in the evening, settle in, and enjoy a dinner at Nefry's. Martha's has a restaurant, but it is closed. Nefry's is kind enough to give us some ice so Eliane and I can enjoy nightcap screwdrivers on the balcony under the stars.

Tuesday, December 27

Today will be a day of adventures. Breakfast at Martha's is a prolonged affair — which is to say we wait seemingly forever to be served and, after eating, to get our check. Then we head for Caracol. The SUV is stick shift, so the driving is left to me, the only one with extensive stick shift experience. Before too long, even I am unsure if this is a blessing or a curse.

For two hours we bounce and lurch over a rough dirt road of ruts and jutting rocks. Old rains have cut gullies here and there in the road's surface. As we make our jaw-wrenching way through the jungle, it must be crossing at least a few minds, particularly those squeezed into the rumble seat over the rear axel, that our goal may not be worth it.

But it is. Caracol is vast, clearly the largest site we've yet visited and still a working archeological dig. We climb pyramids again, peek into hutches where archeologists have left recent finds on their work benches, including the jaw of some herbivorous animal. We explore burial tombs and tunnels under the pyramids. The views from the tops of the pyramids are awe-inspiring. The vastness of the jungle seems eternal from here. Lush green treetops fluff out unbroken in every direction. A mere five kilometers away is Guatemala. And beyond that, the capital Maya city of Tikal. We learn that once a group of Mayans set out on foot from Caracol and traveled some 100 days through the jungle to attack and conquer mighty Tikal.

On the drive back, we want to see a 1,000-foot waterfall. We'd seen the signs for it, heard it was worth seeing, perhaps even a swim. What we don't know is that it is deep within almost impenetrable jungle. We turn off our rutted road back to San Ignacio onto an even worse road of deeply gullied clay pockmarked by rocky outcroppings. After a few miles we meet an oncoming car and inquire; we are told we have about five more miles of this, plus two miles "in" to the falls.

Jolting along at little more than 10 miles per hour for the most part, we finally arrive at the predicted turnoff. This is not a road. It is a cleared strip in the jungle crisscrossed with fissures that would test the shock absorbers of the sturdiest humvee. Instead of dodging rocks and gullies, we are now leaping ravines and trying desperately not to slide off the path into the roadside ditch. We inch our way for about a mile of this. Daylight is dwindling, the gas gauge has dipped below a quarter tank, and the roadway is worsening. I stop the car. "I'm not driving back on this road after dark," I announce.

Eliane and Smaranda walk on to explore ahead while I inch the car back and forth until it is pointed homeward. When the scouts return, they say the road seems to get a little better ahead, but they agree it's too late to go on. The sun is sinking inexorably in the west as we head back to San Ignacio.

In town, I go in search of a cold beer to calm my road-frazzled nerves, but there is no beer to be found except for a Belikin the concierge of Martha's fetches me. I sit sipping it in the lobby, crowded with the luggage of newly arriving guests.

Dinner at Martha's is a repeat of breakfast: a wait of an hour to be served, more than a half hour to get our check after eating. We are nothing if not persistent. We will not allow our spirits to be quashed.

Wednesday, December 28

Our last day in Belize. Natasha, Mihnea and I want one more archeological visit. The others prefer a final morning of shopping. Not willing to test Martha's restaurant service yet again, we all have breakfast at "Pop's," just down the street, where the service is quick and the food wholesome. We archeological explorers are finishing our breakfasts just as the shoppers arrive for theirs.

Cahal Pech is an archeological site perched on a hilltop just outside and above the town of San Ignacio. It is the first really residential Maya "city" we've seen. It has no ceremonial pyramids but many royal quarters, a ball court, other signs of residences. Inside its beehive buildings are rooms with bed-like benches. We three clamber among the ruins until we have peeked into every cranny and crevice.

Back at Martha's, we collect our bags and are at the airport before 11:30 a.m. The trip is over, the adventure finished, the memories starting to meld in our minds. There is nothing left now but last minute souvenir shopping, a snack in the airport, and boarding the plane for the flight home. We have spent all but a little loose change in our pockets, but we are happy, satisfied, tired ... and happy to see Bill waiting for us at the Raleigh-Durham airport.

Appendix D:
Peru, June–July 2007

June 29

Not an auspicious beginning. Our departure is aborted. The flight from Raleigh-Durham to JFK is canceled at the last minute and we are rerouted for tomorrow via Miami. At least American Airlines gives us a voucher for a taxi back to Eliane's house. Downside: our cab driver, from the Congo, preaches all the way home that we must take Jesus for our personal savior. He believes everyone in the university town of Chapel Hill is an atheist. He preaches "neo-evolution," a non-evolutionary theory he appears to have crudely adapted from Francis Collins, the scientist-turned-believer who directed the Human Genome Project.

June 30

In Miami's airport we encounter our first fellow-travelers, including Donna Krabill of Marie Selby Gardens, the one who introduced us to the idea of joining the Environmental Expeditions venture. Then we wait…and wait…and wait…an hour and 15 minutes on the tarmac, without air-conditioning. And our seat mate, a young man from near Wilmington, NC, starts in on the Jesus thing again, although he seems to have a slightly more open mind about science than yesterday's cabbie. At long last, we are in Peru, in Lima, at the Casa Andina hotel. Let the adventure begin.

July 1

We visit an artisan market in Lima — a vast network of stalls. Lots of jewelry, some naughty statuettes in stalls adjoining others with sacred artwork. My big buy: a "Josh Bernstein" leather hat (OK, also like Indiana Jones' hat). Everyone agrees it's "cool," a welcome change from the comments on my headgear in Belize.

After our flight to Iquitos on the Amazon, we ride the "Amazon Queen" downriver to Ceiba Tops. This is roughing it? Air conditioned rooms. Swimming pool. A fully stocked bar. (Scotch is only $3 a shot!) Buffet dinner. Young native dancers put on a show, including acting out how rice is grown and harvested, and a young lady dances with a boa constrictor. The performance includes wrapping the boa around several of the ladies' necks, including Eliane's.

July 2

On the river again, to ExplorNapo Lodge. Now *this* is roughing it. No electricity, no hot water, thatch roofs, only bamboo walls between cubicles, mosquito-netted bunks.

We meet "Charley," a guinea pig on steroids. We're told he's a capybara, the world's largest rodent, and a local "pet." Another pet is a parrot, which sits calmly on the railing waiting to be petted, bowing its head in invitation.

Lucio (one of our guides) says he can arrange for me to buy a real dart blowgun for $40. I explain I don't want one of those toy souvenirs sold everywhere. We seal the deal. Randy Morgan (Cincinnati Zoo) explains all about insects, tarantulas (one hovers overhead on a crossbeam above the bar!) and Eliane gets up close and personal with a tarantula, tickling its fangs at Randy's invitation.

On a forest walk we encounter a fungus that turns the tables on an ant: the ant ate the fungus, the fungus in turn ate the ant from the inside, intelligently eating all the non-vital organs first, then gradually killing the ant and anchoring it to a tree trunk, where the fungus grows and emits a pine-needle-looking thing out of the ant: it looks for all the world as if the fungus has pinned the ant to the tree with a needle.

The "waggle dance," in which Randy has us imitate bees seeking pollen, has us all in stitches. Give me credit: I found the pollen first! After dinner, there's music and dance, thanks to a few guitars. Life is good.

July 3

John and Jim have the cubicle next to ours; they easily overhear me tell Eliane, "Good morning, sweetheart," to which they answer through the wall: "Good morning, sweetheart!" Looks like our fates are entwined for the remainder of the trip. They'll be in the cubicle next to ours at every stop.

We walk to a nearby "ethnobotanical garden" and meet Shaman Guillermo Rodriguez. Lucio gives my arthritic neck and shoulders a rubdown with "cat's claw" camphor and some other substance that penetrates immediately. The muscles there haven't felt that good in years. (The benefits will last a few weeks.)

The shaman does a smoke and leaf-shaking chant over the heads of several in our group, including Eliane, to rid them of evil spirits. Most of us also get temporary tattoos. Mine is an Amazon Bushmaster snake, said to be the most venomous in the Amazon. How appropriate.

We head upriver to ACTS (Amazon Conservatory of Tropical Studies). Rain prohibits us from going to the canopy walk this afternoon, but we walk there at night to get our "sea legs," or more appropriately, our "canopy legs." It is truly amazing — trees loaded with bromeliads and other epiphytes. Unfortunately, on the way back I slip on the mud and have a Humpty-Dumpty style fall. I get zero points for gracefulness but a lot of sympathy and help hobbling back to the lodge.

July 4

We have immersion courses in "wildlife diversity, camouflage and mimicry." Steve Madigosky shows us his research in a "light hole" (an open area where one or more trees has fallen to expose the ground to sunlight). He has sensors strategically placed and takes periodic readings of humidity, temperature and "PAR" (photosynthetic available radiation) to compare with readings in the deeper jungle. Nearby he leads us through a massive, 40-foot wide leaf-cutter ant colony.

On the canopy walkway he demonstrates how "glider ants" find their way back to their home tree: he paints their butts with white-out and has us drop them from the walkway several feet away from their tree; they glide back to their tree. He says they can replicate this from large distances, too far away to "see" their home tree. He says he has discovered they have minute traces of hematite in their brains - suitable for magnetic tracking.

"DC" (Dizzy) Randal has a session showing us the ecological variations of leaf shapes and sizes. Interesting, and DC is fun to be with, hailing from Washington, but I itch to get back into the jungle.

For sunset, we go back to the canopy walkway with a bottle of red wine, thanks to Eliane. We toast the Fourth of July sunset there, at the canopy walk's highest point. Lucio spots two vultures on a treetop on the horizon, two toucans on another treetop in the opposite direction "calling" back and forth with two other toucans, on yet another distant tree.

July 5

On the river again to our next lodge, Explorama, we see a large, three-story "houseboat" beached. It seems palatial in these surroundings and fascinates me.

The women in our group flock to Explorama's large gift shop at the entrance. Back on the Amazon, we are taken to a shallow place and fish for piranha. We all catch one or more. Bottom dwellers, piranha are quite misunderstood, non-dangerous to humans, although voracious for meat on a hook. Afterwards, we swim in the Amazon, not far from some fresh water dolphins, pink and gray, two species that evolved specifically in the Amazon.

At night I go on the night bird-watching cruise, something I'd resisted until now. We must all remain silent for more than an hour as we watch flashlight beams trace eerie patterns through the trees. I don't think I missed much by skipping the other night and daybreak outings.

July 6

We visit Yagua village, our opportunity to engage in trade. But first we have tribal dancing in the community center (a round, thatch-roofed building), in which we all are invited to join. Eliane, of course, is among the first to join in. Next, we are treated to a blowgun demonstration by grass-skirted natives and get to try our hand at it. Proud to say, I came closest to the "bull's eye" on the target post — about three inches below it — with my first dart. Beginner's luck, of course. I didn't even know the post was the target!

Lucio has my new blowgun and darts from the chief ($40). The rest of the time is spent trading tee-shirts, old belts, water bottles and caps for various necklaces, a basket, a toy blowgun for my grandson and "chimes" (rattles, really).

Back at Explorama, we are treated to demonstrations by the natives of their various crafts: weaving, pottery, thatching, making a blowgun, even paddling a dugout canoe, which we get to try. I'm sweating like hell, the heat and humidity are extreme. I've never been so grateful for a cold shower.

We have music and dance late into the night.

July 7

Still at Explorama Lodge, we go by boat to the local "library," run by Nancy Dunn, an American woman who has devoted her life to bringing books and reading to the children of the jungle. As an "exercise," we each interact with one of her kids. Mine is Teddy Diaz Inapi, age 16. He's a bit of a wise guy, I'm told, and I can see it in the glint in his eye. He wants to play professional soccer someday. I challenge him to read more (he's read only 5 books in a year!) and promise to stay in touch. Eliane has photos of us. (I've sent him a copy, as well as an English-Spanish dictionary and a child's story book to the library.)

On the way in, we saw a little girl with what appeared to be a baby crocodile on a leash. On the way out the little girl has a baby sloth. All of our women take turns holding it, cuddling it. The guys take pictures.

We have a brief visit with Linnea Smith at her clinic. She's yet another American woman who decided to jettison modern comforts and live in the jungle, providing basic health services to natives for those things the shamans can't cure. She's proud that she recently acquired a generator. She can now refrigerate drugs and specimens. But our visit is cut short because everyone, including Linnea, wants to get back to Explorama for lunch. And then it's back on the Amazon for the boat ride back to Ceiba Tops.

July 8

It is wonderful to be back in air conditioning, with laundry service, a swimming pool, electricity, hot water. Jungle life is fine, but our creature comforts are now appreciated all the more. We collect our laundry, and inadvertently a bag of laundry belonging to Alexa and Jennifer (referred to by us as the "Bobbsey Twins") is left in our room. We return it to the front desk, not knowing to whom it belongs, but when we discover it's theirs, they seem oddly blasé about their laundry being missing.

We board the boat again, this time for Manco Capac, a jungle village named for the first chief of the Inca Empire. After a get-acquainted session in the communal center, we go to our respective "service projects." Because of my past as a house painter in Spain, I opt for helping paint a classroom of the local school and wind up doing the "high" work, mostly standing on a stool perched perilously atop a small table. We have no ladders. We paint the room a rather deep blue.

Eliane paints a little, plants a garden a little, does roof thatching a little — everything but latrine duty, she says. Afterward, we have lunch in the communal center — fish wrapped in big leaves, chicken and rice wrapped in big leaves, etc. We have a "free for all" exchange between our teachers and theirs, myself and a few others fairly versed in Spanish furiously trying to translate. A good idea gone awry, but fun anyway.

We then adjourn to the newly "roofed" outdoor community center. Donna Krabill breaks out some candy and the kids go wild, swarming around her like bees to pollen. Peace is gradually restored, the native dancing begins, and we are all invited to join. I find myself dancing with Beatriz, the local school librarian. Just like Nancy, she says she needs an English-Spanish dictionary. (After my return to the U.S., I sent her one, too.)

Back at Ceiba Tops, we take a short walk to the Giant Ceiba Tree. Because there are no "seasons" here near the equator, there are no tree rings, so no one knows how old it is, but the guessing is that it is around 150 years old. It is huge, as big around as a cottage. We take group photos at its base.

July 9

Our last day in the jungle. At 6 a.m. I join the early morning birders on the river. We see many of my old friends — the purple martins that used to visit me each year in Chincoteague — plus vultures, kingfishers, snowy egrets, all in a misty rain.

A visit to "Monkey Island" is our final outing: monkeys galore, nine varieties in all, plus parrots, macaws, etc. Monkeys climb through the thatch roof to watch the goings-on inside while the sanctuary is being explained to us. They play and fight with each other outside, pose for our cameras, let themselves be cuddled and fed by the ladies.

We board the Amazon Queen again and head back upriver to Iquitos. We have to hang around its airport from 3:45 p.m. to 8 p.m. Flight delays seem pandemic here. Lucio's son takes us each for a spin around the airport parking lot in his three-wheeled "taxi," the primary mode of transportation in Iquitos. I also manage to talk Eliane into letting me buy a bottle of "Siete Raices" (seven-roots) rum, something DC Randal introduced us to in the jungle. It did not travel well.

My blowgun, wrapped securely in newspaper and cellophane tape, must be checked with my luggage.

July 10

Only six of our group go on to Cusco-Machu Picchu. Our flight out of Lima to Cusco is also delayed. We arrive at Cusco at 11:30 a.m. and are met by Katrina and Fernando. On the plane, I checked out a Spanish-language newspaper and learned that a national strike had been called for the next two days, adding laborers to teachers who had been on strike since last Thursday. I alert the others to this and say it could disrupt travel. The Bobbsey Twins, who have decided to do Cusco and Machu Picchu on their own, seem unfazed. At least they got their laundry back at Ceiba Tops. (I suspected it was theirs by the flower-printed bikini undies.)

Fernando and Jimmy (his driver) take us to Chinchero, where we meet village women who have restored the ancient Inca art of weaving. Their work is incredibly beautiful. Our women buy up lots of it. Laurie in particular buys $800 worth of woolen blankets.

Flora, the head weaver who restarted this ancient craft, invites us into her home for lunch — roast guinea pig. Guinea pigs ("*cui*" in Peruvian, for the sound they make) live in the living room, the only room in the house. The meal is lavish, the roast pig preceded by *quinoa* soup, salads, and any number of other delicacies. Then, while Laurie and Linda continue shopping, Fernando takes Eliane and me to Ollantaytambo, the Inca town where, if you want to go to Machu Picchu, you have to catch the train. Other than hiking over mountaintops on the ancient Inca Trail, it's the only way to get there.

I'm wowed by Ollantaytambo's mountainside "ruins," a virtually intact ancient Inca city. But the altitude is dizzying. We are about 12,000 feet above sea level, well over two miles. Light-headedness is constant, as is heavy breathing and pausing to pant every 10 steps or so. But the Andes are awesome. Words are inadequate to describe it.

Sated with the ruins, we head back, pick up Laurie and Linda, return to Cusco, and check into Novotel, luxury compared to where we've lodged.

July 11

A rough night. I had a headache most of the night, probably the one glass of wine I had with dinner, combined with the altitude. But Eliane was in agony all night — headache (without wine), nausea, chills. Luckily there's no fever. I try to get the hotel doctor for her in the morning, but she insists she's OK. It will be another few days before she is able to eat.

We go for a short walk to see Cusco and run into a lot of demonstrating strikers. Eliane goes back to the hotel. I follow, but go out again with Linda (she needs to find an ATM to buy a memory chip for her camera) and end up getting a load of close-up photos of the strikers in the cathedral square.

Fernando takes us to Qorikancha, which under the Inca was a gold-laced shrine. The Spaniards changed all that, converting it into a Dominican church, Santo Domingo, but much of the original structure remains. From there he takes us to Sacsahuaman, outside of town. It is

Quechua (the Inca language) for "zigzag-head," amazing walls of rocks the size of small rooms, expertly nestled against each other, rocks depicting serpents and other animals. From the air, this site and the original Cusco are supposed to depict a huge puma, part of the Inca zodiac.

Then it is on to Yucay, a suburb of Urubamba, and the Posada hotel, a converted monastery. It takes us more than two hours to drive the 53 kilometers from Cusco, thanks to rocks in the road, either strikers' or rock slides, at this point it isn't clear. (It very much turns out to be the former.) The Posada hotel floor creaks badly, nail heads stick out. Eliane is feeling a little better and eats some alpaca for dinner. Outside our hotel room, on the lawn, there are two aloof alpaca grazing and lazing around. Eliane goes out to meet and pet them.

July 12

Strikers have blocked many roads, including the road to Urubamba, our next stop en route to Machu Picchu. In most places it's with a bunch of rocks and boulders rolled across the pavement. At one spot it's a whole tree across the road. Then it's a kilometer marker post. Jimmy cautiously edges our van around the obstacles, but in Urubamba it becomes impassable. Fernando finds a friend who jumps in with us and directs us over back roads, narrow dirt paths really. These, too, are eventually rock-strewn. For a while Fernando and the friend walk ahead of the van pushing rocks out of the way so Jimmy can inch along. I offer to help but it's felt best that I stay in the van.

In Ollantaytambo, the square is full of tour buses, the tourists crouched fearfully inside. Locals beat on the sides of the buses with palm branches. I'm not sure what they're chanting but it doesn't sound friendly.

Fernando tells us to take from our van only what we need for one night's stay at Machu Picchu, then calls over a couple of uniformed police and tells them to watch our bags for us. He takes us up a side road to visit a woman in her adobe home, complete with the obligatory guinea pigs scurrying about the dirt floor. The home consists of the one room and a loft. This is home for six people, an altar that combines Christian and ancient Indian icons, and I don't know how many dozen guinea pigs.

Back on the square, the police carry our bags at Fernando's instruction the few blocks to where a taxi waits and takes us to the train station. The wait there lasts until 11 p.m. Reports are that strikers are blocking the tracks. A thousand or more tourists are in Machu Picchu unable to get out, another 1,000 here unable to go there. Time crawls along. We see riot-squad police with shields heading for the train station, then returning. We hear one report that some police were injured when strikers started throwing rocks at them.

Fernando goes inside the train station gates. They aren't letting anyone in but he, obviously, knows which strings to pull. He's in touch with Jimmy, our driver, by cell phone and, through him, with us. At long last he tells us to come toward the gate, the first train has come from Machu Picchu and is ready to load for the first return trip. He has seats on it for us.

As a reporter with some experience with crowds both peaceful and not so peaceful, I tell the three ladies to chain behind me, each holding on to the person in front, and we barge in.

I have his long canister that contains his maps and charts. I spot Fernando inside the railroad yard fence and wave his canister to get his attention, then push our way to the small opening of the gate he seems to have created. Miraculously, we are allowed through. We learn he told officials we were "visiting dignitaries." We wind up in first class seats on the train, preferred passengers. I told him he'd forgotten the brandy for our coffee, as a joke. Within five minutes he was back with a flask of brandy, tipping it into my coffee. We arrive at Aguas Calientes, at the base of Machu Picchu, at about 12:20 a.m., dead tired, and crash for a short night's sleep.

July 13

Machu Picchu, at long last. A bus takes us up a switchback road, climbing the mountainside without guardrails, to the gates of the archaeological site. We arrive around 9 a.m. Fernando tells us to follow him but not to look up or out until he instructs us to. When he stops us, he tells us to close our eyes and turn to the left. When we open our eyes we see only a blank wall of stone. He tells us to turn around, and there it is, all of Machu Picchu spread at our feet. This time it isn't the altitude that takes my breath away. I gasp for air, start tearing up. I've been waiting for this moment for 35 years. It is hard to take it all in. It is simply beautiful, grander and more magnificent than even I had imagined. Waynu Picchu rises to the sky beyond it all. Words fail me....

We spend almost four hours touring it. Fernando tells amazing stories. (Among them, how he took Ben Kingsley there to meditate, and how he was Jane Fonda's guide on the Inca Trail a few years ago.) We visit the sun altar, actually an observatory for astronomical readings; the sun temple with windows facing the summer and winter solstice sunrises; "star mirrors" in which the Inca could study the stars' reflected movement in pools of water without breaking their necks looking skyward. A nest of wild chinchilla lives among the stones. Two wild llama scamper through the ruins. The place is enchanted.

The tour ends with an excellent buffet lunch. Goodbye to Machu Picchu.

During the switchback bus ride back down the mountain, a young boy races down paths to meet and wave at us at each turn. At several levels a teenager, apparently American, joins him to wave and scream, but eventually gives up. At the bottom, the young Indian boy gets on the bus to collect tips. His name is Ricardo. I tip him for his successful race against the bus and tell him we share a name.

July 14

Back in Lima, we have a final day of shopping in the artisan markets. After much searching, I find what I want for Eliane: an Andina cross, in Peruvian turquoise. She also loves a necklace in the same shop, so I get her that, too.

One more bit of excitement: eating in the airport while waiting for our plane out, I forget my "Indiana Jones/Josh Bernstein" hat in the restaurant and don't remember it until after going through security. I ask the guards if I can go back to get it without going through security again: no, but they can send for it. The hat has to be scanned and I have to sign for it, but I get it just in time to catch the plane.

July 15

At Raleigh Durham Airport, after our change of planes at JFK, my blowgun fails to arrive on the checked luggage carousel. I wait and wait. Eliane is outside with our ride, Sally. All the luggage has been claimed, but no blowgun. Finally a guy comes in from the tarmac with it in his hand, sees me in my leather hat and grins. It's mine. I can go home now.

Life is, well, you get the point....

www.ingramcontent.com/pod-product-compliance
Lightning Source LLC
Chambersburg PA
CBHW052013070526
44584CB00016B/1738